60 Minute Guide
to Netscape® 2

60 Minute Guide
to Netscape® 2

Dennis Hamilton
and
Craig & Coletta Witherspoon

IDG Books Worldwide, Inc.
Foster City, CA • Chicago, IL • Indianapolis, IN • Braintree, MA • Southlake, TX

60 Minute Guide to Netscape 2

Published by
IDG Books Worldwide, Inc.
An International Data Group Company
919 E. Hillsdale Blvd.
Suite 400
Foster City, CA 94404

Library of Congress Catalog Card No.: 96-75770

ISBN: 0-7645-3008-9

Printed in the United States of America

10 9 8 7 6 5 4 3 2 1

1B/QS/QU/ZW/IN

Distributed in the United States by IDG Books Worldwide, Inc.

Distributed by Macmillan Canada for Canada; by Computer and Technical Books for the Caribbean Basin; by Contemporanea de Ediciones for Venezuela; by Distribuidora Cuspide for Argentina; by CITEC for Brazil; by Ediciones ZETA S.C.R. Ltda. for Peru; by Editorial Limusa SA for Mexico; by Transworld Publishers Limited in the United Kingdom and Europe; by Al-Maiman Publishers & Distributors for Saudi Arabia; by Simron Pty. Ltd. for South Africa; by IDG Communications (HK) Ltd. for Hong Kong; by Toppan Company Ltd. for Japan; by Addison Wesley Publishing Company for Korea; by Longman Singapore Publishers Ltd. for Singapore, Malaysia, Thailand, and Indonesia; by Unalis Corporation for Taiwan; by WS Computer Publishing Company, Inc. for the Philippines; by WoodsLane Pty. Ltd. for Australia; by WoodsLane Enterprises Ltd. for New Zealand.

For general information on IDG Books Worldwide's books in the U.S., please call our Consumer Customer Service department at 800-762-2974. For reseller information, including discounts and premium sales, please call our Reseller Customer Service department at 800-434-3422.

For information on where to purchase IDG Books Worldwide's books outside the U.S., contact IDG Books Worldwide at 415-655-3021 or fax 415-655-3295.

For information on translations, contact Marc Jeffrey Mikulich, Director, Foreign & Subsidiary Rights, at IDG Books Worldwide, 415-655-3018 or fax 415-655-3295.

For sales inquiries and special prices for bulk quantities, write to the address above or call IDG Books Worldwide at 415-655-3200.

For information on using IDG Books Worldwide's books in the classroom, or ordering examination copies, contact the Education Office at 800-434-2086 or fax 817-251-8174.

For authorization to photocopy items for corporate, personal, or educational use, please contact Copyright Clearance Center, 222 Rosewood Drive, Danvers, MA 01923, or fax 508-750-4470.

Published in the United States

 is a trademark under exclusive license to IDG Books Worldwide, Inc., from International Data Group, Inc.

ABOUT IDG BOOKS WORLDWIDE

WINNER
Eighth Annual
Computer Press
Awards ≥ 1992

Welcome to the world of IDG Books Worldwide.

IDG Books Worldwide, Inc., is a subsidiary of International Data Group, the world's largest publisher of computer-related information and the leading global provider of information services on information technology. IDG was founded more than 25 years ago and now employs more than 7,700 people worldwide. IDG publishes more than 250 computer publications in 67 countries (see listing below). More than 70 million people read one or more IDG publications each month.

Launched in 1990, IDG Books Worldwide is today the #1 publisher of best-selling computer books in the United States. We are proud to have received 8 awards from the Computer Press Association in recognition of editorial excellence and three from Computer Currents' First Annual Readers' Choice Awards, and our best-selling ...*For Dummies*® series has more than 19 million copies in print with translations in 28 languages. IDG Books Worldwide, through a joint venture with IDG's Hi-Tech Beijing, became the first U.S. publisher to publish a computer book in the People's Republic of China. In record time, IDG Books Worldwide has become the first choice for millions of readers around the world who want to learn how to better manage their businesses.

Our mission is simple: Every one of our books is designed to bring extra value and skill-building instructions to the reader. Our books are written by experts who understand and care about our readers. The knowledge base of our editorial staff comes from years of experience in publishing, education, and journalism — experience which we use to produce books for the '90s. In short, we care about books, so we attract the best people. We devote special attention to details such as audience, interior design, use of icons, and illustrations. And because we use an efficient process of authoring, editing, and desktop publishing our books electronically, we can spend more time ensuring superior content and spend less time on the technicalities of making books.

You can count on our commitment to deliver high-quality books at competitive prices on topics you want to read about. At IDG Books Worldwide, we continue in the IDG tradition of delivering quality for more than 25 years. You'll find no better book on a subject than one from IDG Books Worldwide.

John J. Kilcullen

John Kilcullen
President and CEO
IDG Books Worldwide, Inc.

WINNER
Ninth Annual
Computer Press
Awards ≥ 1993

IDG Books Worldwide, Inc., is a subsidiary of International Data Group, the world's largest publisher of computer-related information and the leading global provider of information services on information technology. International Data Group publishes over 250 computer publications in 67 countries. Seventy million people read one or more International Data Group publications each month. International Data Group's publications include: **ARGENTINA:** Computerworld Argentina, GamePro, Infoworld, PC World Argentina; **AUSTRALIA:** Australian Macworld, Client/Server Journal, Computer Living, Computerworld, Digital News, Network World, PC World, Publishing Essentials, Reseller; **AUSTRIA:** Computerwelt, PC TEST; **BELARUS:** PC World Belarus; **BELGIUM:** Data News; **BRAZIL:** Annuário de Informática, Computerworld Brazil, Connections, Super Game Power, Macworld, PC World Brazil, Publish Brazil, SUPERGAME; **BULGARIA:** Computerworld Bulgaria, Networkworld/Bulgaria, PC & MacWorld Bulgaria; **CANADA:** CIO Canada, ComputerWorld Canada, InfoCanada, Network World Canada, Reseller World; **CHILE:** Computerworld Chile, GamePro, PC World Chile; **COLUMBIA:** Computerworld Colombia, GamePro, PC World Colombia; **COSTA RICA:** PC World Costa Rica/Nicaragua; **THE CZECH AND SLOVAK REPUBLICS:** Computerworld Czechoslovakia, Elektronika Czechoslovakia, PC World Czechoslovakia; **DENMARK:** Communications World, Computerworld Danmark, Macworld Danmark, PC World Danmark, PC World Danmark Supplements, TECH World; **DOMINICAN REPUBLIC:** PC World Republica Dominicana; **ECUADOR:** PC World Ecuador, GamePro; **EGYPT:** Computerworld Middle East, PC World Middle East; **EL SALVADOR:** PC World Centro America; **FINLAND:** MikroPC, Tietoverkko, Tietoviikko; **FRANCE:** Distributique, Golden, Info PC, Le Guide du Monde Informatique, Le Monde Informatique, Reseaux & Telecoms; **GERMANY:** Computer Business, Computerwoche, Computerwoche Extra, Computerwoche Focus, Electronic Entertainment, GamePro, I/M Information Management, Macwelt, PC Welt; **GREECE:** GamePro, Macworld & Publish; **GUATEMALA:** PC World Centro America; **HONDURAS:** PC World Centro America; **HONG KONG:** Computerworld Hong Kong, PCWorld Hong Kong, Publish in Asia; **HUNGARY:** ABCD CD-ROM, Computerworld Szamitastechnika, PC & Mac World Hungary, PC-X Magazine; **INDIA:** Computerworld India, PC World India, Publish in Asia; **INDONESIA:** InfoKomputer PC World, Komputek Computerworld, Publish in Asia; **IRELAND:** ComputerScope, PC Live!; **ISRAEL:** PC World 32 BIT, People & Computers; **ITALY:** Computerworld Italia, Computerworld Italia Special Editions, Lotus Italia, Macworld Italia, Networking Italia, PC Shopping, PC World Italia, PC World/Walt Disney; **JAPAN:** Macworld Japan, Nikkei Personal Computing, SunWorld Japan, Windows World Japan; **KENYA:** East African Computer News; **KOREA:** Hi-Tech Information/Computerworld, Macworld Korea, PC World Korea; **MACEDONIA:** PC World Macedonia; **MALAYSIA:** Computerworld Malaysia, PC World Malaysia, Publish in Asia; **MEXICO:** Computerworld Mexico, GamePro, Macworld, PC World Mexico; **MYANMAR:** PC World Myanmar; **NETHERLANDS:** Computable, Computer! Totaal, LAN Magazine, Macworld, Net Magazine; **NEW ZEALAND:** Computer'Buyer, Computerworld New Zealand, MTB, Network World, PC World New Zealand; **NICARAGUA:** PC World Costa Rica/Nicaragua; **NIGERIA:** PC World Africa; **NORWAY:** Computerworld Norge, Computerworld Privat, CW Rapport Klient/Tjener, CW Rapport Nettverk & Telecom, CW Rapport Offentlig Sektor, IDG's KURSGUIDE, Macworld Norge, Multimedia World, PC World Ekspress, PC World Nettverk, PC World Norge, PC World's Produktguide, Windows Spesial; **PAKISTAN:** Computerworld Pakistan, PC World Pakistan; **PANAMA:** GamePro, PC World Panama; **PARAGUAY:** PC World Paraguay; **P. R. OF CHINA:** China Computerworld, China Infoworld, Computer & Communication, Electronic Product World, Electronics Today, Game Camp, PC World China, Popular Computer Week, Software World, Telecom Product World; **PERU:** Computerworld Peru, GamePro, PC World Profesional Peru, PC World Peru; **POLAND:** Computerworld Poland, Computerworld Special Report, Macworld, Networld, PC World Komputer; **PHILIPPINES:** Computerworld Philippines, PC Digest, Publish in Asia; **PORTUGAL:** Cerebro/PC World, Correio Informático/Computerworld, Mac•In/PC•In Portugal; **PUERTO RICO:** PC World Puerto Rico; **ROMANIA:** Computerworld Romania, PC World Romania, Telecom Romania; **RUSSIA:** Computerworld Rossiya, Network World Russia, PC World Russia; **SINGAPORE:** Computerworld Singapore, PC World Singapore, Publish in Asia; **SLOVENIA:** MONITOR; **SOUTH AFRICA:** Computing S.A., Network World S.A., Software World; **SPAIN:** Computerworld España, COMUNICACIONES WORLD, Dealer World, Macworld Espana, PC World España; **SWEDEN:** CAP&Design, Computer Sweden, Corporate Computing, MacWorld, Maxi Data, MikroDatorn, Nätverk & Kommunikation, PC/Aktiv, PC World, Windows World; **SWITZERLAND:** Computerworld Schweiz, Macworld Schweiz, PCtip; **TAIWAN:** Computerworld Taiwan, Macworld Taiwan, PC World Taiwan, Publish Taiwan, Windows World; **THAILAND:** Thai Computerworld, Publish in Asia; **TURKEY:** Computerworld Monitör, MACWORLD Turkiye, PC WORLD Turkiye; **UKRAINE:** Computerworld Kiev, Computers & Software Magazine, PC World Ukraine; **UNITED KINGDOM:** Acorn User, Amiga Action, Amiga Computing, Amiga, Appletalk, CD Powerplay, CD-ROM Now, Computing, Connexion, GamePro, Lotus Magazine, Macaction, Macworld, Open Computing, Parents and Computers, PC Home, PC Works, The WEB; **UNITED STATES:** Cable in the Classroom, CD Review, CIO Magazine, Computerworld, Computerworld Client/Server Journal, Digital Video Magazine, DOS World, Electronic, InfoWorld, I-Way, Macworld, Maximize, MULTIMEDIA WORLD, Network World, PC World, PUBLISH, SWATPro Magazine, Video Event, WebMaster; **URUGUAY:** PC World Uruguay; **VENEZUELA:** Computerworld Venezuela, GamePro, PC World Venezuela; and **VIETNAM:** PC World Vietnam   10/17/95a

IDG BOOKS WORLDWIDE

About the Authors

Dennis Hamilton

Dennis Hamilton is president of Software Analytics, Inc., a seven-year-old Indianapolis-based communications and research enterprise. He has written on computer technology and business for 21 years, publishing more than 900 articles on software, hardware, the Internet, and industry issues. His last book, *Jungle Rules,* told the inside story of building from bankruptcy the computer industry giant Management Science America, known today as Dun & Bradstreet Software. He has spent the last two years writing on Internet issues and developing Web sites for businesses. When not writing on technology and business, he has published fiction in the horror, mystery, and espionage genres. He can be reached at cato@iquest.net.

Craig & Coletta Witherspoon

Craig and Coletta Witherspoon are freelance writers and artists. They are the authors of *Optimizing Client/Server Networks,* also published by IDG Books. Their company, Clare Stanley Productions, provides networking and business consulting services to both domestic and international clients. They write fiction on the side.

Credits

IDG Books Worldwide, Inc.

Senior Vice President and Group Publisher
Brenda McLaughlin

Vice President and Group Publisher
Christopher J. Williams

Acquisitions Editor
Ellen Camm

Managing Editor
Andy Cummings

Production Director
Beth Jenkins

Production Assistant
Jacalyn L. Pennywell

Supervisor of Project Coordination
Cindy L. Phipps

Supervisor of Page Layout
Kathie S. Schnorr

Supervisor of Graphics and Design
Shelley Lea

Reprint/Blueline Coordination
Tony Augsburger
Patricia R. Reynolds
Todd Klemme
Theresa Sánchez-Baker

Media/Archive Coordination
Leslie Popplewell
Melissa Stauffer
Jason Marcuson

Development Editor
Nancy Stevenson

Copy Editor
Nate Holdread

Technical Editor
Kevin Hampton

Associate Project Coordinator
Debbie Sharpe

Project Coordination Assistant
Regina Snyder

Graphics Coordination
Gina Scott
Angela F. Hunckler

Production Page Layout
Shawn Aylsworth
Linda M. Boyer
Jane Martin
Anna Rohrer
Michael Sullivan

Proofreaders
Kathy McGuiness
Christine Meloy Beck
Gwenette Gaddis
Dwight Ramsey
Carl Saff
Robert Springer

Indexer
Liz Cunningham

Book & Cover Design
Draper and Liew, Inc.

Dedication

For Margaret Elizabeth Hamilton, world champ in 3-D puzzles and, oh yes, motherhood.

Acknowledgments

If you believe in conspiracy theories, it's easy to understand the kind of collaboration needed to bring off a project such as this one. First, I'd like to thank Ellen Camm of IDG for giving me the chance to write this book. Erik Dafforn's frequent and intelligent words of encouragement were priceless. Nancy Stevenson, my development editor, did just that and much more in organizing the manuscript to be more than the sum of its words. My technical editor, Kevin Hampton, had the omniscience to correct my instructions so that readers didn't detonate their computers when following my guidelines. Nate Holdread's gentle counsel and advice was much appreciated as we raced toward the deadline.

Mostly I want to thank my wife, Jan, and children, David and Whitney, for utterly sacrificing our family life during the writing of this book, wholly without complaint. Small notes of love that floated in over the transom. Warm meals left at the door. Can a writer ask for more?

Table of Contents

Introduction

It will stand as testament to the enterprising cyberneers at Netscape Communications Corporation that they achieved a 70 percent share of the World Wide Web browser market with a terrific product — Netscape Navigator 1.*x* — that pales in comparison to its successor, described in this book. Netscape Navigator 2.0 and its publishing-rich companion, Netscape Navigator Gold 2.0, have managed to pull together in easy-to-use fashion almost every point of functionality that exists on the Internet. From browsing sites to electronic mail, to file transfer, to programming support, to imbedded applications, to a publishing toolbox, the new products put everything under the Navigator banner. As of this writing, no one else is even close. This book explains these new products, how to use them, and what they will mean for Internet users and Web site developers.

The purpose of *60 Minute Guides* is to provide understandable, easily referenced books that put you quickly into the Internet driver's seat. If we've done our jobs right, readers can move from blank tablets to active users well before the book is finished. If you're an old hand at Navigator products, your learning curve is going to be even faster. You have a built-in context to understand just how significant this new generation of tools will be for you. Either way, this book is written for users both new and experienced. It's meant to be both an *introduction* to the Internet, the Web, and the new Netscape software; and a *reference* for users to consult when they wish to explore new facets of this important technology.

Part I

The first section of this book takes you into the basics of the Internet, World Wide Web, browsers, and what you need to know before you actually load up your software and venture into cyberspace.

In **Chapter 1**, you learn how the Internet evolved from a doomsday communications system in the 1960s to the most expansive and exciting source of information in the world today. You're also given a step-by-step guide to selecting your Internet services provider — or ISP — and learn what role a provider plays in your total Internet experience.

Chapter 2 introduces you to Netscape Navigator 2.0. Here you learn just why you need to examine the new generation of browsers — hint: because they do vastly more than let you "browse." You see the new dimensions of this sprawling, constantly evolving wonder called the Internet. The primary advances in Netscape Navigator 2.0 are then examined in easily understood language, illustrating along the way what they are and interesting ways to use them. The book briefly covers the advanced e-mail client application, Navigator's newsreader, its improved browsing facilities, the new level of security, and new plug-ins that add functionality to Navigator 2.0.

In **Chapter 3**, we actually get you up and running. The book takes you through the installation process for Netscape Navigator's products. This book was written primarily using Netscape's Windows 95 version of Navigator 2.0. This chapter details how to get Navigator, how to download it, install it, and configure it for operation. The good news is, even if you aren't a technical person, getting and using Netscape Navigator 2.0 is a relatively easy job. So is using it once you've gotten it up and running.

Chapter 4 illustrates the new electronic mail and newsreader functions that now are controlled from the Navigator "dashboard." You no longer need to leave the browser screen to load a separate program; e-mail can be invoked with a single click right from Navigator. The new newsreader offers access to, and organization of, your newsgroups, again, right from the main Navigator screen.

Chapter 5 details the spectrum of other new features in Navigator 2.0 that help you deal with images and document presentation. This chapter looks at frames, the highly productive new way to view three or more documents simultaneously. You explore Netscape Chat, an interactive, configurable Internet chat product that gives you access to any of a variety of chat rooms and even allows you to create your own. In this chapter you're introduced to the new inline plug-ins that add functionality to Navigator, such as Adobe Acrobat Amber, which allows you to read intact graphic documents, and VRML, which brings virtual reality access to the Internet. You learn about the new levels of security that enable users to transact business or exchange information on the Internet with confidence.

Chapter 6 then takes you on a tutorial walkthrough of everything you've learned about the Internet and Netscape Navigator 2.0. You test all features and functions for yourself, from sending an e-mail message to accessing a newsgroup to downloading a file. When you're done you'll have had, in about 60 minutes, a pretty good look at the possibilities that lie before you on the Internet.

Part II

In the second section we look at Netscape Navigator Gold 2.0, a product that includes all the functionality of Navigator 2.0 but adds a rich array of publishing tools. This is software for people who are developing or maintaining Web sites and want to add all the visual dynamism today's technology affords them. If you are an Internet user but not a Web site builder, you could skip these chapters, but we strongly recommend you read at least Chapter 7. This overview of Navigator Gold 2.0 basics will open your eyes to the marvels you'll be seeing on the Internet: applications (known as "applets"), animation, enhanced images, secure transactions, and more. These marvels could reshape your notions about how deeply you want to be involved in this amazing technology.

Perhaps you'll want to publish your own home page. Maybe you'll want to describe — or demonstrate — your skills, products, and services there. If you have a business, you now can put an autonomously functioning version of it right on the Internet. It can often take customers from contact to contract, order the goods, arrange the delivery, and electronically deposit the money. Last year, $300 million worth of commerce was conducted via the Internet. Can you guess where that figure is headed?

In **Chapter 7**, you learn what Navigator Gold 2.0 is, how it works, and how to determine whether you need it. This chapter also provides an overview of the publishing features found in the software.

Chapter 8 is a practical exercise for creating the 60 minute page. Here you learn the fundamentals of Navigator's HTML editor, how to use the highly functional toolbar, and the creation techniques that can make pages jump off the screen.

Chapter 9 looks in more detail at the inline plug-ins that can bring new depth, motion, sound, and quality to your Web pages. This chapter gives you a description of the applications programming interface technology that makes the world of plug-ins possible. Dozens of inline plug-in products are then listed and briefly described.

Chapter 10 is for Web authors who want to take Navigator Gold beyond the basics in creating their pages. Here you learn the details of how the Navigator programming interface and other features allow you to customize and expand your Navigator and Navigator Gold experience. You get some of Gold's best secrets for developing sites that not only look great but also generate interest, business, and marketing effectiveness.

Throughout the book we try to point to concrete examples and live sites. Just as a vacation is better when you leave the map and actually go somewhere, your 60 minute tour is enhanced when you have a chance to go where the action is. Netscape's new tools are simple to set up, so getting on the on-ramp of the information superhighway is a breeze. Just don't leave your map at home.

Conventions Used in This Book

The *60 Minute Guide* series is designed to share information simply and efficiently. To that end, a word of explanation about the conventions used in the book.

- Whenever possible, we direct you to live sites to allow you a first-hand look at what we consider excellent examples of a given feature or application.

- Whenever there is a procedure, you are shown its sequence in numbered steps.

- Sidebars are used whenever a point of discussion arises that requires some background or clarification. Sometimes a sidebar is simply an interesting side-alley bit of trivia related to the main topic.

Part **One**

Introducing Netscape Navigator 2.0

- Getting Ready to Go Online
- Netscape Navigator 2.0 Basics
- Getting Netscape Navigator 2.0 Up and Running
- Managing E-Mail and Newsgroups
- Images and Document Presentation
- The 60 Minute Navigator Test Run

Chapter 1

Getting Ready to Go Online

T his chapter is intended to serve as a primer on cyberspace, the term for the dynamic world of interconnected computers, communications, documents, databases, and images that lies at your fingertips. You are introduced to the Internet and its exciting new spawn, the World Wide Web. You learn what to consider when selecting your Internet Services Provider (ISP) before you actually install your new Navigator software.

You don't have to be a computer scientist to enjoy the wonders of the Internet. The Netscape Navigator 2.0 software described in this book is extremely user-friendly even to novices — **newbies** as they're called in the jargon of cyberspace. But the fact is that the Internet still is a technology-based medium that has its own vocabulary. Spending a little time in this chapter can help alleviate hunting up terms and concepts later in the book. And it can help you get off on the right foot by showing you how to establish a relationship with an ISP best suited to grow with your Internet needs.

The Internet and the World Wide Web

The Internet, in spite of what the general press may have implied, isn't new. It's actually a thirty-year-old technology. The Internet began life in the 1960s as a communications alternative in the event that a nuclear attack took out conventional communications. For most of the next three decades it served as an electronic mail and file-access system for government, the military, and academicians who wanted to share research. But, because it was text-based, mainframe-dependent, and fairly complex, it languished outside the popular culture. Until the 1990s, it had hardly any role in the lives, businesses, and information of most people. The latest generation of fast personal computers, along with some superb browsing software, changed all that.

The Advent of Browsers and Hypertext

Physically, the Internet today is made up of millions of computers linked to one another. They range in size from huge Cray supercomputers to the personal computer on your desktop. What allows you to become part of the Internet is that you can use tools that enable you to speak the language of the Internet. These tools use standards and protocols called TCP/IP that you will rarely actually see. By using these tools, you gain access to millions of documents, thousands of companies, huge information databases, and tens of thousands of actual people. Once you become familiar with navigating — the verb du jour is "surfing" — the Internet, you can find and organize information on the subjects that interest you. You can even **bookmark** your favorite Internet addresses, called Uniform Resource Locators or URLs, so you can visit them quickly and easily. In many ways, having Internet access is like having a vast electronic library right on your desk, but without the late fees.

The Internet rose to prominence in 1990 when scientists at CERN, the European Laboratory for Particle Physics in Switzerland, came up with the first prototype for a **browser**. A browser is software that uses special commands that enable users to move around the Internet just by clicking on highlighted **hypertext** words. With hypertext, viewers could look, for example, at a document in the category of automobiles, then click on the hypertext word "engines," which took them to a related document; then click on the word "pistons" and get still more information. Still, there were practical limitations to surfing. Everything was pretty much textual, and the slowness of the PCs people used kept more exotic developments, such as graphic images, out of reach.

But the work of the CERN scientists set the stage for the most important catalyst in the history of the Internet — the World Wide Web. When the Web (which is how we refer to it in most of this book) opened the doors to efficient use of hypertext, graphics, sound, animation, and video over the Internet in the early '90s, nothing had changed the world of information so instantly and forever. And nothing has facilitated the growth in the number of Internet users like the Web.

The first Web graphical browser, called NCSA Mosaic, was built at the National Center for Supercomputing Applications (NCSA) and came to market in 1993, capturing two million users within a year. Suddenly, individuals and organizations could see, read, hear, navigate, and participate on the Internet in ways they could easily understand and creatively embrace. What had been a purely textual medium for 30 years was suddenly alive with color and images, along with the information bridges called hypertext links.

The Web and its navigation tools instantly took the Internet from being primarily an electronic mail and file viewing network for academia and the military to a global publishing medium that anyone could use. Today there are more than an estimated 30 million Internet users worldwide. The fastest-growing segment by far are Web users. And the one thing that all Web users have in common is the browser.

Netscape Navigator Enters the Scene

The original Netscape Navigator 1.0 was released in December 1994. Designed chiefly by a student at the University of Illinois named Marc Andreessen (who also was a staff member of the National Center for Supercomputing Applications during the period when NCSA Mosaic was developed), the new browser was an instant hit. Its ability to provide secure transfers of information, present text for viewers to read while waiting for the graphic images to load, color-changes on hypertext links to let you know you'd already been to that site — all won users over in a flash. In addition, Netscape Communications Corporation, which Andreesson founded with Jim Clark, made the Navigator browsers available as **shareware**. Prospective users could try it to see if they liked it before laying out any money — a policy that also applies to the new generation of Navigator products.

One of the most significant aspects of the new Navigator products is that they support what could be called the complete Internet, not just the Web. Millions of users new to the Internet think that what they have seen while surfing the Web is all there is to see and do. It isn't. You probably know about electronic mail, or e-mail, which lets you send messages to people anywhere in the world, as long as they are on the Internet. But with Navigator 2.0, e-mail communications have advanced even further. E-mail can now include hypertext links, secure documents, and more right in the text of your message. There is also file transfer, by which you can send and receive program files, databases, and other coded or formatted information. Newsgroups allow you to subscribe to information sources that post information on the Internet at more than 11,000 sites, including electronic bulletin boards on specific subjects such as Java programming or Madonna.

It's useful, when you're contemplating which browser you're going to go with, to understand that there are many facets to the Internet beyond surfing. This isn't just an information medium: It's also a medium for communication, presentation, and commerce. The more your browser is capable of supporting these activities, the better and more productive your Internet experience will be.

Selecting an Internet Service Provider

Before you can get up and running on the Internet, you need to find an organization that will serve as your Internet service provider, or ISP. If you are already on the Internet and satisfied with your provider, you can skip this section. But if you are just now taking your first tentative steps into cyberspace, you may find this section useful.

This choice is as important as your choice of browser or computer. Instead of a fast, reliable, well-supported, state-of-the-art window to the world, the wrong choice leaves you with eternal congestion at the server, unanswered helplines, confining ISP architectures, limited services, and expired patience.

The problem is the soaring popularity of the Internet, much of it stimulated by the capabilities of World Wide Web browsers that can turn streams of electrons into multimedia extravaganzas. A lot of entrepreneurs are hanging out service provider shingles today to attempt to cash in on that interest — some with only a nodding acquaintance with the needs of Net users. That makes your job of selection vital, and sometimes a little tricky.

The competition has produced a mixed bag of results. It has dramatically driven down connect charges, slashing them by two-thirds in some regions. The downside of the lower prices is that ISPs are competing for less money per user and trying to boost profits with market share. This sometimes means shaving expenditures in areas such as helplines, programming support, and equipment upgrades. That makes for a troublesome tradeoff.

What Should You Expect from an ISP?

One common mistake individual users make is thinking the Internet connection they have at work or school is the one they will enjoy on their home PC. It's not. Corporations and colleges — where many users are introduced to the Net — often come armed with fast communication links such as T1 or even T3 lines and frequently have their own networks and servers. This is all supplemented by speedy 486- or Pentium-class machines.

On systems such as these, downloading graphics from Web sites is almost as fast as changing channels on your TV. When you get home and try to do the same thing on your 386/33 with your 2400-baud modem, it's like waiting for Michelangelo to finish the Sistine Chapel. You spend more time treading water than surfing and end up turning off the graphics just so you can get a look at the text sometime before it goes out of date.

Beware of the fact that no ISP can compensate for antiquated equipment on your end. Think of the bottleneck metaphor. If transmission gets squeezed anywhere enroute, you end up with slower response times and a diminished experience on the Net.

Thus, before you search for a local provider, you should bring as much power to the party as you can afford, especially if you intend to become a serious Internet user. This is especially true if you want to use the World Wide Web, which has colorful graphics, video clips, animation, and sound, all in addition to the text. Of course, all of that takes up memory and processing time, which an older, slower personal computer won't handle well.

Minimum Requirements

If you want to use the Web, you need a minimum of a 486/60-class computer, 14.4 modem, and eight megabytes of RAM (Random Access Memory). That configuration enables you to navigate effectively and download most of what you'll find on the Web. You can help your cause considerably by committing fully to a Pentium-class machine with 100 MHz bus, 16 megabytes of RAM, and a 28.8 modem.

What Kind of User Will I Be?

After you've made the equipment commitment, it's time to figure out what kind of user you will be. It isn't hard and will save you a lot of grief. When you know how you'll use the Net, you can better find someone who will support that use.

If you're just playing around, checking out chat rooms and looking for Web pages celebrating '57 Chevies, you do not have to be particularly picky. Look for the lowest-cost option, but check with some existing users first to make sure peak-time congestion and helplines are not a problem. Make sure the ISP supports the World Wide Web and the various media that make it as colorful and valuable as it can be, such as e-mail, graphics, video, and audio.

If you're more serious about using the Net, you'll want to take advantage of the other facilities it offers, such as electronic mail, file transfer, and newsgroup access. All these facilities come with Navigator 2.0, but some providers (increasingly a minority) don't support them. Using these requires an upgrade in your choice of providers.

If you think you may want to establish your own Web page, you will want only the best area provider. Answer this question before you start looking for your ISP.

What Is the Reputation of the Company?

Now you're ready to begin your search. Start with a general business evaluation. Look for companies that have been in business for awhile. But only look for those that have had both new customer growth and good retention of old customers. Defections from an Internet provider are a red flag for high costs and poor service. Find out whether the ISP, as its business grew, added servers and improved its network by adding, for example, a high-quality commercial router instead of using aging hardware. Or is it squeezing everyone onto its original configuration? Time in business alone isn't enough; a good ISP will demonstrate growth and undiminished service. Your local computer club will have a boatload of Net users, and it would be an excellent place to ask these fundamental questions. You can track down computer clubs through the Yellow Pages, various gratis publications you can find at local newsstands, or even your prospective ISP.

Who Are the Customers?

Find a customer base that looks like who you are and what kind of Internet user you want to be. If you're a casual user, you probably don't need endless raw power, multiple helplines, and a Web site development staff. But if you're a serious user, these factors are important. When you find an ISP candidate, speak with others who already use the service. Talk to those who have needs similar to your own. Are they satisfied? Find out if the ISP is dependent upon one or two large companies and their user bases to stay in business. Most ISPs have hypertext links to sites they've developed for individuals and businesses. Use those links to locate customers and ask questions. Is the ISP responsive? Do users often get "can't access" or "busy signal" messages? Is its billing as advertised, or are there hidden charges? Can you reach a person when automated messages don't have an answer to your problem?

A good ISP also allows you to grow on the Internet. How easy has it been for users to add new services? How expensive has it been? Will you need to switch providers if you want a state-of-the-art service level? If you're a user, changing ISPs usually isn't difficult. If you have a Web site your current ISP is maintaining, you need to find out what is involved in transferring your old site to your new ISP if your current ISP isn't providing the service you need.

Is the ISP a Member of Professional Associations?

ISPs can join professional associations that promote customer service, new technology, and professional management within their rapidly growing market. The Commercial Internet Exchange Association (**http:// www.cix.org/**) is one group that offers this type of membership. It also apprises members of regulatory issues and provides a forum for them to stay abreast of — and even recommend the formulation of — laws and regulations that affect Internet use. Conscientious ISPs then pass that information along to their users.

Understanding the ISP's Network

If you intend to be a serious user, it's important that you find out about the ISP's physical network topology and strategy. These are fancy terms they may use that refer to how much data traffic their computers and communications lines can handle. Some things to consider:

- How many computers does the ISP have on its network?
- How many computers are accepting modem phone calls?
- How many modems do the computers have?
- Is the bandwidth sufficient to handle all of the calls?
- Can the bandwidth support large data transfers such as a large Web site may need?
- How many users are on a single line?

Good ISPs are usually free with this information. But make sure the ISP is giving you a map of its physical network, not its virtual network. The physical network represents the real-life paths of Internet usage. The virtual network represents all possible routes in the area that the ISP services in theory and can be used to make the ISP's services appear more extensive than they actually are.

This information is important because it tells you how intelligently the ISP has designed its network to move information quickly. For example, if the ISP has a slow link sending data out — say, 56 Kbps (extremely slow for an ISP) — then you'll receive that data slowly, no matter what computer and modem you have at home. You'll receive information at the maximum speed the ISP offers and your modem accepts (although factors such as the number of users logged on and the quality of the ISP's hardware slow down the real-world speed you see). Thus, your system and the ISP's need to have some harmony. A system is only as fast as its slowest bottleneck.

Understanding Your ISP's Backbone

The key area to inquire about is the network **backbone**. This is the main artery of communications to which all other computers, networks, routers, and other devices are attached. Many of today's ISP's use at least one T1 link as a backbone. A T1 link can transfer data at the rate of 1.54 megabits per second. Even faster is a T3 link, which can transfer data many times faster, at 45 megabits per second. These rates represent the **bandwidth**. You may find ISPs that have bandwidth ranging from 56 kilobits per second (as noted, extremely slow for an ISP) to four T3s, as my own provider has. Generally, the greater the bandwidth, the fewer bottlenecks you'll run into sending and receiving information. Here's a good situation, although one you'll likely only find with large ISPs:

- **An operational T3 high-speed backbone.** Just make certain it is installed and not merely "planned."

- **Multiple external links.** Be sure the ISP has more than one link to the world; a single connection means total shutdown when the connection fails and, sooner or later, it will.

- **We never close support.** Is the Network Support desk staffed constantly? It should be. "On Call" support isn't good enough for a serious Internet user. The Internet is global and not subject to time zones for its operation. Not every provider will have the resources for 24-hour/7-day onsite support; but if you have a globally-used Web site, you need to find one that does.

Understanding Your Options

When you find the ISPs that have the right business equation, you need to learn which services they offer. Choosing among them will again depend on which services you need. Here are some points to consider.

Should You Choose a Local or National Provider?

The types of ISPs entering the business range from one-server, two-man local operations to national outlets that can put you on the Net from anywhere for the price of a local call by using their 800 number. Your local ISP could be either one or something in between. There is no universal answer. Your choice should depend on how you intend to use the Internet.

If you go with a large national company because of its name and security, you could be well-served but sometimes pay more than you need to (conversely, you could pay less, too; knowing your regional rate structures is imperative when comparing them to national rates). This is because national providers compete in a national market and price their service based on broad market averages. That average could be more or less than the structure that exists in your particular market.

A local provider with reliable service and lower costs may be the better choice. On the other hand, if you travel a lot, are likely to use the service on the road, and the pricing is acceptable, a national provider such as Total Internet Access (info@earthlink.net), whose Internet software we have included in this book, could save you dramatically on long-distance charges and give you nationwide access instantly.

Should I Buy My Internet Services from a Commercial Provider?

Don't do this unless you are independently wealthy. Once commercial providers such as CompuServe, America Online, The Microsoft Network, and Prodigy saw themselves losing customers to Internet service providers, all developed Web browsers and Net connectivity. The problem is the cost. All these providers have nifty and useful services in their basic service lineups. They have accumulated millions of users worldwide because they have made online information simple and organized in a way that the Internet is not, and they demand no technical knowledge while boasting great 24-hour support. But they tend to charge way too much for volume Internet usage and restrict some of the places you can visit; for example, CompuServe banned access to certain non-adult-oriented gay and lesbian newsgroups and some adult-oriented Web services on the Internet because of complaints from German authorities. AOL caused a big stir when it banned the word "breast" on its services in an overzealous attempt to curb "indecent" communications. Unfortunately it also curbed needed discussions among breast cancer survivors. Since then, these situations have been addressed, but the shadow of censorship remains.

If you are going to be a limited Internet user who would use the friendly non-Internet services of the commercial providers, then getting your Internet access through them would be a good choice. But if you're going to be even a semi-serious Internet user, find an ISP. You don't have to give up your commercial account (they are terrific for many things), just don't use it for the Internet.

What's a Shell Account and Should I Buy It?

You may hear the words **shell access** and **shell account** when you start talking to ISPs. This is a low-cost (as low as $5/month) account that you'll see running only on terminal emulators by using UNIX command lines. Simply put, shell accounts are text-based, while SLIP/PPP accounts are graphical. These accounts are called shell because you aren't connected directly to the Internet. You send UNIX commands to the ISP host, which connects you to the Internet. Your PC just displays the communications between the ISP's computer and other hosts. Some Windows programs can run over the shell's UNIX interfaces.

Shell accounts are fine for technical people who want to create programs, or individuals who want only text. Some ISPs use the term shell account to mean you can use their service in conjunction with your new ISP's better Web services. But the advice here is that shell access should not be considered if you can possibly go with another option such as PPP or SLIP. Shell access doesn't allow you to run most of the excellent supplemental applications that you can get with other accounts. There are some helpful programs, however. A relatively new add-on is called The Internet Adapter (TIA). TIA runs over the shell account and acts like a SLIP account. It does a pretty good job of making it seamless, but a **WinSock**-based connection (WinSock means "Windows Socket" and is the standard TCP/IP connection for Windows-based computers) still gives you the most flexibility with far less clumsiness and with only a little more cost.

Pricing for Your Internet Service

In your search for an ISP, look for a flat-rate account. Here you pay one monthly charge, usually for unlimited access. A pseudo flat-rate (not an option everywhere; usually in urban centers) account gives you a flat rate for something like 120 hours a month (it might as well be unlimited; if you're spending more time than that on the Net, you're losing your humanity). After that an ISP charges per hour.

Bear in mind that some access providers don't bill their Internet usage the same way they bill access to their regular services. So when you think you are getting "10 free hours" per month, that may be referring to regular services, while Internet access charges accumulate from the first hour.

You may run into variations, some of which you should be aware of. Restricted flat-rate accounts impose policies whereby you might be on for two hours, then off for two. The idea is to prevent abuse by someone logging on and staying inactive, while tying up a modem for long periods. Other systems log you out if there is no connection traffic passing for some period of minutes.

You want to avoid the per-hour accounts if you think you will become a serious Internet user. The bill can get out of hand quickly, and it is distracting always worrying about the meter running. Of course, if you're a casual user racking up only a few hours a week, it can be more cost-effective just to use the "free" hours usually provided in the basic service fee of a commercial provider, such as CompuServe.

In most markets, Internet users can expect to get connected for a small start-up fee (in the $20 to $50 range, although sometimes it is waived to get the customer) and a monthly flat rate or pseudo-flat rate where you can be connected for 100 or more hours for $15 to $30. If you have a 28.8 modem instead of the 14.4 modem, which most individuals have, the charge could be slightly higher. In some markets, eager entrepreneurs have lowered costs to as little as $7.50 a month for unlimited access. It's appealing, but you have to be careful that the business equation of your ISP supports a technical staff and equipment upgrades.

Some ISPs may require you to maintain service with them for a given period of time, but this is the exception. Even large commercial providers stop billing when you tell them to. Given today's technology and competitive environment, Internet access should be easy to start and easy to stop.

Map Your Internet Alternatives

The following table provides a worksheet to help you with your selection process.

Selecting an Internet Service Provider

Criterion	Provider A	Provider B	Provider C	Provider D
Monthly fee				
Free hours per month				
Charge for additional hours				
Number of customers				
Number of modems				
Customers per modem				
Bandwidth to Internet				
E-mail provided				
FTP provided				
Newsreader provided				
24-hour tech support				

Look for Lots of Service and Functionality

In the end, you should expect a lot from your ISP. Much of what you need to have fruitful Internet access is either extremely cheap or completely free. By asking a few questions beforehand and adhering to your baseline expectations, you can bring the window to the world into your home, and it costs precious little to open it. Let no one tell you otherwise.

The Mechanics of Connecting to the Internet

One of the first things you should consider in establishing your connection to the Internet is how you will interface with it. For that you need to understand something about various access options and protocols.

What Are TCP/IP and WinSock?

If you're a Windows user (WinSock doesn't apply to Macintosh or UNIX machines), you'll want to seriously consider using WinSock, the standard for Windows-based Internet access. It comes in various implementations — for example, Trumpet WinSock, NEWT, Chameleon, Internet Chameleon, and Internet In A Box — but the idea is the same. They all allow your Windows PC to speak **TCP/IP**, the language of the Internet. TCP/IP (Transfer Control Protocol/Internet Protocol) is just a way to move information and without WinSock, the information is simply gibberish.

A good ISP probably will provide you with a copy of free WinSock software, or you can buy more sophisticated versions in a bookstore or software shop. This software must be installed with great care (no, you don't need a technician, just attention to detail). But after that, you probably won't know it's there. Prices range from around $500 to low-cost shareware to free (Trumpet WinSock, for example, is a free program and often is distributed on a disk by the ISP, or can be downloaded). NetManage's Internet Chameleon, on the other hand, comes with more WinSock applications than the shareware (such as a good Archie client, which is a file-searching utility). Your choice, again, depends on how you will use the Internet.

SLIP and PPP

Serial Line Internet Protocol (SLIP) and **Point to Point Protocol** (PPP) were developed because millions of people who didn't have network access wanted to get on the Internet. They are communication protocols (or languages) that make your PC operate as if it is attached to a network connected to the Internet. Instead, of course, you are just using a modem, not a network. SLIP and PPP access is vastly slower than network access but, nevertheless, they provide the missing link.

If you are connected to a network directly, for example, through a university, then of course you don't need SLIP or PPP. A network connection at this level, through what's known as a T1 line is not something an individual would normally have at home (as nice as that would be). It's just too expensive. T1 lines move data at 1.54 megabits per second, meaning one and a half million bits of information every second. Their faster cousins are called T3 lines; these move data at 45 megabits per second and are designed for handling a large number of users linked in at a single site, such as a business. When you don't have this kind of network access, you use the alternatives designed for at-home users, such as SLIP and PPP.

There are a number of differences between SLIP and PPP, although both work well. PPP is the recommended choice because it is more flexible in its support of various network protocols (for example, NetBEUI, IPX, TCP/IP, and even AppleTalk) at the same time over the same connection. SLIP was designed with much more simplicity, which many users find appealing (it is reputed to have been designed on an envelope, then built in an afternoon). That simplicity has made it the most prevalent account, but not the most functional. If your ISP offers only SLIP, and your applications work well with it, there is no reason to change service providers just to get PPP. There are several commercial implementations of SLIP and PPP.

If your ISP and local telephone company both offer Integrated Services Digital Network (ISDN) service, you can get a big speed boost by using your regular PPP or SLIP access on it instead of by using a regular phone line and modem. In essence, ISDN is a digital telephone system. Your current telephone system is probably an analog. An ISDN connection would give you a speed boost from the current top analog speed of 28.8 Kbps to the top digital speed of 128 Kbps. It usually costs more, but the jump in speed might be worth it for you. As a rule of thumb, anything you can do to speed up your Internet service is a good idea.

Be warned that not all ISPs are set up to offer ISDN. About three-quarters of the country's area codes are being offered ISDN service. The cost to get started is about $200 on the low end with a $40 monthly charge, plus a small online fee — so it isn't a casual expenditure. Some providers have dropped the online fee in favor of a high installation cost of $500 or more.

Your User ID, Password, and Domain Name

ISPs need to be able to distinguish you and your account, and **user IDs** —
user identification names — are how they do it. User IDs are for logging
on to your account and using your e-mail. User-friendly ISPs enable you to
pick a user ID name (as long as it's not already in use) that is closely identi-
fied with you — for example, "bill" for William Jefferson Clinton. Other
ISPs just assign you a name, such as "bclinton." A few still like to play
pointless technoid games and give you a computer-generated handle such
as "87urfn93."

You also need to obtain a password to go with your user ID. It should be
at least eight characters in length (fewer than that and your password is too
easily cracked) and should contain at least one number. Don't use your
name or your birthdate or anything else that might be conspicuously
associated with you. Your ISP will probably give you a temporary password. It's up to you to change it.

The **domain name** is the name of your ISP's network. You use it to send
electronic mail, among other things. For example, if your provider is
Iquest, the domain name might be iquest.com. Your e-mail name would
then be something such as user ID@iquest.com. If you want to create your
own Web page on the Internet, you could be issued a domain name for
your own address — for example, mycompany.com. And your e-mail
address there would be user ID@mycompany.com. However, you don't
have to have a domain name to have your own Web page. Most full-service
ISPs allow you to set up a page either way. The difference is whether you
have a domain name formally registered with InterNIC, the sanctioning
organization. You can do this registration yourself with InterNIC (for a $50
annual fee), and no one else can use the name.

Internet Protocol Addresses

With some 30 million Internet users worldwide, a numerical scheme had
to be devised to identify each machine on the Net. This scheme is called
the **Internet Protocol address** (IP). There are more than four billion
combinations, but that hasn't stopped the same number from being
mistakenly issued to more than one person on a few occasions. You need to
request that your ISP provide you with an IP address for your computer.

The two types of IP addressing are dynamic and static. In all likelihood
you will receive dynamic addressing from your ISP. If you are a dial-up
user, which most individuals are, this means that the ISP's host

computer will assign you a unique IP address for the particular session you are in. When you log off, that address will be available again. When you connect later, dynamic addressing gives you a new IP address.

In some rare circumstances, an ISP will provide you with a static IP address which will be used every time you log on to the Internet. But this is by far the exception and not the rule. Of course, if you want to create a Web page with a domain name, a static IP address is necessary so that people can find your page. You can technically have a Web page without your own domain name and have a dynamic address. While having a static IP address is not required in order for people to find a publisher's Web page, it is useful. Because purchasing usage of a single static IP address usually comes with a user-specified domain name attached to it, it can make for a more easily accessed site. Make certain you request complete information about this from your ISP. If you're just surfing, a dynamic address is fine.

Internet Applications

If you are a serious user, your ISP should support some of the standard applications that really make the Internet a fantastic resource. With a small amount of reasonably priced (or free) software, you can send e-mail to any other Net user anywhere in the world, download and upload program files, and access information from all newsgroups that interest you.

Electronic Mail

The most common application on the Internet is **electronic mail** or e-mail. Avoid an ISP that doesn't support it with both products and expertise. Even if you're not a person of letters, so to speak, the nature of the Internet is such that you are in company with many people and organizations and, sooner or later, you'll want to say something to them. E-mail products such as Eudora (which is free) make both the installation and use of the product simple. Navigator 2.0 includes a new e-mail application you can invoke right from the Navigator "dashboard." Most direct Internet e-mail costs nothing.

Newsreaders

Think of these programs as special-interest access tools. They allow you to link into newsgroups and electronic bulletin boards (BBSs) where users discuss (sometimes with volcanic tension) specific subjects. A variety of newsreaders is available, but one public domain application that can make your Internet news exploration worthwhile is called News XPress. Because it is a public domain product, ask your ISP if it is provided along with the basic service. It is loaded right along with your e-mail, WinSock (or connectivity software), and other applications. Navigator 2.0 provides newsgroup access as part of its new functionality. If you are installing Navigator, you don't need another newsgroup access application.

Another useful question to ask your prospective ISP is whether it restricts access to certain newsgroups, either for storage reasons (there are several thousand groups on Usenet, for example) or for content reasons. Because access to information is one of the main reasons that people use the Internet, the filtering out of certain groups may impact a user's choice of an ISP.

File Transfer Protocol (FTP)

FTP is the protocol or set of commands used to translate file formats and send them from one place to another. More data is fired through the Internet every day via FTP than even e-mail (though the latter is a more common application, the former is used for much bigger transfers). Any serious user will most likely use FTP to send or receive all types of files. Like e-mail and newsreaders, FTP should be considered a basic part of your Internet service. Again, there are low-cost and no-cost options for FTP. WS_FTP is available free (you can download it from: **ftp:// ftp.usma.edu/pub/msdos/ws_ftp.zip**), though there are commercial FTP products available that enable you to move files a little more simply. A good ISP bundles FTP software into its basic service.

Summary

If you are a first-time Internet user, or are looking at reasons to upgrade your ISP, this chapter helped answer some of your more important questions and considerations. Nothing improves your understanding of the look, feel, and potential of the Internet like actually getting onto it. But the points touched on here — understanding what the Internet and World Wide Web are, getting some command of the jargon of cyberspace, and learning the critical aspects of selecting your ISP — can prepare you to sit back, buckle up, and step on the gas with a degree of comfort.

Once you've selected your ISP and looked at some software tools, your Internet adventure is ready to begin. Now it's a matter of which software you choose to navigate through that adventure. The rest of this book is devoted to explaining the software that many users believe is the best on the market, Netscape Navigator 2.0.

Chapter 2

Netscape Navigator 2.0 Basics

T his chapter gives you an overview of what all the fuss is about with Netscape Navigator 2.0. The product boasts an array of new features and support for helper applications called **plug-ins** that are designed to complement Navigator's functionality. This chapter introduces you to client applications such as e-mail and newsreaders. You begin to see the exciting new ways in which you can view and interact with the Internet and the World Wide Web because of the support for a technology called **frames**, and programming languages such as Java and JavaScript.

While the discrete components of Navigator make interesting stories individually, it is the fact that so much of the Internet's functionality has been pulled together into one place that makes the total package so compelling. Where once you would have had to leave your browser to send e-mail or visit a newsgroup, now that and more can be done right from your Navigator screen. You learn how the world of 3D and animation are now coming of age on the Web, thanks to technologies and tools supported by Navigator 2.0. And you find out why Web publishing — that is, the creation of the pages you see on the World Wide Web — has been made simultaneously simpler and more versatile with the features incorporated into Netscape Navigator Gold 2.0, the publisher's version of this new software.

> ## Just What Is a Client?
>
> You will often see references to three terms in learning more about Navigator 2.0: Clients, servers, and client applications. It's useful to understand these three fundamental aspects of Internet technology.
>
> **Server.** This refers to the computer that is sending, or "serving up," the information that is being sent out over the Internet. It can refer to any sending computer on the route, meaning the computer of origination or the server at your Internet service provider that provides the last link in the chain to you.
>
> **Client.** The client is the computer that sends out requests for something to be done over the Internet; for example, access to a newsgroup or a page on the Web. The computer you operate at home or work generally is regarded as the client because it is from there that you issue instructions to server computers. However, depending on whether you have Internet-accessible information on your computer, it could also be a server as well.
>
> **Client application.** These are the functional applications that work either inside Navigator or as a complement to it on your client computer. For example, you can send and receive e-mail right from the Navigator screen. You can access newsgroups, engage in chatroom conversations, and open portable documents via tools such as Adobe Acrobat Amber. All of these represent client applications that can be invoked from Navigator 2.0's screen.

Why Do I Need a New Navigator?

If you have been using the Internet with an earlier version of Navigator (1.x) or with one of the other browsers on the market such as Spry Mosaic, you have at least a vague sense of the changes that have taken place in Net technology. You've found yourself unable to access some Web sites because of messages saying something like: "This site was developed using Netscape Navigator 2.0," accompanied by an icon you can click on to download the software. You've seen references to applets and Java and JavaScript and frames. After a while, you get this gnawing sense that you're missing out on a lot of the Internet's most interesting advances.

You are.

When Netscape Communications introduced the beta versions of Navigator 2.0, it was immediately clear that the face of the Internet and the World Wide Web was making a quantum leap forward. The enhancements were so compelling that Netscape ceased referring to Navigator as a browser — a term indicating software that can move viewers from site to site around the Internet — and adopted the term **client**, because Navigator 2.0 utilized a range of new client applications within its framework. The control bar you can see near the top of the screen in Figure 2-1 provides instant access to a range of these client applications.

Useful Internet functions you previously had to perform with separate applications — e-mail, file transfer, newsreading — can be invoked from the primary Navigator browsing screen. In addition, heretofore unavailable goodies such as 3D graphics, interactive screens, and realtime displays have gone live. This is an umbrella product that can support the breakneck evolution of the Internet.

Figure 2-1: The Navigator 2.0 primary screen has evolved from a browser into a kind of Internet dashboard that lets you control all of the primary functions available to Internet users.

Navigator Gold 2.0 Is Navigator 2.0 Plus Web Publishing Tools

In the course of this book, references are made to features of two products: Navigator 2.0 and Navigator Gold 2.0. The former is Netscape Communications' product for conventional users of the Internet and the World Wide Web. The latter, Navigator Gold 2.0, refers to Netscape's product for Web developers and authors. It has all of the features contained in Navigator 2.0, but also contains a toolbox of utilities expressly designed for publishing Web pages. Whenever referring to a facility in Navigator 2.0, that facility is also a part of Navigator Gold 2.0. Facilities found only in Navigator Gold 2.0 are focused on in Part 2 of this book.

Netscape, despite being only a couple of years old, has done a good job of mastering life at the leading edge. Its 70 percent share of the browser market owes much to Netscape's quest to add extensions to HTML — HyperText Markup Language, the format language with which most Web pages are designed. Another significant factor is the company's policy of making the software available for downloading on a free trial basis.

But it's the improving functionality that keeps the Internet world interested. Navigator's browser client has evolved to a point where it leads every other browser, if only because it supports new languages such as Sun's Java and the embedding of HTML and live objects into what had been standard text. Other clients running under Navigator — such as e-mail and the newsreader — are also nice packages, even if they are not at the top of the functionality charts in their respective categories. There are more advanced commercial versions of both e-mail and newsreaders on the market, should your use of such applications demand them. But after running Navigator's, it's clear these versions will more than satisfy the average Internet user (see Figure 2-2).

These oft-used functions are now incorporated into the Navigator package, so you can get to them without having to switch out to a separate application. This makes Navigator 2.0 more of an Internet dashboard that allows users to do the three most popular Internet activities — browsing, e-mailing, and newsreading — from a common interface.

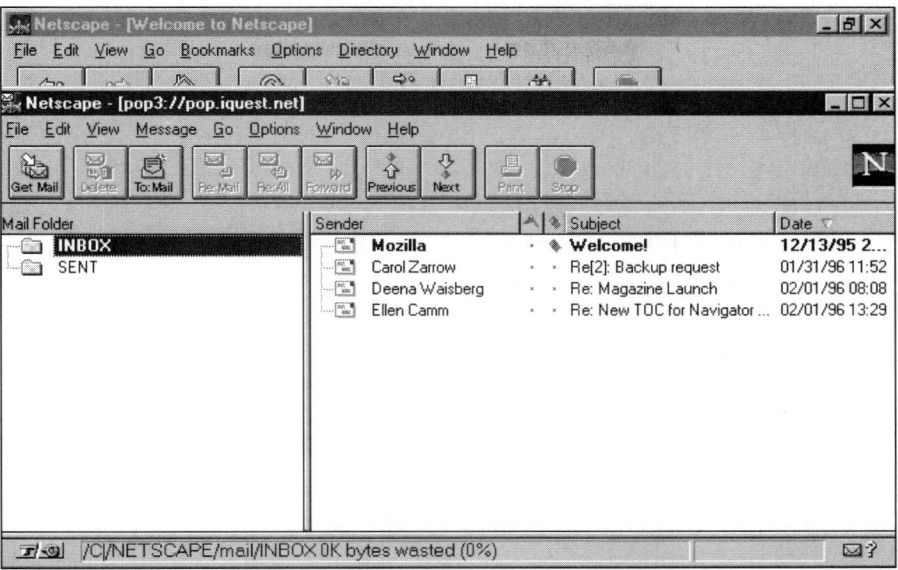

Figure 2-2: The new e-mail client presents a series of framed, scrollable information panes. The new newsreader utilizes the identical format to make finding, browsing, reading, and responding to mail and news simple.

Major Features of Netscape Navigator 2.0 and Navigator Gold 2.0

Beyond the incorporation of a range of convenient client applications into Navigator 2.0, Netscape's browser for normal Web users, and Navigator Gold 2.0, its publishing-rich product for Web authors and developers, there are other reasons to think about moving to the software. Browsing isn't just browsing anymore. As the page development technology has evolved, pages now incorporate motion (curious patriots can see the flags waving at **http://www.whitehouse.gov**), applications, problem-solving, split and coordinated frames, forms, financial transactions, 3D images, real-time displays, and CD-ROM-level color and interactivity. Before, a browser could take you to a page to see whatever text and (usually) primitive graphics were there, then let you make a hypertext jump to another document. That was pretty much it. It was essentially the cyberspace equivalent of window shopping.

The new world of the Internet — and particularly the World Wide Web — more closely approximates a hands-on shopping spree. Once you get to a site developed with Java, the revolutionary programming language developed by Sun Microsystems, or the inline plug-ins from Netscape, you're likely to find animation, working applications, realtime updating and interactivity, all awash in color and imagery you had thought was reserved for compact discs. As you can see in Figure 2-3, the Internet has gotten a facelift.

Realistically, Internet users dialing up with a 14.4 modem and visiting heavily trafficked sites could end up waiting several minutes for some pages to download into their computers. There is more and more density, functionality, and complexity being loaded into Web pages, and waiting is the price you pay. But if it's a site — or sight — you really want to see, you'll see it as never before.

VRML: Graphics Coming at You

One of the most promising concepts — although it still is in its infancy for Web use — is that of exotic three-dimensional images. The Web has evolved as a medium for presenting information, and many sites have used imaginative images to grab and keep Internet users. Until recently, those images were confined to two-dimensional representations. Now the advent of **VRML** — Virtual Reality Modeling Language — has opened up a world of possibilities for how Internet travelers will view and interact with sites on the Web (see Figure 2-4).

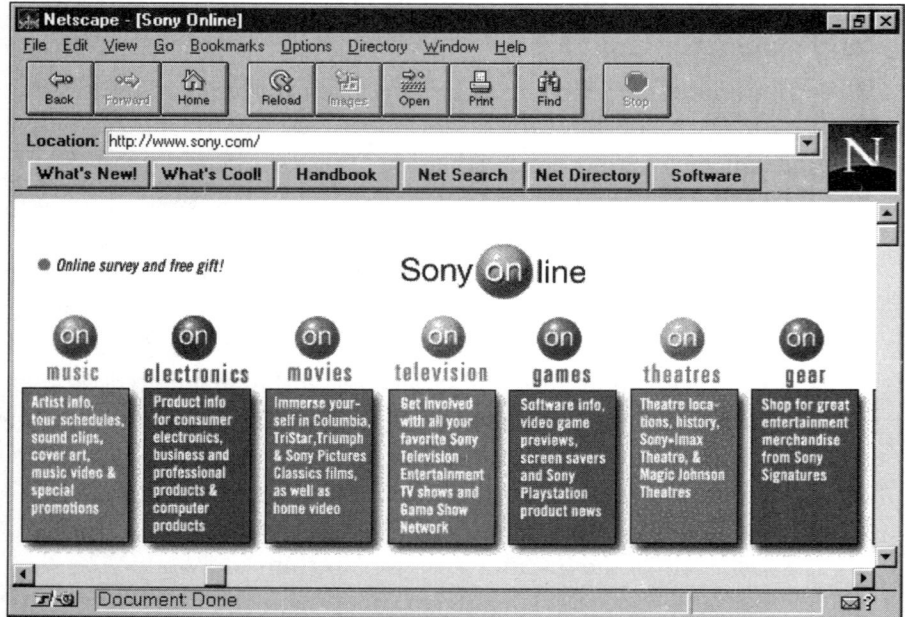

Figure 2-3: No longer just a medium for sending text and files, the Internet's World Wide Web is delivering every visual and aural medium than can be put on a computer.

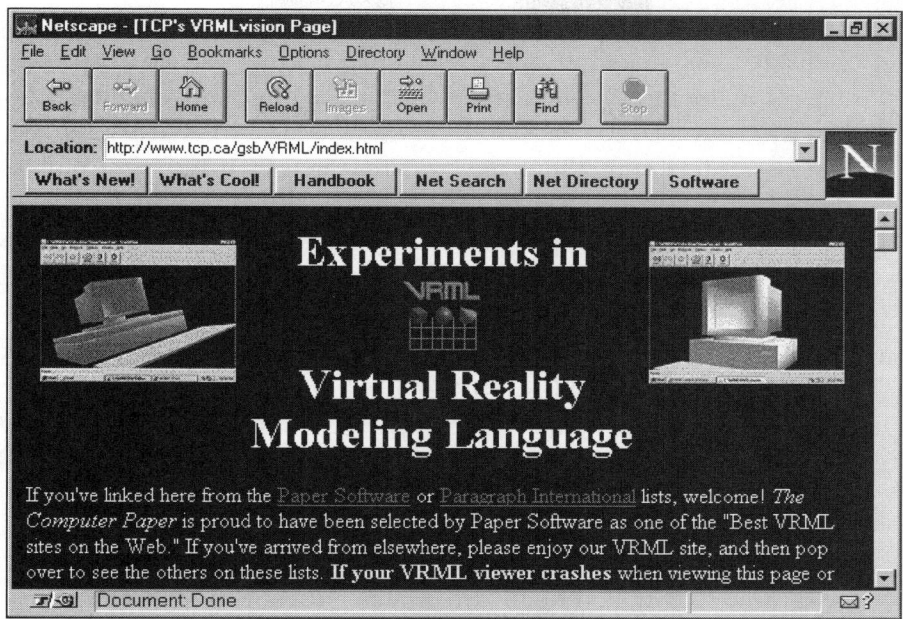

Figure 2-4: With only a VRML viewer, Navigator 2.0 can take you into the woolliest creations of virtual reality that have made it to the Internet — though at this writing they are still few and far between.

For those unfamiliar with virtual reality, it is the concept of putting you into a computerized "virtual" world and, by using graphical headsets to see and special gloves to manipulate objects in the virtual world, you can perform functions, access information, shoot bad guys — anything that has been programmed.

VRML-developed sites, which Navigator 2.0 allows you to visit with the assistance of software helpers called **plug-ins**, could be games, storefronts, real-time conferencing, or libraries, as long as you have the necessary viewing and interacting equipment. With VRML, you can go shopping and never leave home. The technology is still in its nascent stages, but already VRML is making an impact on Web site developers who are trying to figure out what kind of face they want on their site. The VRML answer is one that talks back.

Faster Browsing

Fast browsing is the sacred goal of everyone in the Web world, but it has been hindered by a range of bottlenecks. The Internet service provider's bandwidth is insufficient; your modem is too slow; your computer is too slow; your browser is too slow. Sometimes all of the above. The result is often a tedious wait while the browser sends a signal to a separate document or image in a distant server, where traffic might be congesting, and then tries to relay it to your screen over slow lines and modems. But Navigator 2.0 is streamlining the way it interacts with Web sites, and that means faster navigation for you.

In truth, most browsing you do from your PC will never be an exercise in lightspeed linking. As more people come onto the Internet and congest communications lines and servers, access speeds will be diminished. As graphics get more ponderous and complex (if more interesting), loading will take more time. Realistic expectations should be that navigating around the Web just isn't going to be like changing channels on your TV. Navigator 2.0 isn't a panacea for performance; the product delivers as much boost as you can get given the realities of the pages and people on the Net.

From the way it handles memory caches to its synergistic inline plug-ins, Navigator 2.0 has made significant strides in the technology that affects the speed, productivity, and fun of the browsing experience. Even client applications such as Navigator 2.0's newsreader load all information into a Navigator directory, so it doesn't have to keep making time-consuming circuits back to the news server. High performance is part of the Navigator 2.0 package.

New E-Mail Functionality and Simplicity

From the Internet dashboard of Navigator, you can send e-mail messages, program and graphics files, and even embedded HTML addresses — all without leaving Navigator. Historically, e-mail was sent by using a companion product such as Eudora. To use it, you had to alt-tab away from the browser screen, load the e-mail package, and send your messages. Navigator has brought both a new simplicity and new face to the e-mail function on the Internet (see Figure 2-5).

Instead of leaving your browser, Navigator 2.0 enables you to invoke e-mail right from the screen. Then you get a fully organized, three-pane window containing a variety of tools for managing your messages. You get an address book, file attachment facility, HTML support, mail list organizer, mail security features, and more. When you're done sending messages, close with a click and you're back into your Web page.

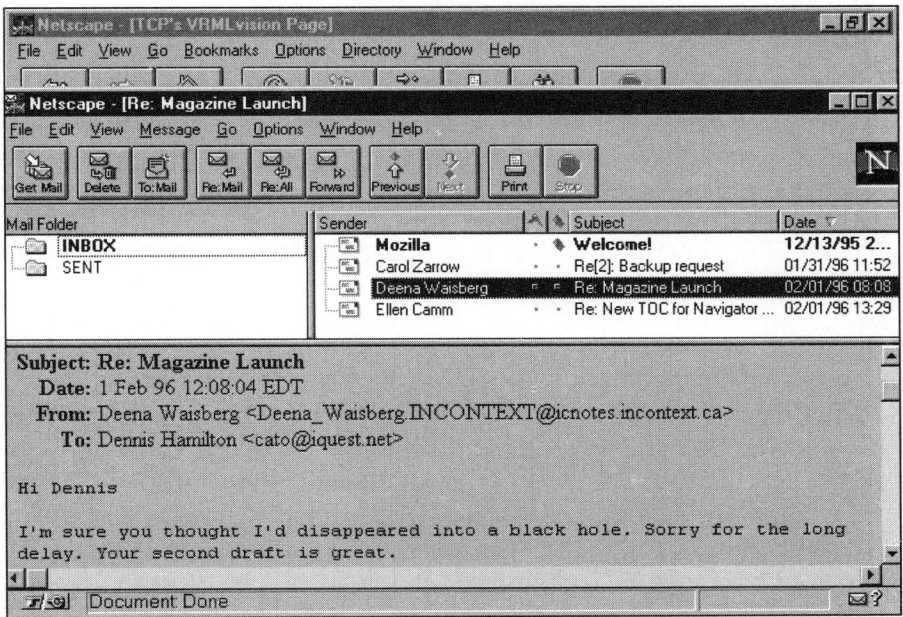

Figure 2-5: Just a click on the Navigator dashboard and your e-mail screen appears with information segregated into three panes.

Improved Newsreader

If you take part in newsgroups — Internet forums that share news, information, software, jobs, and more in just about any field — Navigator 2.0's new newsreader facilities give you another browser extra. Two-click access to your news subscriptions means you no longer need to invoke another application outside of Navigator 2.0. (See Figure 2-6.)

A three-pane window presents information by using the identical screen you find in your e-mail client. The **MIME**-compliant (Multipurpose Internet Mail Extensions) newsreader gives you the ability to bring your news postings to life with URLs, live objects, and images.

Improved Information Security

Security on the Internet has provoked a whirlwind of debate. If the public deemed the Net to be riddled with weaknesses, much of its potential never would be realized. Financial transactions would dry up, confidential information sharing would vanish, and the general sense of privacy, anonymity, and freedom the Internet was built on would be dead. Last year, $300 million dollars worth of commerce was conducted on the Internet,

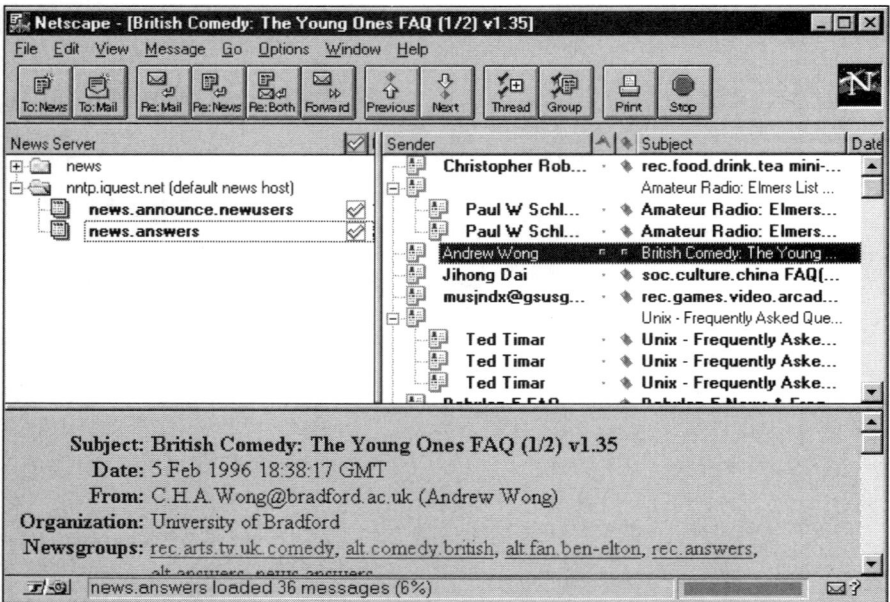

Figure 2-6: The Navigator newsreader organizes information in three panes, just as e-mail does. Files can be threaded to keep subjects logically grouped.

according to a year-end report from ABC News. While a great number for a new (the Web is essentially three years old) technology, some observers said it would have been far more had the general using public not feared security weaknesses.

Navigator 2.0 has implemented the Secure Courier open protocol to help raise the security bar to a higher level than ever (Internet communications, in truth, never have been terribly vulnerable; this makes them even less so now). This protection, in addition to the use of the Secure Sockets Layer (SSL) protocol through Navigator 2.0, assures that your e-mail, newsgroup articles and messages, and financial transactions move in special, untouchable electronic **envelopes** that, just like paper envelopes, shield the contents from prying eyes.

Inline Plug-Ins Go Online

As more Web pages come on stream around the world, Web authors attempt to incorporate more exotic elements such as sound, animation, and video. In the past, Web browsers could deliver these media only if the resident computer was using helper applications that supported those modes. Most often, a user would have to leave the browser screen to invoke the helper application.

Navigator 2.0 delivers what it has called **inline plug-in support**. This means that some plug-ins can actually be referenced in the HTML coding, providing the Web page viewer with a means of viewing files, such as MPEG videos, without having to resort to switching to helper applications outside of the browser. Other plug-ins, called full-screen plug-ins, require helper-like applications, but these can be invoked right from the Navigator screen.

Navigator 2.0's support of these plug-ins means that more viewers will be able to enjoy a fuller experience on their Internet journeys and that developers will have more options for creative expression.

Functioning Frames

Much of the usability of the Web depends upon how much information someone can access from a single screen. Frames is a new Navigator feature that incorporates sizable (at the option of the developer) frames that resemble windows on many Windows programs. Integrated spreadsheet users will recognize the look and feel of these frames, which help improve Web usability. Figure 2-7 shows how information manipulation is made easier by using Navigator's frames.

Figure 2-7: Frames make information windows not only more plentiful on a Web page, but more useful. Each frame is scrollable, with its own hypertext links.

The frames screens can be considered separate, scrollable windows into which information can be put that may or may not be related. For example, you could see text in one, images in another, and hot buttons in another. From each of the three frames you could gather different elements of related (or unrelated, if the developer wishes) information. Whereas before users may have had to make three hypertext jumps to take in the same information, now they can see it all on one page at a glance, then jump in the direction they wish.

Better Bookmarks

Putting your favorite URLs into a bookmarked file for easy access always has been a strong feature of Navigator. In Navigator 2.0, what was good has gotten better. The bookmarks facility has been enhanced to include new organizational capabilities that allow you to logically group hundreds, or even thousands, of Internet site addresses. Even better is a new facility called SmartMarks, an intelligent bookmarking tool that comes as a helper application for Navigator 2.0 (see Figure 2-8). It does for bookmarks what the Navigator did for newsreading and e-mail — it lets you organize them into logical groups. Even better, it monitors your designated Web sites and tells you if content or addresses have changed anywhere.

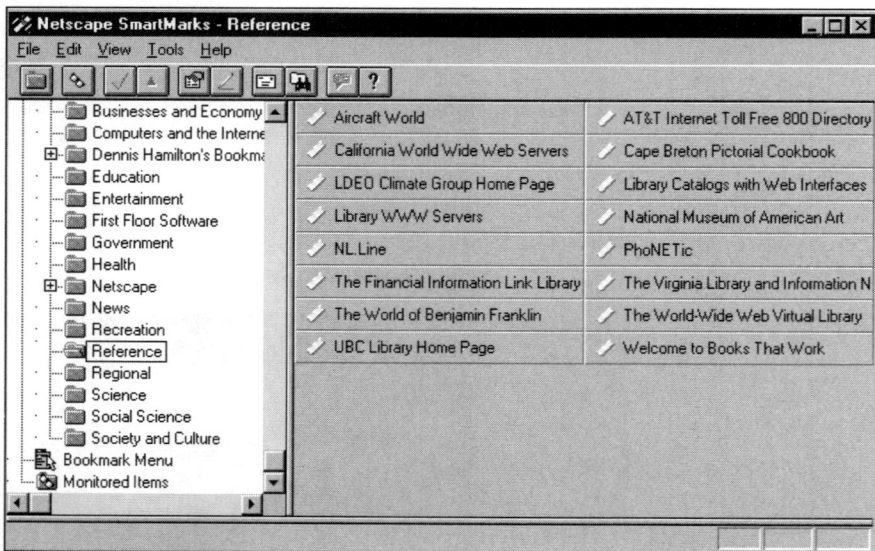

Figure 2-8: SmartMarks not only lets you organize your bookmarks into hierarchical groups, but also does periodic fly-bys of your designated Web pages to see if either the content or the addresses have changed.

New Developer Tools

Sun Microsystems put the finishing touches on a new programming language called Java without even having the Internet specifically in mind. But development of Java applications took off in new Web pages, and now it looms as one of the most interesting and versatile tools for Web developers and authors.

Java isn't alone as a newly supported programming tool in Navigator. Netscape engineers developed JavaScript, a scripting language that allows authors to script certain events on their Web pages. The new HTML editor in Navigator Gold 2.0 enables developers to create what-you-see-is-what-you-get pages and turn them into HTML.

Java

The fastest rising star in Internet programming is Java, an object-oriented programming language from Sun Microsystems. Navigator 2.0 — as well as Navigator Gold 2.0 — supports Java and its applications (known as applets because they tend to be smaller than normal applications).

Java's applets are suited perfectly to the Web's diverse platforms. They can run on most of the computers that are linked to the Internet, a portability that has made them increasingly popular with developers who don't want to shut anyone out of their site.

JavaScript

For developers on the run, or those authors who aren't as technical as a Java programmer might be, Navigator 2.0 also brings support for a new scripting language called JavaScript.

JavaScript lets developers script some action on the Web page — that is, it can sequence events or actions to happen whenever a given command is invoked. What this means for both new and experienced developers is that they don't have to resort to more complex coding and, instead, can quickly assemble a script to handle the action. JavaScript, as you probably inferred, is based loosely on Java.

HTML Editor

In Navigator Gold 2.0 — a version of Navigator 2.0 that contains advanced Web publishing tools and is targeted at developers — creation of Web pages has been made strikingly simpler. Thanks to HTML editing tools that can produce, among other things, what-you-see-is-what-you-get (WYSIWYG) pages from original sources such as Microsoft Word, some of the HTML coding and mapping drudgery has been eliminated.

While a number of developer tools are found in Navigator 2.0, it is Navigator Gold that delivers most of this terrific new array of development products. (See Part II of this book for more about Gold).

Summary

Clearly, browsing has radically changed since the first primitive graphics were downloaded a few years ago. The rate of evolution is nothing short of phenomenal. The exploration of the World Wide Web now requires a versatile, powerful client manager that was unimagined even 24 months ago. And the next 24 months likely will see even further developments in image quality, motion, sophisticated applications, and screen management.

Navigator 2.0 and Navigator Gold 2.0, for the moment, have the lead in the browser market, mostly because Netscape has recognized that browsing itself has evolved. There are not only more types of images to see, but also different types of information to communicate, and different types of creativity to express it all. The ability to wrap up into a single product features and support that can accommodate virtually everything that might appear on the Web is a significant achievement.

Chapter 3

Getting Netscape Navigator 2.0 Up and Running

T his chapter explains where you can get your Navigator 2.0 software and how to set it up to begin your Internet travels. Getting the software up and running has moved sharply toward a refined science. In the early days (that is, a couple of years ago), when users had to determine a lot of custom settings and assemble the various and vaguely compatible supporting and helper applications, the process could range from tedious to exasperating. But the popularity of the Internet, and the explosion of nontechnical users, dictated the development of a simplified set-up procedure.

Thus, users coming onto the Internet today are treated to more self-installation of their browsers, help "wizards" that guide them through, default suggestions, and generally more friendliness than the pioneers enjoyed.

This chapter shows you where to get the software, what kind of computer would optimally support it (and which wouldn't), and how to actually install it. You learn how to configure the software, and you discover the fastest installation options — including some that can have you on the Internet within minutes of inserting your disks.

Getting the Navigator Software

If you are new to the Internet, there are a number of ways to acquire Netscape Navigator 2.0. Some are wondrously simple, and none is difficult. You can get Navigator

- Directly from the Netscape home page
- From the Netscape FTP server
- From CDs or floppies from commercial providers (ISPs, publishers, book and media stores, and so on)

Navigator 2.0 is not a free product, but it can be downloaded from a Netscape server for a 90-day free trial. Figure 3-1 shows you what that important Netscape home page looks like.

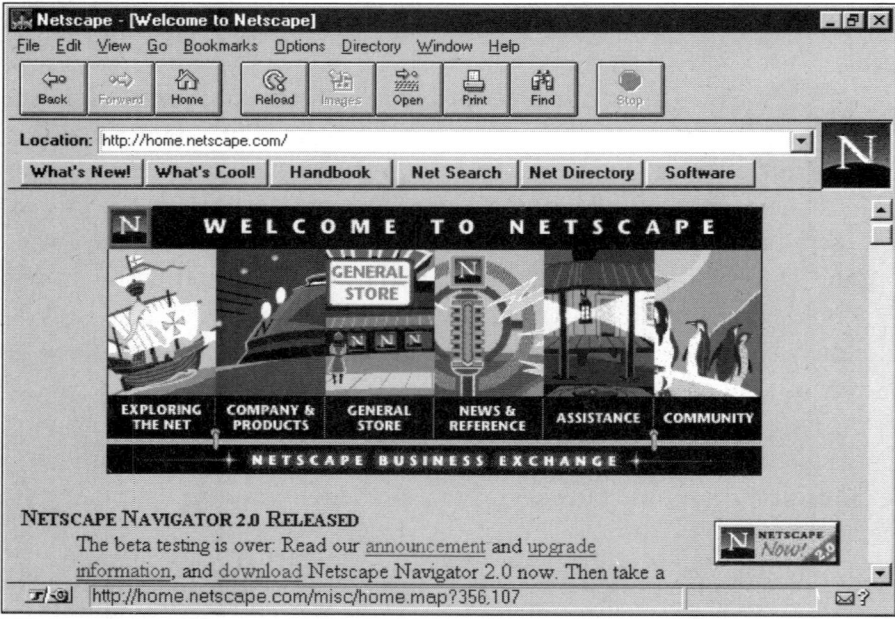

Figure 3-1: The Netscape Home Page is the mecca for getting to downloadable software, both from Netscape and the companies that provide supporting applications.

At the end of that trial period, Netscape Communications asks for $49 for a copy of Netscape Navigator 2.0, and $79 for a copy of Netscape Navigator Gold 2.0, the version for Web authors and developers. Often you can purchase a copy in another context, such as on a CD-ROM, from a software store or in the back of a book such as this one. But the latest versions usually are found on the Netscape download servers.

If you have a CD-ROM or floppy disk from your ISP or other source, but don't have the Navigator 2.0 or the other Netscape software on it, you need to load the CD or floppy to install your File Transfer Protocol (FTP) software, which was described in Chapter 1. This is a simple process for anyone. Existing users probably have FTP software up and running. New users can get this software from most of the Internet service providers (ISPs) who sell the connect services. ISPs have found that they can greatly speed up installation and improve customer satisfaction by providing — usually gratis — a floppy disk or CD containing popular applications such as e-mail, FTP, TCP/IP software, a newsreader, and sometimes even the Navigator software itself. If they do, you can be live on the Internet literally in a matter of minutes. EarthLink Network's Total Internet Access disks, which you'll find in the back of this book, provide much of this package.

Why Get the Complete Package?

A complete package from an ISP whose service and prices you like is an excellent way to go for both new and experienced users. You usually have a setup wizard to guide you through the installation process, complete with help screens and fill-in-the-blank dialog boxes with recommendations on the best or most popular choices. You also have the CD with all the software, so if anything causes a system crash later on, you can load up again in minutes.

Of course, many Internet users, especially more advanced ones, have their own choices for e-mail, FTP, and other applications. While many of these products are available free from a variety of sources on the Internet, other commercial versions with more exotic features are also on the market. Navigator 2.0 contains its own e-mail, file transfer, and newsreader facilities that, while extremely well crafted, are not among the most sophisticated available. Until you get your feet wet in the subtleties of the Internet, the excellent free versions you can get over the Internet or within Navigator are more than up to the tasks you'll have.

Netscape Navigator 2.0 is an example of a quickly evolving product (it is in Version 2, Beta 6, at this writing), so users who want to stay current with the latest features may want to download the software right off of the Internet. Netscape has made this an easy task. Here is what to do.

If you have a CD or floppy from an ISP or other source, just load it and let the prompts take you through the simple installation process.

If you have a Web browser already up, follow these steps:

1. Go to

   http://home.netscape.com

2. Click on the "Netscape Now!" button, as shown in Figure 3-1. This takes you to a simple option list that asks you to select three things: Your **operating system, location,** and **which Netscape product you want.**

3. Once you have selected these, click on the bar that says "Click to display download sites." You will then have a range of hosts to access. If one is busy (they often are), try another.

4. Create a temporary directory to store the downloaded file (for example, "Nettemp"), or load it into your permanent Internet directory. Figure 3-2 shows you what Netscape's useful download site asks for: Three easy questions.

If you need to use FTP because you're having trouble with the Netscape download page, contact one of the Netscape FTP sites. It has 11 sites, so finding one that's not busy is pretty easy. They are numbered sequentially, for example, `ftp2.netscape.com`, `ftp3.netscape.com`, and so on, up through FTP12. A user wanting Navigator 2.0 would click on a site and then follow the prompts (it asks whether you have Windows, Macintosh, and so on) to FTP the correct file directly to your computer.

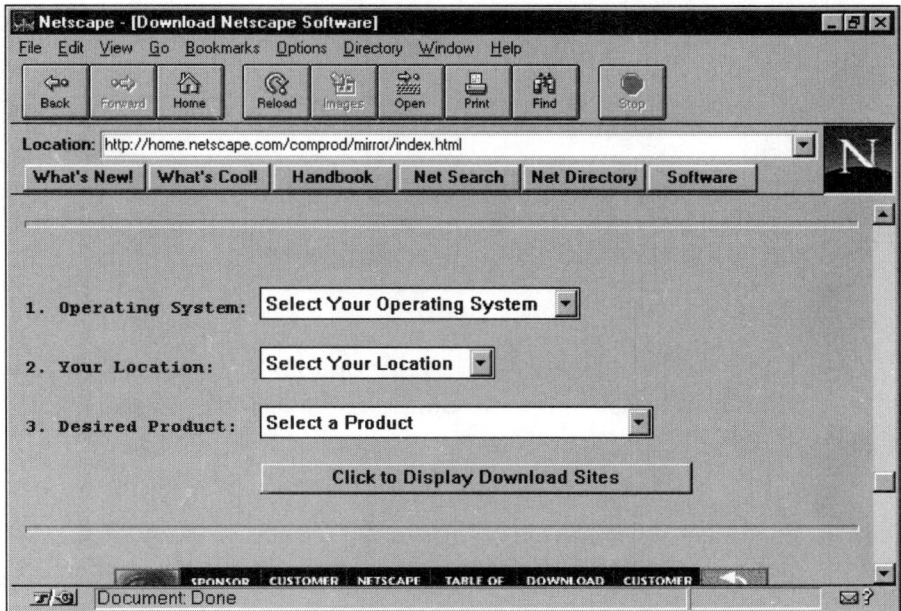

Figure 3-2: When you reach the download site from the Netscape Home Page, answering these three questions quickly gets the download process underway.

If you have only FTP software and no browser access, follow these steps:

1. Bring up your FTP menu.

2. Type **Netscape** in the Name field.

3. Type **ftp:netscape.com** in the host field.

4. Select Anonymous for the login ID (many FTP sites don't ask you to identify yourself; Netscape's is one). You might also input your e-mail address in the password field. While many FTP sites don't require this, it is commonly requested for anonymous users.

5. Type **/2.0/windows/** in the Initial Directory (**/2.0beta6/windows/** if you want the latest version). In this example, we are assuming you are a Windows user. If you want the latest *released* version, type **netscape/**.

Some Variations of Note

Note that the filenames differ for different operating systems: Macintosh versions end with hqx. Windows 3.1 versions end with n16. And Windows 95 and Windows NT versions of Navigator end with n32. One important note: If you have Windows 95 but are running a 16-bit WinSock stack, you need to download the Windows 3.1 version. The 32-bit Windows 95 software can't utilize the 16-bit stack.

---

6. Click on Save (if your FTP has that option) to retain the designations in the dialog box; you can bring the dialog box up later for other FTP transactions with Netscape.

7. Click on OK to link into the Netscape download directory.

8. Highlight the Netscape Navigator 2.0 file and click on the download arrow to move the file to your directory. (A message should tell you if the download is underway and when it is complete.)

With the file in your computer's directory, you can double-click on it and bring it up. Depending on the speed of your computer and modem, transferring a file can take from a few minutes to 45. If your ISP and Internet access account are in place, you're ready to install the software.

Installing Navigator 2.0 for Windows 95

Once you have downloaded the Navigator software, it's necessary to install it into its working directory and then configure it for your use. This process is automated to a large extent no matter how you got the software. CD-ROM installations are fastest because they usually include wizard guides as well as the necessary supporting software, such as a TCP/IP stack to connect to your ISP. But even the downloaded versions have decent prompts to get you up and running.

System Requirements for Windows

As mentioned in the introduction, having enough power in your PC is imperative. Navigator and its associated applications take a good share, as does navigating around the Internet. Table 2-1 shows the minimum to optimum configuration a Windows-based computer should have.

Table 3-1: Minimum to optimum configuration for a Windows computer

HARDWARE	FAIR	BETTER	BEST
Computer	386/SX	486	Pentium (586)
Available Hard Disk Space	2MB		
RAM	4MB	8MB	16MB
Operating System	Windows 3.1	Windows 95	
Modem	14.4	28	ISDN or better (T1 or T3 Access)
ISP Account	SLIP	PPP	Direct Network

The more power and memory you have, the more productive your Internet experience is likely to be. Navigator 2.0's facilities are such that it can access extremely involved pages of graphics and applications, and that translates into heavy memory and processing requirements. Minimum requirements get you onto the Information Superhighway, but memory and power truly get you into the fast lane.

Installing the Software

If you are using the diskettes from EarthLink found in the back of this book, follow the simple prompting instructions:

1. Close any other Windows or MS-DOS applications that are running.
2. Insert disk 1 into drive a: or b:.
3. Open the floppy folder (a: or b:) inside the "My Computer" folder.
4. Double-click on the "Setup" icon.
5. Follow the instructions to register the new account.

If you are using another CD-ROM or floppy with the software on it, follow the setup instructions that accompany it. More than likely they will ask you to

1. Close any other Windows or MS-DOS applications that are running.
2. Put the CD-ROM or floppy into the appropriate drive.
3. Click on the Start button and select Run.
4. Type: **C:\temp\setup.exe** (or any other specified setup instruction) into the Open field.

5. Click on OK to begin the installation.

6. Follow the intuitive prompts until the installation is complete.

If you're installing the software from a downloaded file, locate the file in the folder you created earlier to place it in (for example, Nettemp).

7. Double-click on the file to have it run its self-extraction routine.

8. Click on setup.exe.

9. Follow the prompts.

A status bar on the screen indicates how the installation is progressing. When it indicates that it is 100%, a message will state that all went well and the software has been installed. You then have the option of looking at the README document. It's a good idea to read through the document and, perhaps, even print it out for a more patient perusal later on.

Is It Free or Just Shared?

The terms **freeware** and **shareware** have gotten confused more and more as new users join the ranks of the Internet. They are not the same thing. Freeware refers to software that usually can be downloaded from one or more sites on the Internet or from FTP servers and for which there is no cost. While the software is free, the support for it is often thin. Shareware — for example, Netscape Navigator 2.0 — refers to software that can be used free for a period of time, but then must be paid for. You often cannot get shareware via an anonymous FTP the way you can freeware (Navigator is the exception), although you can with a user-identified FTP. But there often is more support available for shareware than freeware. For example, you cannot get documentation or technical support for Navigator 2.0 until the copy you have has a paid-up license. Netiquette on the Web says that shareware fees should always be honored as long as you find value in the software. Navigator's $49 asking price is one of the great deals in the history of software.

If You Are Having Problems with Installation

You can turn to a couple places for help if problems do occur during the installation process.

- **EarthLink's Support**
  Automated information via e-mail: info@earthlink.net
  Technical support: support@earthlink.net
  Voice: 213-644-9500

- **Netscape Support**
  Technical support for Navigator (automated and voice):
  1-800-320-2099
  Technical support for servers: 1-415-528-2727
  Technical support for Navigator Personal Edition: 1-503-626-5475
  Technical support for Navigator via e-mail: client@netscape

Often, the technical support personnel at your ISP can assist you via telephone or e-mail in solving installation or performance problems. On the Internet itself, a range of Usenet newsgroups post both FAQs (frequently asked questions) and answer specific problems sent to them via e-mail. The most effective policy is to begin at the source of the problem: Contact the source that provided the installation instructions that don't seem to work. Even if that doesn't pan out (and it usually does), you can always rest assured that you're not the only one to have your particular problem and that the mutual caretaking mentality of Internet users is to share information, including solutions.

Summary

Navigator 2.0 is, in general, an extremely simple piece of software to find and install. Its popularity is such that technical people, the original Internet and Web users, now constitute only a small portion of the total user universe. This is not to say that you won't encounter the occasional stumbling block. Sometimes an unclear term may lead you to put incorrect information into a certain field, rendering the feature inoperable.

Just bear in mind that literally millions of people, including many novices and nontechies, have installed this software, including the Navigator browser, WinSock communications software that links you to the Internet, e-mail for sending and receiving messages, file transfer for moving files around, and such helper applications as SmartMarks, Adobe Acrobat Amber, and Netscape Chat — which you'll read about in Chapter 4. Check with the most knowledgeable sources, such as your ISP or the Netscape hotlines.

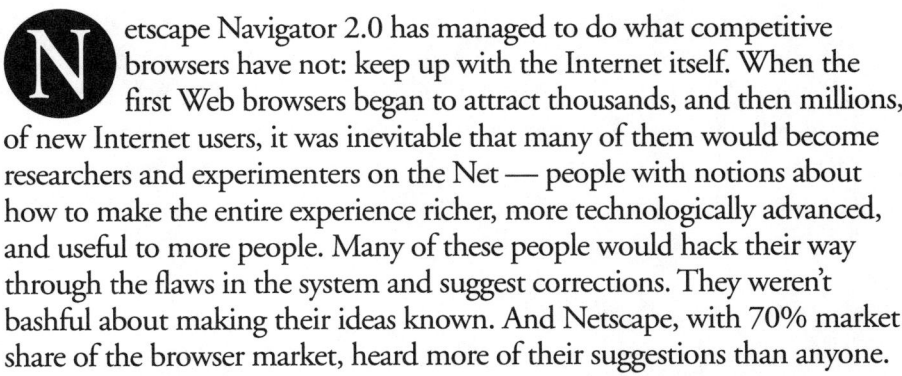

Chapter 4

Managing E-Mail and Newsgroups

etscape Navigator 2.0 has managed to do what competitive browsers have not: keep up with the Internet itself. When the first Web browsers began to attract thousands, and then millions, of new Internet users, it was inevitable that many of them would become researchers and experimenters on the Net — people with notions about how to make the entire experience richer, more technologically advanced, and useful to more people. Many of these people would hack their way through the flaws in the system and suggest corrections. They weren't bashful about making their ideas known. And Netscape, with 70% market share of the browser market, heard more of their suggestions than anyone.

The Internet, at 30 million-plus users, boasts the largest user group in the world. It is also the fastest-growing user group in the world. It represents a cultural phenomenon as much as a technical one. While the Internet doesn't demand great technical knowledge to use, many of its users are indeed technical and, thus, looking at the Internet's potential from a technological standpoint and posing the question: What else is possible?

Navigator 2.0 incorporates more of what is possible than any other similar system we have seen. In fact, Netscape Communications feels it has made Navigator so versatile that the word "browser" is no longer adequate to describe what the product does. Netscape's preferred word now is "client," and we honor that when possible, although we use the word browser when it is necessary to describe a specific function or class of software. This chapter describes the new advancements in the Navigator 2.0 client, especially in the area of managing e-mail and newsgroups. Chapter 5 then looks at the strides Netscape has made in Image and Document Presentation.

What's New and Why Is It Important?

Let's take an overview look at what e-mail and newsgroup functions are incorporated into the Navigator 2.0 browser.

The most useful new features are

- HTML 3.0 Support
- E-mail
- Threaded newsgroups

HTML 3.0 Support

HTML 3.0 support refers to the latest version of Hypertext Markup Language, the programming language used to create the text on the vast majority of pages on the World Wide Web. By using HTML, users have been able to jump from document to document, site to site, by clicking on text or graphics that contain links to locations on the Internet. New facilities in Navigator 2.0 allow it to display textured backgrounds, tables, blinking text, colored hypertext links, and transparencies.

Easy to Use E-Mail

Full **e-mail** has been a while coming, but was worth the wait. It boasts a personal address book and drag-and-drop features. Plus, in Navigator 2.0 mail, it's not just simple text anymore. You can actually embed URLs and pages to create HTML mail — for example, a recipient can click on an embedded link and go right to the site from their e-mail.

Threaded Newsgroups

Threaded newsgroups greatly simplify the process of sorting, reading, and posting **threads**, which are series of responses to items that have been posted in the newsgroups. You can subscribe to a newsgroup as before but, instead of a loosely (if at all) organized list of articles and responses, you can quickly scan the articles and their threads (indented below them) by title.

E-Mail

One of the most logical extensions of Navigator in its evolution from a browser to a full-featured client was the addition of electronic mail, or e-mail. This facility enables users to compose and send messages, programs, and other attachments directly over the Internet so that they arrive seconds after being sent. No stamps, no postage meters, no snow delays. For 25 years, e-mail was the primary reason people used the Internet, and it remains the most frequently used Internet application.

The Internet exists to inform, present, entertain, and communicate. E-mail is the principal means of that communication, and its value increased with the introduction of the World Wide Web. Suddenly, there were tens of thousands of Web sites and millions of users, all increasingly clamoring for interaction. E-mail was principally how they interacted.

The earlier version of Navigator (1.*x*) possessed the ability to send e-mail, but not to receive it. This was a glaring deficiency for Internet users because almost all meaningful e-mail requires interaction and response. If there is a Web site whose products or information you are interested in, or a newsgroup or forum whose members could help you solve a problem, e-mail is how you would contact them and how they would contact you. If you wanted complete e-mail facilities with Navigator 1.*x*, you had to use a separate e-mail application such as Eudora, then switch back and forth between e-mail and the Web. You could mail from the Web, but had to move to your e-mail application to check your responses. It was awkward if you had an active dialog going on.

In Navigator 2.0, Netscape has put together a solid e-mail component that lets users enjoy most of the send/receive functionality that the better e-mail applications offer. Its greatest asset is one that none of the others possess: Navigator's e-mail was built in harmony with the other advancements in this new version of Navigator and can recognize embedded HTML. The mail reader can spot any URL in the text, and viewers of the text can click on it to go to that site.

Netscape is faced with surging competition from companies such as Microsoft Corporation and Lotus Development, which would love to have their e-mail software become the Internet standard. To combat that competition, Netscape's engineers added Reply To, Forward, and Carbon Copy facilities to its new e-mail, all popular facilities in other e-mail packages.

While Navigator's e-mail facilities are a major leap forward from earlier versions, only the HTML recognition capability dramatically sets it apart from other good e-mail products. Netscape engineers are intent on continuing to raise the bar, however, so whatever facilities Navigator lacks in this version will almost certainly be addressed in later ones.

How to Set Mail Preferences

As always, when setting up an e-mail system, you have to take some time out to supply name and address information (in several forms) and design the kind of e-mail you want to send and receive. The information is pretty fundamental and can be obtained with a phone call to your ISP or system administrator. After that, you just fill in the blanks and make some choices.

1. First, bring up your Navigator screen and click on the Options menu at the top.

2. From there, select Mail and News Preferences. You get a tabbed screen with five marked tabs on it: Appearance, Composition, Servers, Identity, and Organization (see Figure 4-1).

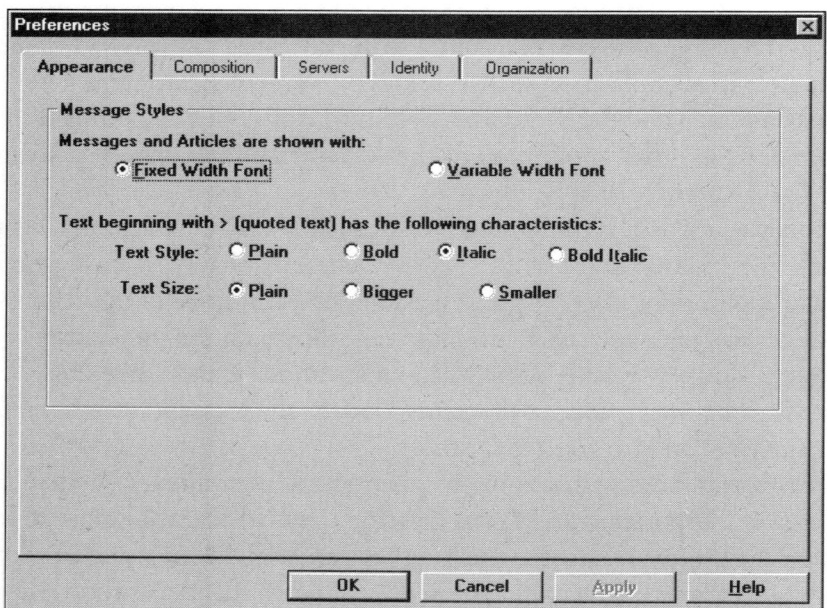

Figure 4-1: Setting the News preferences up front is necessary for users to take full advantage of the new Navigator features — including installation help from fellow users.

Appearance

Here you find a series of options that determine the appearance of e-mail text and documents you send and receive. You probably want to select the box for Fixed Width Font (see Figure 4-1). This assures that messages sent to you and from you stay in a fixed width across the screen. This generally makes it simpler to read and scroll messages. Variable width fonts, the alternative selection, can play havoc with the formatting of messages.

Beneath this selection is another options list: "Text beginning with > (quoted text), which has the following characteristics:".

These selections allow you to determine the appearance of text within the body of the messages. If you have stylistic preferences, go ahead and designate the fonts you want. If not, click on Plain in both Text Style and Text Size, then go back later and make changes when you've had a chance to view the various looks.

Beneath these selections you see a choice for: When sending and receiving electronic mail:. If you choose Use Netscape Mail and News, you will be using Navigator's facilities; if you select Exchange Client for Mail and News, you will be choosing the Microsoft Exchange facilities.

Composition

From the Composition tab, you will be making settings that will determine some important automatic functions (see Figure 4-2).

The Send and Post selection establishes how file attachments are coded. You should probably choose the 8-bit default because it is the most common form.

With the next selection, Mail Messages, you can determine whether Navigator will save a copy of your messages and documents, as seen in Figure 4-2. If there is a repository you wish to have messages stored in, enter the address in that field. Do this both for Mail Messages and News Messages.

In the Mail File field, you find the default address where Navigator's e-mail stores your messages on disk. If you don't want any outgoing mail stored on disk, just delete the pathname from this field. Similarly, if you want news stored on disk in a location that's different from the default, you must determine where you want it and enter the information into the field.

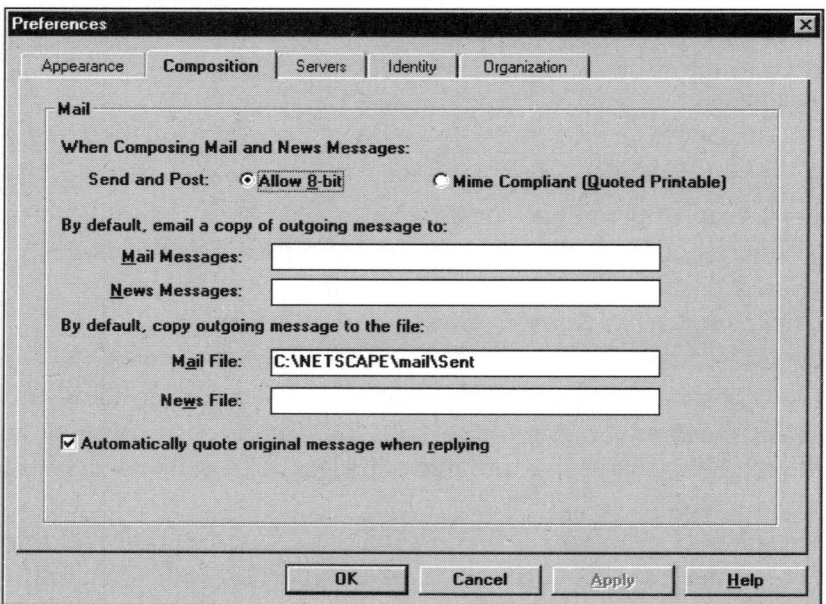

Figure 4-2: If you wish to have your news messages routed automatically, you can designate the path in the News Messages box.

The final selection to make on the Composition tab has to do with choosing whether you want to automatically quote the original message back to someone when you reply to them. Many e-mail users do this, but it is not necessary, and the text can get somewhat cluttered on your reply.

E-Mail Netiquette

E-mail netiquette, especially when responding to someone not familiar with you or who has a range of items he or she would like responses to, says to copy back the original message on your reply. That way the recipient of your reply can more clearly see to what you are responding. In the case of someone with a list of items to be answered, you can space them out on e-mail by hitting the return key between items and entering the text of your response right after each question. Thus the response comes back as question: answer: question: answer, and so on. But if you don't want an automatic inclusion of this text in every reply (some are extremely long), you can always copy and paste.

Servers

The Servers tab requires that you input some precise and important information, as indicated in Figure 4-3. Before you enter this information, you have to get certain data from your ISP or system administrator (if you don't already have it).

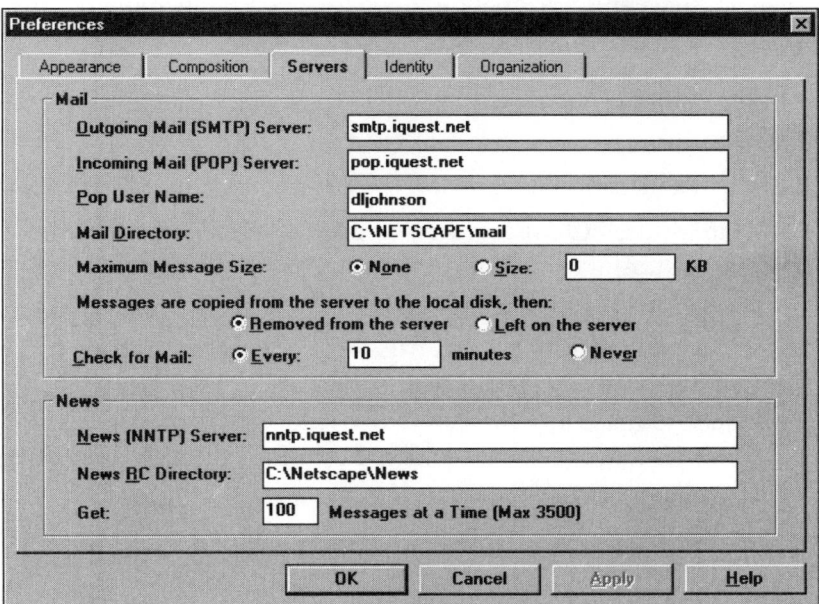

Figure 4-3: The important SMTP and POP addresses have to be entered into the respective fields on the Servers information screen.

The information to enter includes

- Your ISP's SMTP (Simple Mail Transfer Protocol). This is a Send Mail address, where the ISP's mail server is doing the sending. The address enables the ISP to route mail around the Internet.

- Your ISP's POP (Post Office Protocol). This is a Retrieve Mail address that enables mail to come from the Internet to the ISP's customers.

- Your e-mail name.

- Maximum Message Size ensures that any e-mail message will reach you in its entirety. The default is None and should be accepted unless you want to screen large messages.

- Messages are copied... asks whether you want e-mail retained on or deleted from the mail server. It's a good idea to have messages automatically deleted, which is the default.

- Check for Mail indicates how often the server is checked for your e-mail messages. The 10-minute default is good for most users.

When you have this information, open the Servers tab and enter the information in the designated fields:

1. In the field for Outgoing Mail (SMTP) Server, type the SMTP address.

2. In the field for incoming mail (POP) Server, type the POP address.

3. In field for the POP user name, type your e-mail name (not the whole address). For example, the name "bill" in the address bill@inett.net is the POP user name.

4. In the Mail Directory field, Navigator should have provided you with a directory where your mail folders are located. You probably do not need to make any changes to this field. If you do, use Windows Explorer to find the correct folder, then return to the Mail Directory field and enter the correct path.

Note that this path and the path in the Mail File field of the Composition tab should match.

Identity

The information you enter here personalizes, to whatever extent you want, all messages you send out. This is illustrated in Figure 4-4. You can add your name, your company name, and your e-mail **signature**.

Online Signatures

Signatures are little sign-offs that many e-mail users use to illustrate their wit, politics, philosophy, individualism, jokes du jour, and so on. Signatures such as "No Matter where you go, there you are" or "Happiness is found along the way, not at the end of the road" are typical. These phrases should not be more than 80 characters long.

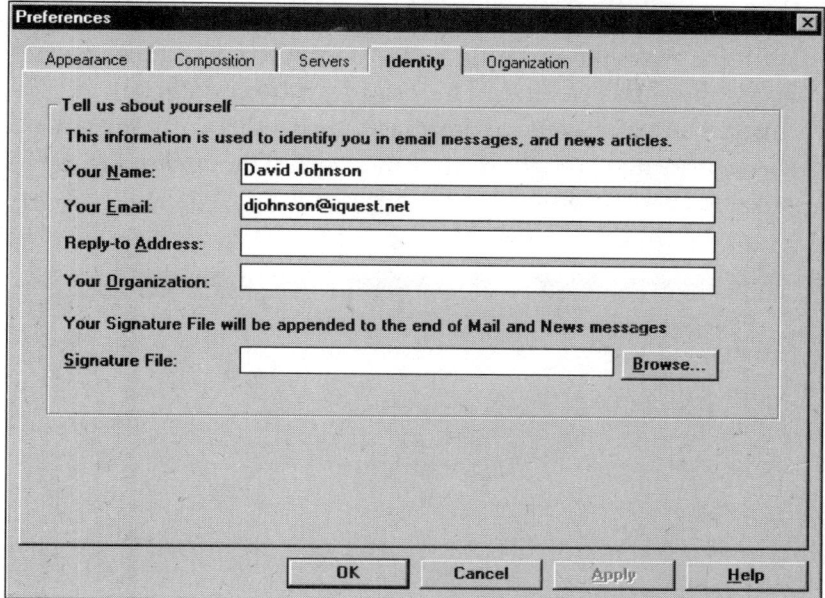

Figure 4-4: Your name and e-mail address are the minimal bits of information you're required to submit on this page. The rest is optional.

1. In the Your Name field, enter your name.

2. In the Your E-mail field, enter your complete e-mail address.

3. In the Reply-to Address field, enter the address (if any) where you wish your outgoing messages sent, if that address is different than the address designated in the e-mail. For instance, if you wanted your secretary to see all your replies, this is where you would designate his or her address.

4. In the Your Organization field, enter your company's name if you wish it automatically attached.

5. In the Signature File field (see the sidebar titled "Online Signatures"), you can designate a signature file to be attached to any message you send. Just click on the Browse button and select a signature file.

Organization

The selections on the Organization tab allow e-mail users to designate password usage and threading of news and mail.

1. Click in the Remember Mail Password box (see Figure 4-5) if you want the system to prompt you for your password each time you access the e-mail facilities. This provides protection from e-mail intruders. If your work environment is such that you want to skip the security and go right to your messages without entering the password each session, leave the box blank.

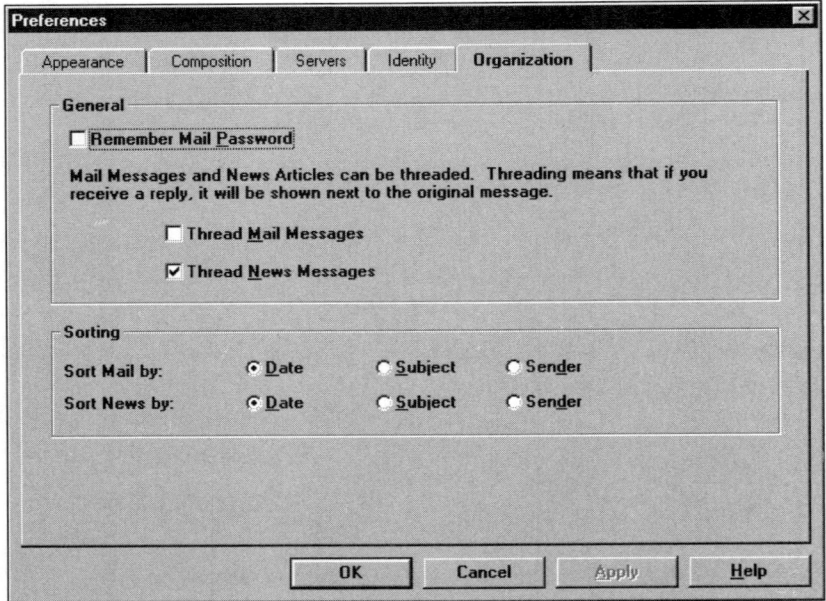

Figure 4-5: This screen allows you to organize incoming information in the way you like to sift through it. Threading lets you organize by subject.

Note that early beta versions of Navigator 2.0 do not have the Remember Mail Password option, thus there is no box to click. The e-mail automatically prompts you for your password each session with these versions.

2. Click in the Thread Mail Messages box if you want your messages threaded. This selection means that if you receive a reply, it is shown with the original message along with other replies to that message.

3. Under the Sorting options, click on the way you want the mail sorted. You can choose Date, Subject, or Sender. Date is the default

and simply presents e-mail to you in the order it was received. Subject organizes mail by information in the Subject line of the message. Sender organizes mail by the sender's e-mail address.

4. Click on Thread News Messages if you want news items threaded.

5. Under sorting options, click on the way you want news threaded.

When you've completed making your selections, click on OK to save your settings. Any of these settings can be changed at a later date just by clicking again on the Mail and News Preferences selection under the Options heading of the Navigator page. If you have any doubts about any of the information, just go with the defaults until you've had time to work out more specific preferences.

Using Navigator's E-Mail

Now that you've set up Navigator's e-mail client, you can start sending messages. The general principal is simple: Start with small messages the first couple of times — just to test your configuration and connections — and then move up to whatever length messages you wish to send.

When you want to invoke e-mail, there are two ways to do it: You can click on the envelope icon in the lower-right corner of the Navigator screen; or you just click on the Windows button on your Navigator page and select Netscape Mail, as shown in Figure 4-6. Enter your password. Then click on OK.

Figure 4-6: The password facility maintains privacy in the blizzard of e-mail messages sent globally every day.

The first page you see is Navigator Mailbox (see Figure 4-7), which gives you a great deal of information about locations, senders, times sent, dates, and the total number of unread messages awaiting your perusal.

Mail Folder
shows locations
of messages

Sender identifies
person sending
the message

Subject tells you
what it's about

Date tells you
when it arrived

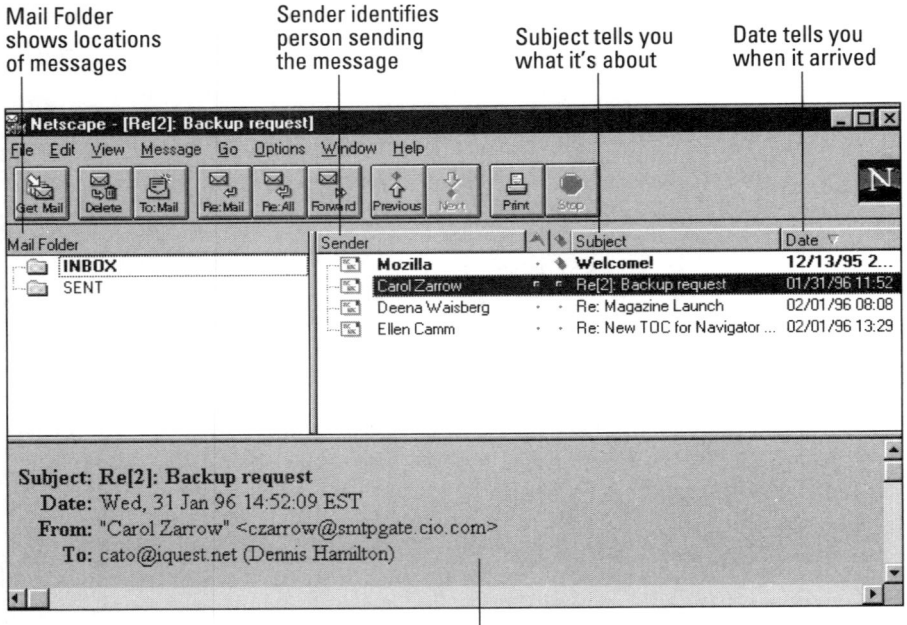

The message text window displays the text
of a message when you double-click on it

Figure 4-7: The Mailbox contains a wealth of information about who is mailing you and why.

Use the scroll bars to scan down the messages for any that you are
particularly interested in. Double-click to retrieve any message. You don't
have to do this in any particular order.

All panes in the Mailbox window change sizes on you from time to time,
obscuring information that is contained within them. You can expand the
frame sizes by clicking and dragging on the edges of the panes until all
information is shown.

Sending E-Mail

You can start composing an e-mail message very simply. Begin by clicking
on the New Mail Message selection from the File menu or by clicking on
the To: Mail button on the control bar. This opens your message form (see
Figure 4-8). If the message form is partially off the screen, click on the blue
bar at the top of the form and drag it until the form is centered. You always
want to be able to see the whole text of your message.

A basic message is extremely simple to do.

1. In the Mail To field at the top, enter the exact e-mail address of the individual or site you are sending this document to.

2. If you want to copy the message to a third party, click on the View menu and select Cc — the designation for Carbon Copy.

3. In the Cc field, enter the exact e-mail address of the destination. If you frequently use carbon copies, you can keep the Cc field on your message form just by not clicking off of it when you've completed the message.

For E-Mail Novices Only

If this represents your first experience with e-mail, remember that this mail doesn't have a chance of getting through if even one character of the recipient's address is incorrect. Unlike snail mail, there are no postal carriers who know the neighborhood and can interpret where a letter should go by partial or close-enough address information. Keep the names of frequent recipients in the address book, then you can just call them up instead of rekeying them. This helps minimize typing errors. If you do enter an incorrect address, the system notifies you later that it has been unable to find the recipient's location. Check the address and send the message again.

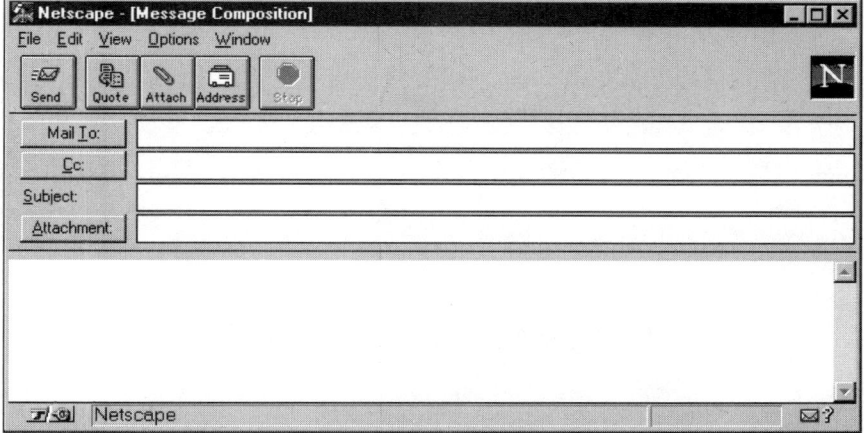

Figure 4-8: Sending e-mail is no more complicated than writing a message into the text box, filling in an address, and clicking on Send.

4. Next, enter a brief description of what the message is about in the Subject box.

5. Put your arrow into the upper-right corner of the text composition page — the large box at the bottom half of the screen — and click once to place your cursor there.

6. Start typing your message.

When you've completed writing your message, click on the Send button in the upper-left corner of the message screen. If you have designated automatic mailing in your Preferences, the mail is dispatched instantly (usually the best choice). If you chose to have your messages queued up to be sent manually, the message goes to the disk to await your sending instructions.

Attachments

Navigator's e-mail client has the capability of sending more than just text. It can also mail binary files over the same Internet lines (most other e-mail packages have this capability too). Thus, if you want to send Java program files or some other ASCII-coded files, you can attach them to your e-mail and fire them out just like a simple text message. Figure 4-9 shows you where to go to attach your file.

What none of the other e-mail products can do is attach URLs to an e-mail message.

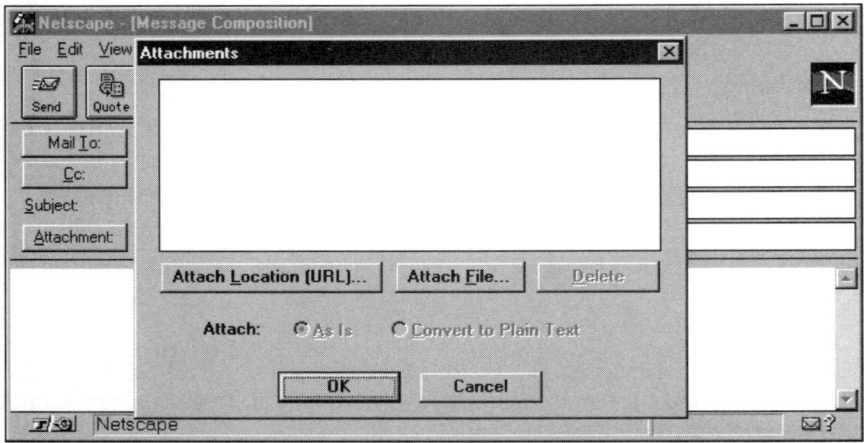

Figure 4-9: Navigator can send an embedded URL link or can attach an entire file.

Open the Attachments box by clicking on the Attachments button. You'll see two additional buttons below the screen designated Attach Location (URL) and Attach File. You can perform the following actions:

- If you want to attach a file, click on the Attach File button. You then select the file you want from the Enter File to Attach dialog box. The designated file should then appear in the Attachments box. If you highlight it to tell Navigator this is the file you want included, then click on OK.

- If you want to attach a URL, click on the Attach Location (URL) button, as shown in Figure 4-10. This opens a location box with a one-line field in it called Location (URL). In that field you enter the URL of the Internet page you wish to have attached. If you are mailing the URL to another Navigator 2.0 mail reader, click on the As-Is radio button on the Attachments page before you send the message. The recipients then can do things they never dreamed of with other browsers. The Navigator reader, interpreting the HTML source code from the site you attached, can write a complete Web page for the recipient to see. That page also links directly to any other Web page whose links are mentioned in the source code.

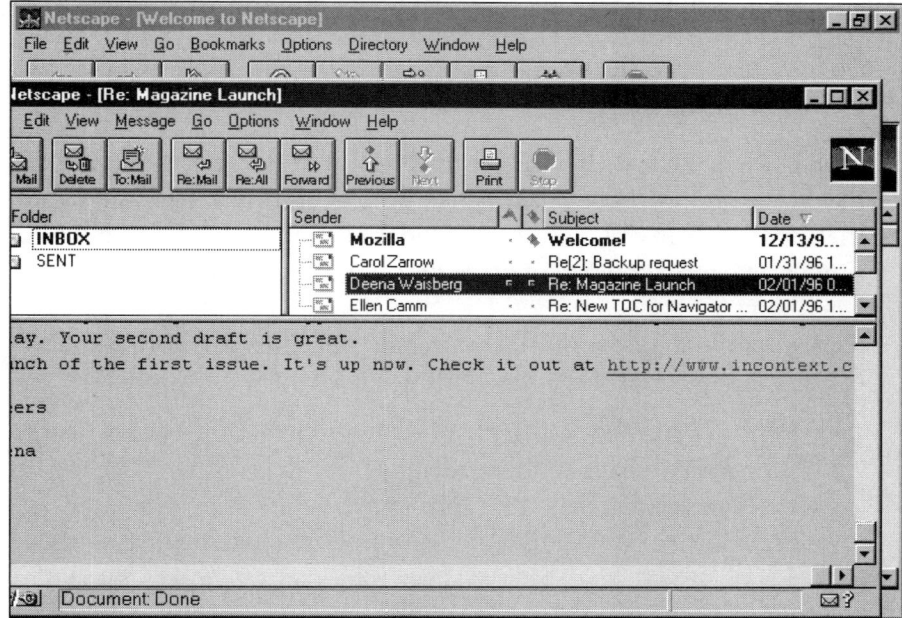

Figure 4-10: The bonus of being able to send live URLs via e-mail is available because Navigator treats the whole e-mail message like an HTML document.

For recipients who haven't made the transition yet to Navigator 2.0's mail reader, you need to check the Convert To Plain Text box (instead of the As Is box) on the attachments page. Unfortunately, recipients will not be able to make hypertext jumps from e-mail since the conversion removes the HTML tags. But they will still receive the text of the page.

Receiving E-Mail

Receiving and retrieving e-mail from Navigator's e-mail client is designed to be simple. E-mail can arrive for you at any time and is stored on your ISP's mail server. It is available whenever you want to open e-mail and look at what you've received.

When you open the Netscape Mail window, e-mail tries to log on automatically to see if you have any messages waiting. Assuming you have set the designations correctly in the Preferences box discussed earlier, e-mail will report back to you that you have new mail waiting or that there are no new messages.

You can also retrieve your new mail from the Netscape Mail window by clicking on the File menu and selecting Get New Mail, or by clicking on the Get Mail button on the control bar at the top of the screen. From the list of messages, just highlight the one you wish to open, then double-click on it. The e-mail opens and the text displays in the frame at the bottom of the window.

Responding to E-Mail

One of the attractions of e-mail is that it is so simple to respond to that dialog can almost become interactive. E-mail on Navigator offers most of the features commonly found on standard e-mail packages, even if it lacks some of the more sophisticated features found on products such as Microsoft's.

Most of the response menu commands are self-explanatory, but here's an explanation of some of the functions you'll have at your disposal:

- **Reply.** If you click on Reply or Reply All, you can return a pre-addressed message to the sender by using the address at the top of the page (see Figure 4-11). You have the choice of including or excluding the text of the message you were sent. By pressing the return key, you can create your own message at the top of the message sent to you. Then you can press the Send button and mail it.

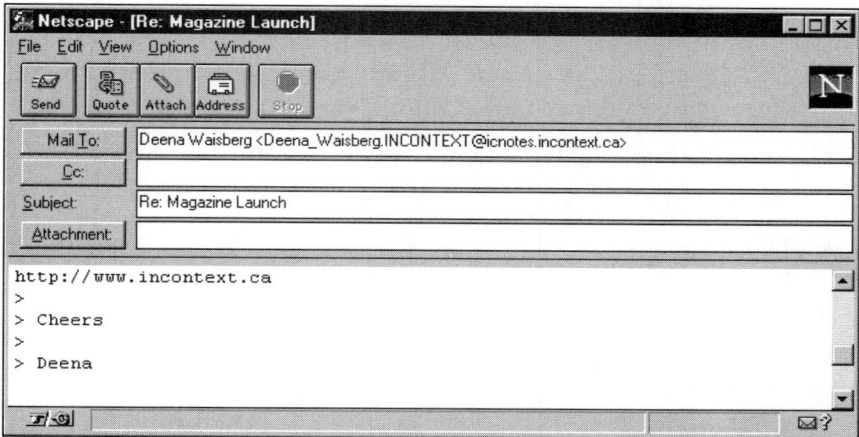

Figure 4-11: Just by clicking on Message - Reply you can automatically address an e-mail reply to a letter that has been sent to you.

- **Attach.** If you wish to attach files or URLs to your response, just press the Attachment button and follow the same procedure described in the section on composing e-mail documents.

- **Forward.** If you want to forward the message you received to a third party, the Forward button creates another message with the text of the received message, but no address. You then fill in the address of the recipient you want to forward the message to. Forward also includes any attachments you designate; or you can delete the attachments before you send the message.

Storing and Retrieving Addresses

Virtually every e-mail package comes with an address repository, and Navigator's e-mail is no exception. These directories contain addresses of recipients you frequently (or even not so frequently) send e-mail to. They are useful because e-mail addresses often can be complex, which leads to errors when you key them in manually. With an address book, you can just designate the recipient — or multiple recipients — of a message right out of the repository. It saves time and assures accuracy.

The best way to add addresses to the address book is to lift them right off of messages people have sent you. Just click on the Message menu, then select Add to Address Book. This adds the sender's name to the repository. As you receive more mail, build your book.

There are four fields to an entry:

- Nick Name asks for a name that serves as a shortcut to finding a given address (all nicknames must be written in lower-case only).
- Name is the actual name of the person or entity you are adding.
- E-mail Address is the precise address the system will use.
- Description asks for a brief description, which is optional (see Figure 4-12).

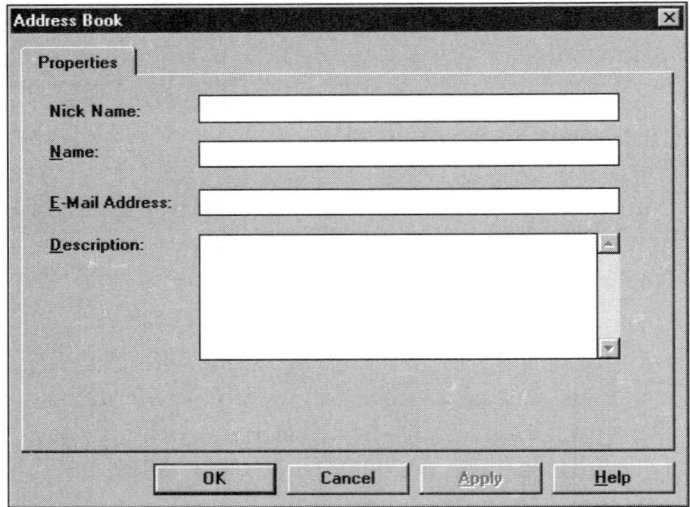

Figure 4-12: The Address Book has a box for adding descriptive information about the individual you are mailing to.

The Description information won't show up anywhere but on your screen. You may simply want to write in the company and business title, or the subject about which the two of you generally correspond.

If you don't have a message from which to lift the address, you can add entries to the address book by clicking on the Window menu and selecting Address Book. From the new screen, click on Item and select Add User. A Properties form will appear; simply fill in the blanks.

Using the Address Book

Once you've begun building your address book, using it is simple.

1. Place the cursor in the Text Composition window's Mail To field.

2. Click on the control bar's Address button to open a window displaying your list of addresses.

3. Highlight the address you wish to place in the Mail To field and double click. The Mail To field will be completed automatically with the name and e-mail address of the designated recipient.

For speedy addressing, the Nick Name facility allows you to shortcut all of that by entering the nickname of the recipient (the one you entered in the Properties form) in the Mail To field. If you want to copy someone, enter the nickname into the Cc (carbon copy) field or the Blind Cc field (if you want to send a blind carbon copy).

Using Newsgroups with Navigator

One of the Internet's most popular features is something called a USENET newsgroup. This is an electronic forum where special-interest Internet users gather to provide and access information on specific subjects — and almost any subject anyone can imagine has a newsgroup. From Amiga owners to JFK assassination buffs to mathematics problem solvers, newsgroups post articles, state problems, provide answers, share wisdom (and sometimes folly), and generally have become as ingrained a part of the Internet's usefulness as anything else it offers.

Newsgroups have also provided fodder for much of the antagonism that has arisen toward an unregulated Internet. The alt.sex designation, for example, became a byword (or by address) for legislators wanting to impose their views of morality on Internet users. Because no one owns the Internet, and because it is global in its reach (and therefore potentially subject to laws, regulations, and mores from the more than 100 countries it reaches), efforts to knock out undesirable newsgroups and sites have been largely unsuccessful. Which nation's standards do we impose on the world?

CompuServe, at this writing, is in the midst of a dispute with German authorities, which deemed some sex-oriented newsgroups off-limits to German Internauts. The consequence: Lacking the technology to shut down the newsgroups just for Germany, CompuServe had to shut them down for all the world's CompuServe/Internet users (that is, those accessing the Internet through CompuServe's facilities). They faced losing German business (or going to German court) for keeping them online; or antagonism from the rest of the world for taking them off.

Still, the disputes coming from the newsgroup debates truly pale compared to the popularity and usefulness that most Internet users find in newsgroups — with a little effort. There are homes for everyone. You can't be too radical, too religious, too militant, too smart, or too dumb. If you are into a subject with some passion and don't mind the occasional excesses someone else's passion might produce — such as profanity — newsgroups can be interesting places to visit.

How Newsgroups Work

Newsgroups are all linked to special network servers by using the Network News Transfer Protocol (NNTP) to move the information around. When news is posted, it travels over the network and is stored on news servers, where your computer goes to retrieve it.

Because there are almost 11,000 newsgroups, the storing of that much constantly changing information is a huge task. It is shared by many servers on many networks whose only task is moving and storing news. Your computer accesses the news servers much as they do the e-mail POP servers of your ISP. The difference is that your computer is only sent news from the newsgroups to which you've subscribed, while your e-mail server sends you everything it has collected in your name.

Types of Newsgroups

There is a simple way of dividing the types of newsgroups: Moderated and unmoderated. Because there is no regulating body, most of the alternative — containing the alt. designation — newsgroups are reigned over by their members. In other words, they are unmoderated. Thus, some of them are civil and others are raucous. Some information is worthwhile, while other information is utter tripe. The variety makes for some memorable experiences one way or the other, so you just have to find those that fit your style.

Other newsgroups, called moderated newsgroups, have editors who control the content of what appears. They read all articles and notices, then decide which should be posted. This sits well with people who don't like the blather they sometimes have to tolerate in the unmoderated newsgroups. Conversely, others call the editors' decisions censorship.

In the end, it comes down to the individual newsgroup and the members and editors. Some unmoderated newsgroups thrive on their editorial freedom, and word of them spreads around the Internet (often via newsgroups). A good editor can make an unmoderated newsgroup a superb forum for information; a poor one can turn the exchange of ideas into sterile farce.

Your newsgroup experience will almost certainly be rewarding if you invest the time to sample a variety of newsgroups and subscribe to those that, in your view alone, have something to offer you.

Using the Navigator Newsreader

Now that you have an idea about how newsgroups work, take a moment to get acquainted with the software that lets you interact with them. This type of software is called a newsreader. What distinguishes one newsreader from another is not that it can get access to newsgroups — all can do that — but what it does to organize the news for you once it retrieves it. Too often, finding useful nuggets of information in newsgroups is like sifting through a ton of pitchblend to find a gram of radium. Navigator's excellent newsreader lets you get out to find and interact with all the news providers you can wish for (and maybe a few you didn't).

Setting the Preferences

You must set the preferences for Navigator 2.0's newsreader to get at your news the way you want to. Here is where you determine where your messages are retrieved from, how many you will receive, whether they will be threaded, and how they will appear. You can do it in moments by following the instructions below.

1. Click on Options on the control bar, and then select Mail and News Preferences.
2. Click on the Servers tab.
3. Complete the field for your NNTP server address, as shown in Figure 4-13. (If you haven't completed the field for your SMTP server when you configured your e-mail, you must do this now. All this address information is available from your ISP.)

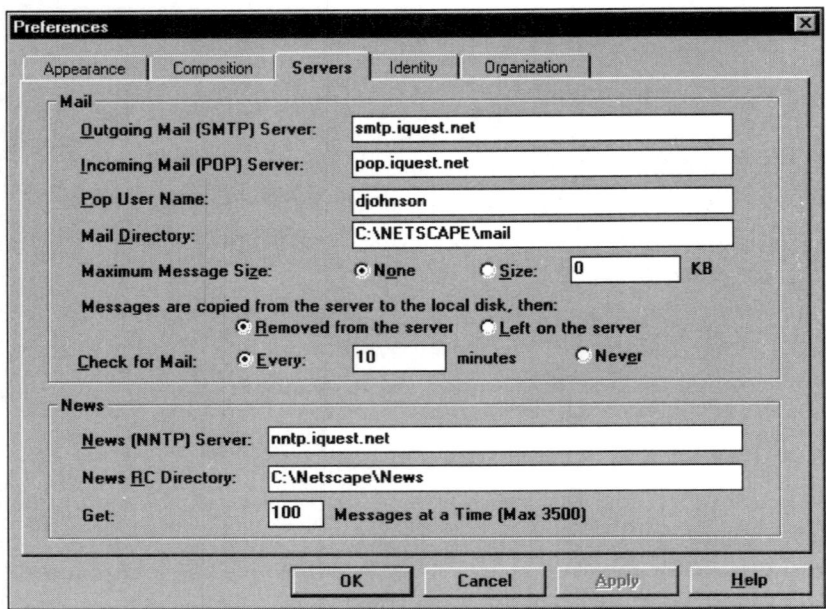

Figure 4-13: Completing the Servers fields provides Navigator's news client with directions to your ISP's news server. Call your ISP for the address.

4. If the default address is missing in the News RC Directory field, enter **C:\Netscape\News**.

5. If you have a preference for receiving only a specific number of messages, designate a number in the Get Messages at a Time box. The default is 100 messages at a time.

6. Click on the Identity tab.

7. Complete the fields for your name, e-mail address, and reply-to address. Optionally, you can also add your signature file to news you send. If you did not do this during e-mail setup, do so now, if you wish to. (See Figure 4-14.)

8. Click OK to save your information.

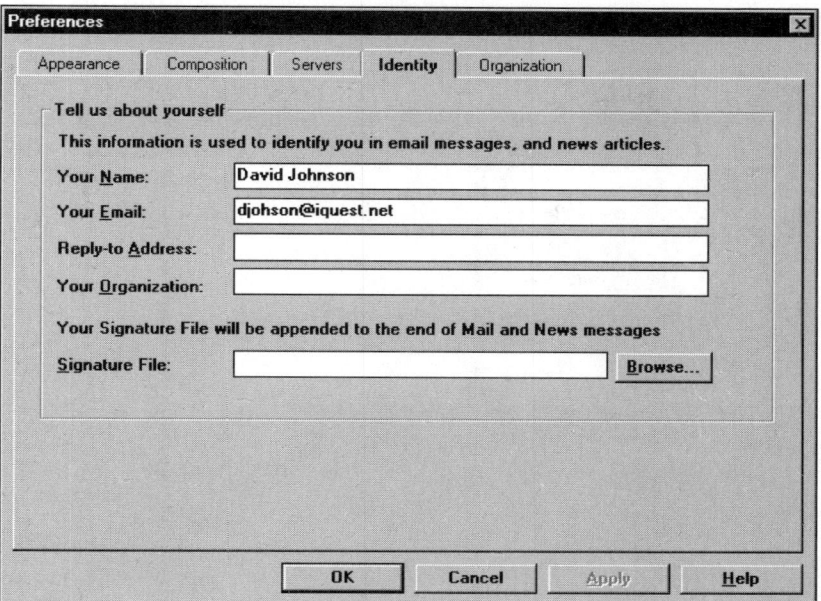

Figure 4-14: If you completed the Identity information when configuring your e-mail, you won't have to do it again for News.

Checking Out the Newsgroups

There are several ways to find newsgroups. One is to get onto the Web, use one of several search engines, enter the keywords "newsgroups" and "(your subject)," then see what turns up. Sometimes the newsgroups are given arcane names and their usefulness isn't apparent in the title. Search engines that look at some descriptive text beyond the title can track down specific groups. You also can ask around among Internet-using peers who share your interests. Often they have discarded the frivolous and tied into the good ones. The most thorough way, in the end, is to plunge right in and load the names of all newsgroups directly from the server, then see what strikes a chord as you read through them (see Figure 4-15).

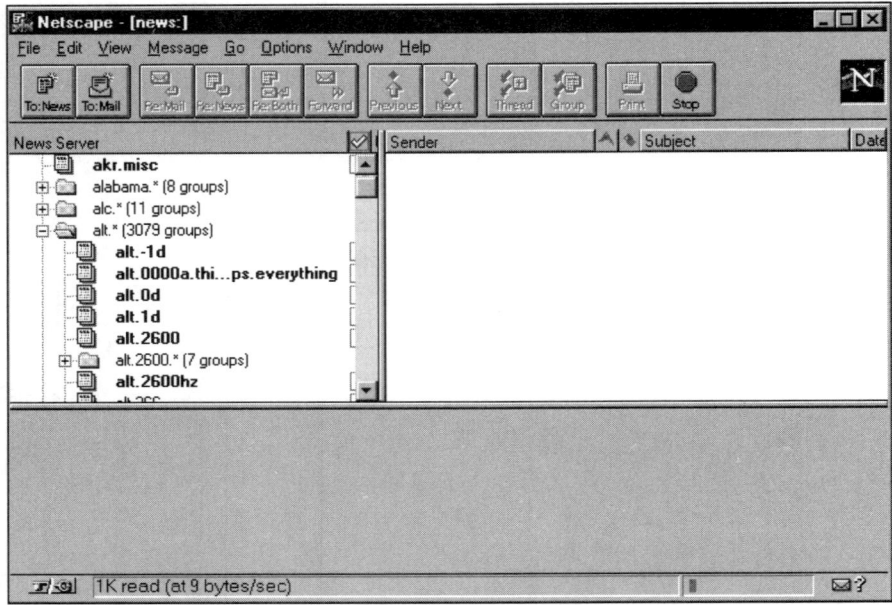

Figure 4-15: When you click on Show All Newsgroups, be prepared to wait several minutes while the server loads them. Then you can search for those that interest you.

1. Click on the Options menu at the top of your Netscape News page.
2. Select Show All Newsgroups from the menu.
3. Click on OK.

Newsgroups are always listed alphabetically, so while you have to scroll through many of them, you're spared the agony of trying to figure them out line by line. Just move down the list by using the scroll bar until you reach the likely alphabetical location of the newsgroup in which you're interested. It doesn't take long to get the sense of how they are organized.

Basically, newsgroups are organized in folders and subfolders. When you receive the list of newsgroups, it will be in the first-level hierarchy — that is, in alphabetical order, the most generic names that can be applied to a category of newsgroups. For example, if you want to test the waters with the alternative newsgroups, with a special interest in comedy, the sequence would look like this:

1. Click on **alt**. This takes you to a list of all alt. categories.

2. Click on the subcategory alt.comedy. This takes you to a further list of subcategories. Scroll down until you locate the type of comedy you're interested in; for example, improvisation.

3. Click on **alt.comedy.improvisation**.

That's how it works. Once you understand the newsgroup system, testing the various groups becomes simple. In most cases, you have to subscribe to the newsgroup to take part in it. This usually involves clicking on a box and means only that you are instructing the news server that you are now a subscriber and want the news from that newsgroup downloaded to your computer whenever you logon to the server.

For example, if you want to subscribe to **alt.comedy.improvisation**, follow these steps:

1. Click on the top-tier alt. newsgroup.

2. Scroll down and click on alt.comedy.

3. Find alt.comedy.improvisation and check the box to the right.

4. From the control bar, click on Options and select Show Subscribed Newsgroups.

After that, Navigator's newsreader will show you only news from the newsgroups you've designated.

When you enter a newsgroup (via the news server pane at the top left of the newsreader window), you are given a list of all articles and messages that have been posted (in the article pane at the top right).

To extract the text of an article, highlight the selected article and double click. The text of the article will appear in the text pane at the bottom of the window.

You can navigate around the news panes with great ease by using the control bar at the top of the screen. On the control bar itself, you'll find the Previous and Next buttons. These open articles in the queue that you have not yet seen.

The Go menu lets you select articles in a variety of ways:

- **Next Message** opens the next article (read or unread).

- **Previous Message** opens the previous article (read or unread).

- **First Unread** goes to the first unread message.

- **Next Unread** goes to the next unread message.
- **Previous Unread** goes to the previous unread message.
- **First Flagged** goes to the first flagged message.
- **Next Flagged** goes to the next flagged message.
- **Previous Flagged** goes to the previous flagged message.
- **Stop Loading** interrupts the current transfer.

Note that some transfers of newsgroup lists, because of their size, can take several minutes, depending on the speed of your computer and modem.

Posting an Article

Reading articles posted in your newsgroups is only half the fun of subscribing. In fact, the culture of the Internet invites joining in — interacting with various sites, forums, newsgroups, and so on. If you have an answer to a problem someone else in the newsgroup is faced with, your membership in the group demands that you share the solution. That, in the world of the Internet, is how you pay for your subscription.

You participate in a newsgroup by posting an article of your own, which can be either an original discussion or a response to a previous article.

Article Defined

While the word **post** frequently is used to describe information in a newsgroup posting, another word has come into the vernacular. The word **article** is used in many newsgroups to describe a variety of messages you might post. Obviously, it could be an article as you normally understand it — a discussion or analysis of a subject in some depth. In other cases, article could refer to a one-paragraph answer to someone's problem (you could also e-mail this response personally to the recipient, but posting it usually makes for a better dissemination of the solution). Or it could be a statement of your own problem, asking for help to fix it. It could be a job posting, where you describe help wanted or available. As you read more articles from newsgroups, you'll get a sense of the breadth of the notices and be able to respond in kind.

Threaded Responses

Threading is one of the central features of the statement/response metaphor used in newsgroups. It means that when you respond to a certain article — a statement or question someone poses — your response is then placed in the thread that groups all responses to that same article. This makes your search more logical by allowing you to compare responses.

To post an article, you must first go to the new article screen. There are a couple of ways to get to a new article screen. From the main Navigator screen

1. Click on the Windows menu and select Netscape News.
2. Click on File and select New News Message (this can also be done from the newsgroup window).

Or, if you're already in the news application, you begin at this point.

3. Click on the To: News button on the control bar. This brings up the message composition window.
4. From the message composition window, complete the fields — Mail To, Cc, Subject, Attachment — exactly as described in sending e-mail. Be certain the Mail To address is that of the correct newsgroup.
5. In the text pane, write your response.
6. To mail it, click on the Send button.

To reply to an article, follow these steps:

1. Click on Window and select Netscape News.
2. Access the message to which you wish to reply.
3. Click on Message and select Post Reply.
4. Complete your response in the text window.
5. Click on Send.

Like e-mail, news responses can use the text from the original article and then intersperse answers between questions or paragraphs. When you look at the text window for a reply, you will see the text of the original message. You can keep all of it, delete portions that are not to the point, or leave just enough for the original author to recognize that this is a response to him or her. It is often useful as a reference point for a reply to answer each question in turn.

Summary

E-mail and newsreading are among the most frequently-used facilities available to Internet users. Virtually every person using the Net has instances where he or she needs to communicate with someone else, or some organization, that is also online. E-mail and newsreading are the two most interactive modes of Internet communications. Thus, taking a few moments to learn and configure your e-mail and newsreader will help assure a more complete Internet experience for you.

E-mail users will find Navigator's new newsreader similar to the easiest-to-use e-mail readers. That quickly intuitive layout of the screen makes for a product that makes finding, reading, and responding to the news easy for new and experienced users alike.

Navigator 2.0's newsreader is not among the top echelon of newsreaders that exist, but it is quite capable of handling the newsreading tasks of most Internet users. The best features of the newsreader are in the presentation of information. The excellent organization of the new newsreading window gives a clear but concise view of the news hosts, newsgroups, articles, subjects, dates, threads, and text.

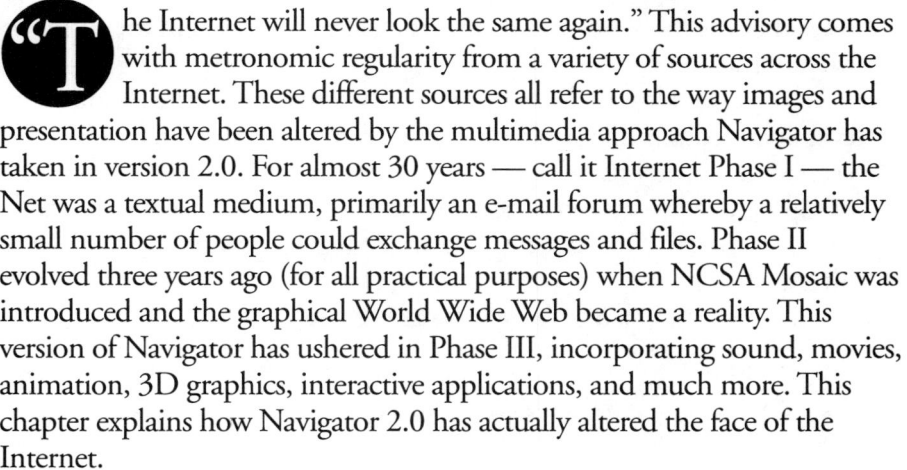

Chapter 5

Images and Document Presentation

"T he Internet will never look the same again." This advisory comes with metronomic regularity from a variety of sources across the Internet. These different sources all refer to the way images and presentation have been altered by the multimedia approach Navigator has taken in version 2.0. For almost 30 years — call it Internet Phase I — the Net was a textual medium, primarily an e-mail forum whereby a relatively small number of people could exchange messages and files. Phase II evolved three years ago (for all practical purposes) when NCSA Mosaic was introduced and the graphical World Wide Web became a reality. This version of Navigator has ushered in Phase III, incorporating sound, movies, animation, 3D graphics, interactive applications, and much more. This chapter explains how Navigator 2.0 has actually altered the face of the Internet.

Much of that alteration has come in the form of new creative modes of expression. But Navigator 2.0 has also changed the way you can look at information from a practical standpoint. For example, it has added a technology called Frames that allows several screens to be presented in the Navigator window simultaneously. This often saves vast amounts of time lost switching back and forth among pages, such as an index, information, and images.

Support for new Internet programming languages such as Java and JavaScript enables viewers to see and use working applications on what had once been relatively static screens. To date, more than 1,000 Java applications — called applets — have been developed.

Additionally, this chapter tells you about Netscape Chat, a tool that enables you to carry on interactive dialog in chatrooms around the world. The face of the Internet now has a voice to go with it.

New Image and Document Presentation Features

Tenured users of the Internet and Netscape Navigator will have a better perspective about Navigator's newly available functions in 2.0 than a brand-new user will. While much of what is now supported appeals to the eye, it also appears to have been designed for the mind: The productivity value of Frames, the interactive dialog features of Chat, the peace of mind with new security features. Taken in sum, they represent a notable forward thrust in Netscape's attempt to grab "mindshare" — the feeling among users that the tools are both comfortable and functional in their support of the Internet.

It hasn't been lost on Netscape cyberneers that the Net is a rapidly evolving medium that could do perhaps a billion dollars in commerce this year alone. To do business on that scale requires use by customers of a piece of software that is easy to handle, broadly functional, and utterly safe from threats to privacy. The bottom line is that Navigator isn't just a pretty face, it's a secure one.

The major points of this evolution are these:

- Frames
- Chat functions
- Java and JavaScript support
- Support for live and embedded objects
- Security
- File transfer

Frames Make Interaction Easier

Frames refers to a feature that allows sites to publish information in several interactive windows simultaneously although they are part of the same

HTML page. At first glance it appears to be a Windows type of application, but Frames is more analogous to picture-within-a-picture television, where several things can not only be seen, but interacted with.

Chat from Any Web Page

Chat features enable users who want to maintain interactive chat to do so within a frame on any given Web page. A chat client, which Netscape markets separately (usually to chataholics) in Navigator Power Pack, provides facilities for embedding links and objects in e-mail.

Support for the Java Programming Language

Java support is one of the most exciting features of Navigator 2.0. Java, a programming language and environment, is being used to develop applications called **applets**, which are finding their way onto the Web in the forms of animation, interactive games, video, audio, and more. When you come upon an applet while browsing, you can just click on it to start it. In addition, JavaScript, a companion tool under Navigator 2.0, is a scripting language that is not as complex as Java to use, but lets Web page developers create a whole new variety of feature-rich pages.

Embedding Live Objects

Live objects support refers to objects such as the URLs you can embed in e-mail, news and chat, but also more visually dramatic applications called **in-line plug-ins**, which enable you to view, for example, multimedia presentations created in Macromedia Director or documents published in Adobe Acrobat. Click on the embedded object and it starts automatically. This functionality will dramatically alter the way the Web looks — and performs.

Improved Security

Security has always been a concern for people on the Internet, especially in the areas of financial transactions, bugged chats, and individual vulnerability (whether someone can move through the Web to penetrate your PC). Netscape asked hackers to break its security, and they did, exposing fatal weaknesses. These weaknesses have since been patched, and Navigator 2.0 security is the soundest of any commercial browser.

Built-In File Transfer Capabilities

File transfer is an example of an application (e-mail is another) for which you previously had to have a separate piece of software in addition to your browser. Before, you could access FTP sites, but the server administrator had to create a WWW front end for the FTP server. And to upload files, you had to use file attachment features of your e-mail or newsreader. But Navigator 2.0 incorporates FTP into its array of functions, allowing users to both find and transfer files — up and down — with great ease.

And More...

In addition to all these new features, Navigator 2.0 boasts improvements in other areas, such as graphics handling via Progressive JPEG. JPEG (Joint Photographic Experts Group) refers to the way images appear on your screen. A baseline JPEG image — the old technique — rendered the image line by line, starting at the top. Progressive JPEG renders the image in whole-image layers, enabling the viewer to see the image in its entirety as even more detail is added.

Another advance is in what are called client side image maps. Image maps are graphic images that have Internet locations mapped into them, allowing you to click on an image to move to a particular location. The latest version of Navigator allows you to download image maps to the Navigator instead of keeping them on the server. This saves time running back and forth from client to server and back again for the information.

Navigator's Frames

One of the most interesting features in Navigator 2.0 is called Frames. Whether you are a new Web user or a tenured Web site developer, Frames has implications for how you will interact with pages on the Internet. It provides, in effect, a way for you to look at two, three, or more Web documents at one time on the screen.

Frames is a feature that allows your Navigator window to be segmented into multiple viewing windows or frames. A frame is an independent, scrollable window that appears with other frames on the same Navigator screen. Frames use the format now prevalent in many Windows 95 applications where separate, controllable frames pop up to provide information about various aspects of a subject. Frames uses (usually) sizable panes — developers can also choose frames with fixed sizes — like those you have seen in Navigator's e-mail client. The page in Figure 5-1 illustrates how the screen can be divided.

What you can do with the panes is mostly up to the developer of the Web page you are viewing. Some of the panes are fixed in size, while others can be sized by clicking and dragging the borders of the frames, allowing you to incorporate the elements within the various frames — for example, text in one, GIF image graphics in another, JPEG images in another, and so on.

Each frame can also present the page of an entirely different URL. This capability gives developers great opportunities to have what have been called **sticky crawlers** in earlier technology — that is, a frame that follows, or sticks to you as you navigate around a site. You could have a table of contents in one frame and text in another. You could find an ad, a message from the chairman, a control bar, and a warning, for example.

Frames are a way of specifying multiple, independent, scrollable regions within a display window. As such, they are pretty much limited only by the Web developer's imagination and objectives.

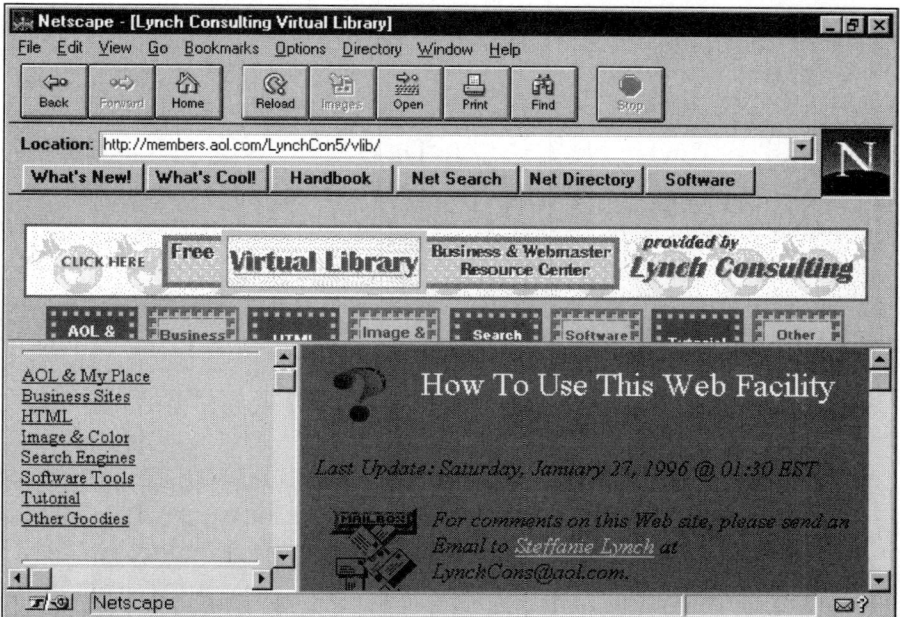

Figure 5-1: Navigator's Frames boast scrollable cells that allow you to navigate more logically and quickly to the information you're seeking. With an index on the left and text on the right, there's no more switching back and forth between pages.

Frame Frustration

At this writing, no other browser incorporates Frames-type technology. This fact alone has implications for how you will view many Internet pages because literally thousands of them now have incorporated Frames and other Navigator-specific features. The consequence is a little problematic. If you have Navigator 1.x, and especially if you have a non-Navigator browser, many pages on the Web are simply unavailable to you. You will click to a site, only to see a message saying something like: "You don't have Navigator 2.0! It is required to view this site. Click here to download Navigator 2.0." Other Web pages don't shut you out completely, but will limit what you can see and do. The message there will be: "This site is best viewed with Navigator 2.0."

The result is a period of transition that is frustrating for both users and Web sites. Users who haven't upgraded to Navigator 2.0 can't see a lot of the niftiest sites; and Web sites that have upgraded by using the newest features are losing traffic to their sites until significant numbers of people make the transition. Frames is one of the features that can shut you out of a site completely if you don't have Navigator 2.0.

Targeted Windows

Each window, or frame, can be given a NAME value. These are called targeted windows in Navigator 2.0. These windows can be targeted by links in other documents, such as other frames on the same screen. Say you wanted the text of the history on B-52 bombers in one frame. NAMEing allows that text to be linked to an image of the bomber in another frame. In a third frame you could even see a motion video of bombs being dropped. If you scrolled the images frame down to an image of the F-14 Tomcat, the text window would bring up the text on the F-14, the motion frame would bring up the video, and so on. In Figure 5-2 you see an example of targeted windows being used on a cyber-shopping trip.

With the capability of having NAMES associated with different browser windows, users can choose where text or images appear just by designating a NAME. Links in any window can refer to another window by NAME. When you click on the link, the document you asked for appears in that named window. If the window is not already open, Navigator opens and names a new window for you.

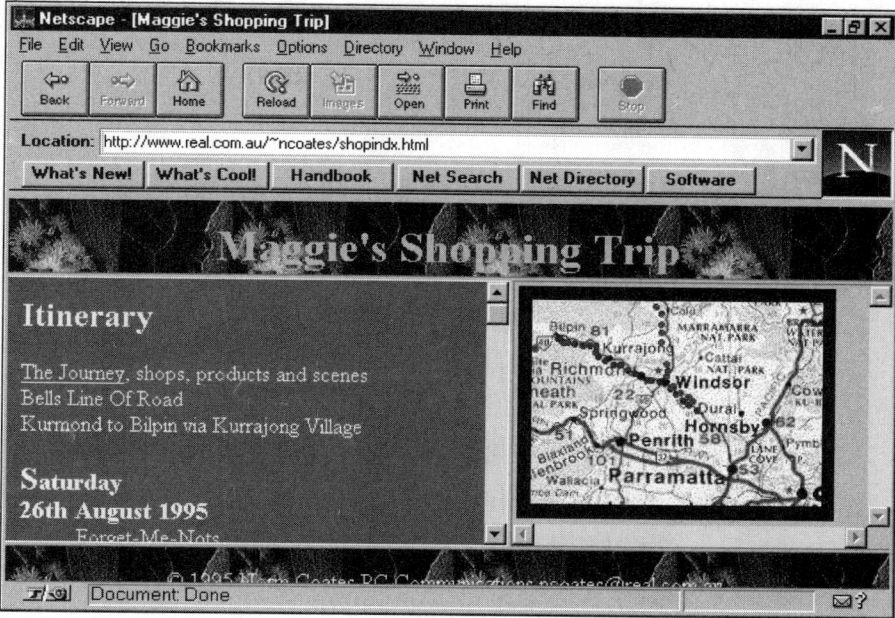

Figure 5-2: Targeted windows means that you can specify a URL in one frame to open up a document in another frame.

Client Side Image Maps

Client side image maps represent a performance enhancement for users of Navigator 2.0. If you have a graphics-capable browser, you probably have come across what have been known as server-side ISMAP images when you were accessing Web pages. An excellent example is Time-Warner's page at **http://www.pathfinder.com**, as shown in Figure 5-3. (Netscape's home page — **http://home.netscape.com/** — is also good.)

Image maps are graphic images into which hypertext links have been mapped. While most of the hypertext jumps on the Web are made from the more common blue-colored link words, this color is user-definable and links can be other colors as well. In addition to these colored text links, Web page developers can embed URLs directly into a portion of a graphic. It's a process similar to mapping precise coordinates on a paper map. Where the coordinates join, the developer can plant his URL so that viewers can pull up a much more dynamic and interesting representation of a site. Instead of clicking on a blue link, they could click on an object, a graphically represented word, a picture — whatever image has been mapped.

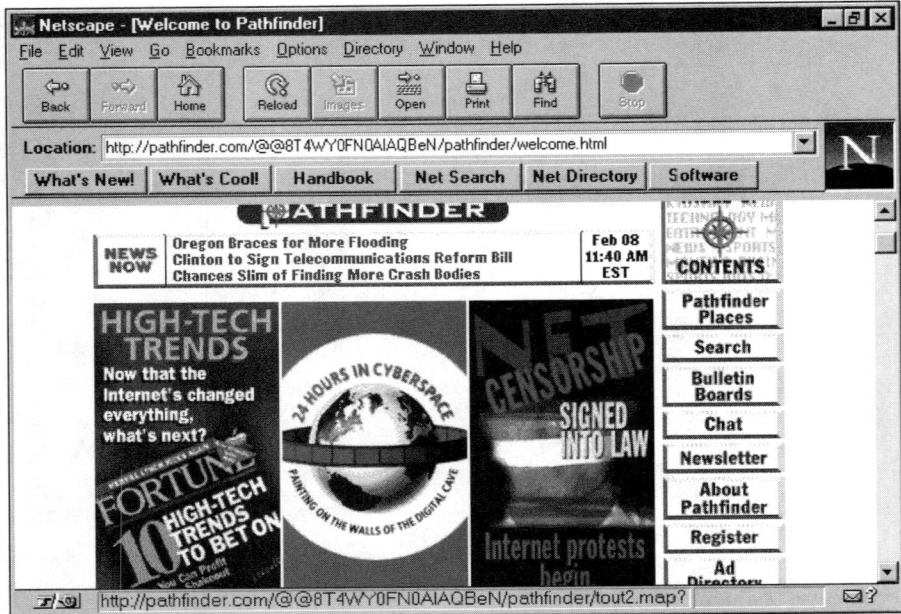

Figure 5-3: A deliciously varied image map such as Time-Warner's can please the eye but not the patience. Because of this, the company also offers a text-only alternative.

The difference between server side image maps and client side image maps is one of file location. Improvements here give Navigator a performance boost. Server side image maps are kept on a server. Whenever someone comes across a mapped image and clicks on one of its elements, the link sends a out a request to the server and the server then loads the image. This could be a tedious process, especially if you have a 14.4 Kbps modem or slower (which most users, regrettably, have to tolerate).

Client side image maps found in Navigator 2.0 shift the file location. The map that relates parts of the image to different URLs is stored in the current file. This saves a round trip to the server and should present your documents faster. Because the map information is stored in the document you are viewing, the destination URLs can be displayed in the status area along the bottom of the screen as you pass the mouse over the image map.

Client side image maps also give developers a chance to present object-oriented views of their information. For example, a page using frames and image maps could provide a map in one frame, text in a second, and icons in a third. You could click on a portion of the map you want information about; click on an icon representing the type of information you want (for example, population, per capita income) and read the textual output in the third frame. This versatility allows viewers a one-screen, multi-dimensional look at data that might have required several hypertext jumps before, with all the downloading that would entail.

Developer Considerations

Developers contemplating the use of image maps — and, in truth, many of the other more exotic presentation media — have both practical and artistic considerations to weigh. Navigator's use of client side image maps puts some speed to what has been a molasses-slow process in many instances (the aforementioned Time-Warner site is a good example). When the graphics are so large that their download time tries the patience of a stone, viewers sometimes turn off the graphics and therefore subvert the developer's use of any page design.

An interesting dichotomy is growing in the Web page design community. One school takes utter advantage of every evolving graphic image that is supported. This can make for visually stunning pages, but sometimes slows the Internet navigation to a crawl. These developers are not taking into account a kind of internal clock that grows in Internet users. Once this clock tells them they've been waiting too long, they simply leave a page if it isn't yet completely loaded.

At the other end of the spectrum are the Web's artistic minimalists who have concluded that fast sites packed with evident information are more important to many Internauts. The Technology Information Centre KnowledgeBase in England (**http://www.tickit.com**) is one example of the minimalist approach, as shown in Figure 5-4.

The organization that created the page shown in Figure 5-4 grudgingly conceded a small (but creative) home page graphic, then undertook the challenge of aggregating a wealth of technology information, organized in most of the ways users might wish to search. At this writing, no other graphic is to be found.

Thus, while Navigator 2.0's features have improved the productivity of Web browsing, even great image maps require some recognition of the viewer's internal clock. The style outlook will always be a mixed bag because of the sheer number of developers and their preferences. Navigator's support will assure better performance and more varied and striking images. But look for the examples of more intelligent application of this new array of visual images.

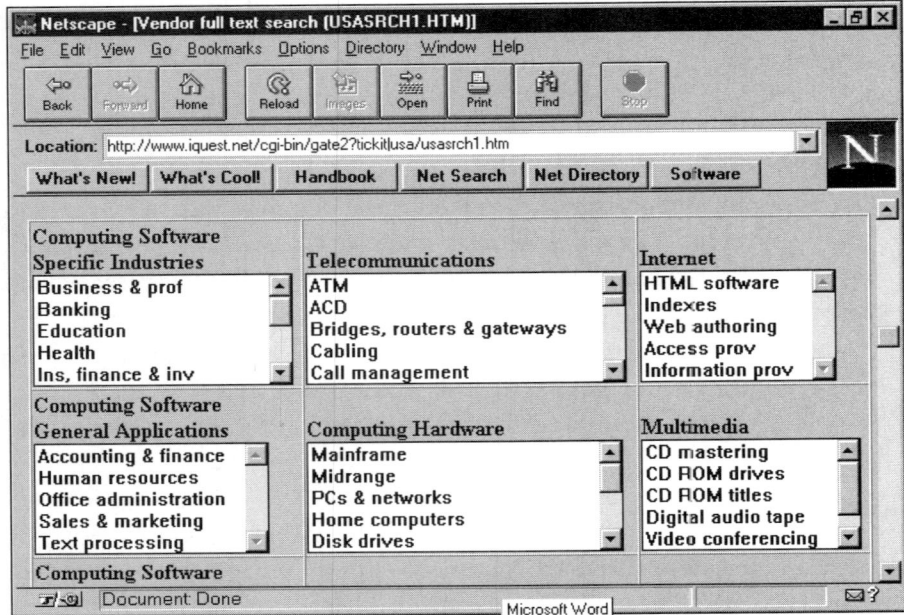

Figure 5-4: The TicK site took the minimalist approach to graphics, opting instead for a fast-loading wealth of information accessible from scrollable frames.

Inline Plug-Ins

The rapid evolution of presentation technology on the World Wide Web induced Netscape Communications to begin support for some of a more exotic type of file called live objects. For the most part, these are files that have motion or sound. That support, in the form of what Netscape calls plug-ins, is the equivalent of mini-helper applications embedded right into the Navigator software. Plug-ins allow the user to view or hear the action right from the client window.

In the past, whenever you came across a page that carried something such as an MPEG video or a MIDI sound file, you couldn't run it unless you had already installed a separate helper application. Now Navigator allows the development and viewing of a wide range of these more exotic presentations by letting developers embed plug-ins directly into an HTML document. The user no longer needs to go outside the browser to the helper application; in fact, he never needs to leave his screen. The result is a quick and easy integration of many existing technologies that you might have found only in media such as CD-ROM.

Some plug-ins allow you to view and hear such things as Apple QuickTime movies, Adobe Acrobat PDF — Portable Document File — documents, and Macromedia Director presentations. A partial list of outside plug-in suppliers can be found at the end of this section.

In addition to the embedded inline plug-ins that Navigator 2.0 supports, it also provides support for full-screen plug-ins. These are being sold by a variety of manufacturers with the idea of turning the Web into a five-star media center. Acrobat Amber, for example, lets you view, navigate, and print PDF files right in your Navigator window. This means you could view something such as a vivid, four-color brochure with all fonts, graphics, and layouts that would be unavailable in most HTML text.

Navigator's plug-ins go a long way toward taking the Internet to the goal of a super-visual, multimedia, real-time, interactive technology. Hypertext links or expandable JPEG images sometimes give the impression that the Web is a dynamic place, but in reality, it hasn't been. The plug-in technology changes that. It instantly takes the Web pages from static to dynamic in the purest sense.

Plug-In Levels

It is necessary for users to understand the three levels of plug-ins:

- embedded
- full screen
- hidden

Embedded plug-ins are built right into the Web pages by the developer. When the user clicks on the icon that invokes the plug-in — for example, if you wanted to view the animated recreation of the Kennedy assassination or a scene from Star Wars — you simply click on the image or text that starts the application. The embedded, in-line plug-in activates it without your having to do anything further.

Full-screen plug-ins, like helper applications, become screen managers when they are invoked. By using the Acrobat Amber product, which is based on the popular Acrobat software from Adobe, you can search through software documentation by using hypertext links or page numbers to move on, but without the compromises of HTML-only presentation.

Hidden plug-ins operate in the background to provide support for objects that might come up with some frequency, such as MIDI files. None of the plug-ins will alter the basic appearance of the Navigator's screen.

Plug-In Suppliers

At this writing, Navigator was gathering steam for its plug-in facilities by lining up support from a variety of sources. Most of these companies offer free looks at beta versions of their products, which can be downloaded from servers on the Internet.

A partial list of plug-in suppliers follows:

- **Adobe Acrobat Amber.** This plug-in lets you view, navigate, and print PDF files right in your Navigator 2.0 window. It's one of the hottest plug-ins. (**http://www.adobe.com/Amber/Download.html**)

- **Apple QuickTime.** Apple's plug-in lets viewers get a full multimedia experience, including movies. This plug-in is not available at this writing, but is coming soon.

- **Corel Vector Graphics.** Corel's CMX Viewer is available for Windows 95 and NT only. (**http://www.corel.com/corelcmx/**)

- **Envoy.** This plug-in from Tumbleweed, which runs on Windows 3.1, Windows 95, Macintosh, and Power Mac, is primarily for viewing Envoy documents.

- **Formula One/NET.** This product from Visual Components is an Excel-compatible spreadsheet with built-in Internet functionality (you can include live charts, links to URLs, and clickable controls and buttons). (**http://www.visualcomp.com**)

- **Lightning Strike.** This plug-in professes to be a better way than JPEG to compress images. (**http://wwwinfinop.com**)

- **OLE Control.** From NCompass, this plug-in lets you embed OLE (Object Linking and Embedding) controls as applets created by using standard programming languages like C++. (**http://www.excite.sfu.ca/NCompass/**)

- **OpenScape.** Object Power's OpenScape delivers OLE/OCX compatibility and enterprise application development facilities. It uses a visual drag-and-drop environment and Visual Basic scripting. (**http://www.opower.com/**)

- **RealAudio.** This plug-in from Progressive Networks supports live and on-demand real-time audio over 14.4 Kbps or faster connections. (**http://www.realaudio.com/**)

- **VDOLive.** VDOnet's plug-in compresses video images and works well on 28.8 and faster modems. (**http://www.vdolive.com/ newplug.htm**)

- **VR Scout.** This VRML plug-in from Chaco Communications lets users move through 3D graphical scenes. (**http://www.chaco.com**)

- **WebFX.** Paper Software's plug-in is another VRML-support tool. (**http://www.paperinc.com**)

The number of plug-in suppliers grows constantly and at such a rapid rate that the number as you read this will be greater than there are at this writing. Check out the products from the URLs mentioned above, but be sure to look at the latest list from Netscape's Plug-ins page: **http://home.netscape.com/comprod/products/navigator/version_2.0/ plugins/index.html**

A Word about Navigator's Plug-Ins

The idea behind plug-ins, whether inline, full-screen, or hidden, is to enhance the experience of the World Wide Web. They take screens from static to dynamic, and Navigator's support means you rarely have to leave your browser window in order to enjoy video, animation, sound, or other special effects. Netscape's efforts here are being complemented by an eager array of plug-in providers. The number of Web pages utilizing sound or motion are still relatively few, but the support in Navigator 2.0 will launch that number dramatically skyward. In Netscape Navigator Gold 2.0, the Web author's version of this software examined in Part II of this book, the comparatively simple process of embedding plug-ins makes it clear that Web authors and developers will be incorporating these features widely.

It's a good idea to sample the commercial plug-ins by using their downloadable betas. Many of the products perform similar functions, and their effectiveness can vary from platform to platform.

Using Portable Document Format with Navigator

Portable Document Format, or PDF, provides a means of preserving the integrity and appearance of a precisely designed page as it is transferred from one point to another. While pages designed in HTML are *open* — that is, they can be read by any Web browser on the market — each browser interprets the elements of the page differently. Thus a page designed to look best in Navigator 2.0, a notation you will see frequently on Web pages, could look entirely different on NCSA Mosaic or one of the other browsers. Some will not handle graphics at all, thus jeopardizing the sometimes important look and feel of a company's carefully crafted image. PDF can help.

How PDF Works

PDF files can capture an image and, regardless of the HTML interpretation constraints of a given browser, present a page exactly as it was designed. While Navigator's support of a range of graphics formats enables you to design pages that will generally look and feel exactly the way you intended, some pages will require that you consider other factors:

- Are you transferring documentation of other material where the integrity of schematics and diagrams must be preserved?

- Are you transferring forms whose layout must always be consistent?

- Are you transferring brochures or catalogs whose print and electronic versions must always match, as shown in Figure 5-5?

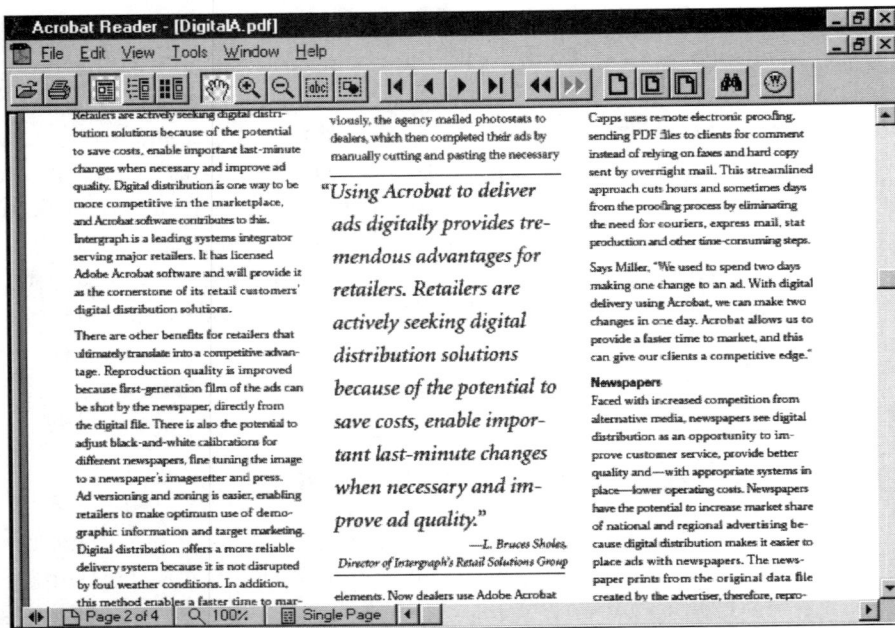

Figure 5-5: When documentation and other textual information must retain their format, no matter what browser they are read in, PDF files maintain the integrity.

In any situation where appearance must be preserved, PDF files are how it is done with consistency. To do this with Navigator, you need to download or otherwise acquire PDF plug-ins or helper applications. Several PDF tools are on the market — Novell's WordPerfect Envoy, Common Ground's Mini Viewer, and others; consult the section "Plug-in suppliers" in this chapter to stay current — but the most prominent is Adobe Acrobat Amber, a version of Adobe Acrobat that is specially integrated to run with Navigator 2.0. Adobe Acrobat Amber can be downloaded from the following Web page: **http://www.adobe.com/Amber/Download.html.** It also is available on Netscape's PowerPack CD.

Installing Adobe Acrobat Amber

After you've downloaded the software, you need to install and configure it to work with Navigator. At this writing, it should be noted, the Amber product was only available for Windows. However, Adobe Acrobat, its predecessor, has versions for a wide range of platforms.

To install the Windows version, click on the icon for the self-extracting file **ambr32D1.exe**. When the file has extracted,

1. Click on the setup.exe and run through the setup process.
2. When setup is complete, click on Edit and select Preferences from the menu.
3. Select Weblink from the menu.
4. Click on Browse to find your path and filename for Navigator.
5. Highlight the filename and click on OK.
6. Click on OK on the Weblink Preferences window, as shown in Figure 5-6.

This process enables the Adobe Acrobat Amber software to run automatically whenever Navigator comes across a PDF file that could not otherwise be read by Navigator.

If, after downloading and installing the Acrobat Amber plug-in, you want to see PDF in action, you can get a good picture of PDF files by going to Adobe's home page (**http://www.adobe.com**) and linking to any of its own PDF pages or visiting various PDF Web sites you can jump to from Adobe's home page.

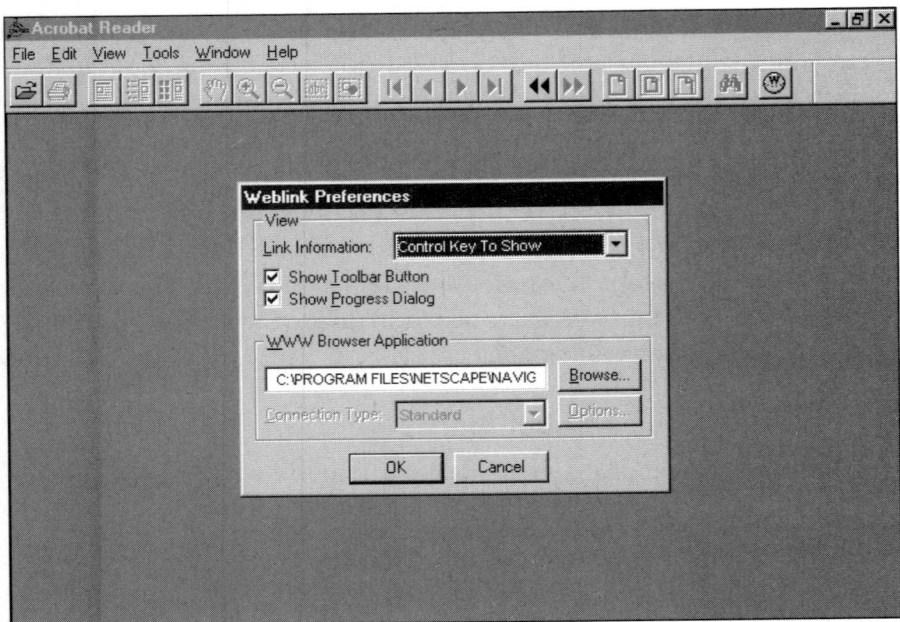

Figure 5-6: The WebLink plug-in allows you to hook up Acrobat Amber to run automatically with Navigator 2.0.

Bookmarks

Bookmarks have always been one of Navigator's strengths. One of the common complaints users voice about the Internet is the complexity it seems to have, starting with URL addresses that can exceed 40 characters in length. Finding where you want to go, then getting there in some reasonable fashion, has frequently been where commercial services such as CompuServe and America Online got higher marks as information services. Everything was tidy and headlined and categorized. It is that kind of organization that Navigator's Bookmarks feature attempts to bring at a handy, if extremely rudimentary, level.

The idea behind Bookmarks is simple: If you find a site on the Internet that you will visit frequently, you click to add it to your Bookmark file. Navigator 2.0 adds the URL and its site-specific information (such as the site name) to the file. After that, you simply open your Bookmark file and click on the site's name to visit. No tedious URLs, no roaming with search engines; just click and go.

Capturing a Web Address in Bookmarks

You capture a Web address with two simple clicks directly from the control bar at the top of Navigator's screen. The process is simple: You never even have to leave the screen to save an address. From the site itself, simply follow these steps:

1. Go to Bookmarks on the control bar and open the menu.
2. Click on Add Bookmark to add the URL and site information to your file.

If you want to add a bookmark for a page you aren't on — for example, you might be reading about a certain address in a book such as this and want to add it without actually going to it — you can do that by another process, illustrated in Figure 5-7.

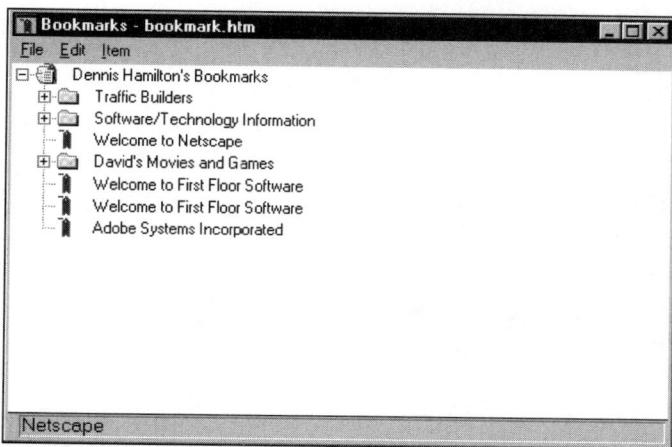

Figure 5-7: Open the Bookmark file from the control bar, then select Go to Bookmarks to open a URL or add a URL for a site you're not currently visiting.

1. Click on Bookmarks and open the menu.
2. Select Go to Bookmarks.
3. Select Item.
4. Click on Insert Bookmark.
5. Complete the fields as described: The name of the site, the URL, and a description.
6. Click on OK.

This process adds the bookmark to your Bookmarks file. When you are ready to visit the site, just select the Go to Bookmarks button, then double-click on the name of the site you wish to visit. Navigator opens it automatically.

Removing a Web Address

It is as easy to remove an address from your Bookmarks as it is to add one.

1. Open the Bookmarks menu.

2. Select Go to Bookmarks.

3. Highlight the address to be deleted by clicking on it once.

4. Click on the Edit menu and select Delete.

The bookmark will disappear from your Bookmark file.

Bookmarking from Navigator History

Each time you use Netscape Navigator 2.0, the system automatically creates a list of all sites you visited during that particular session. If you get busy moving around the Internet during a session and forget to create a bookmark for a site you liked, you can return to it via the History list and enter the site into your Bookmark file, as illustrated in Figure 5-8.

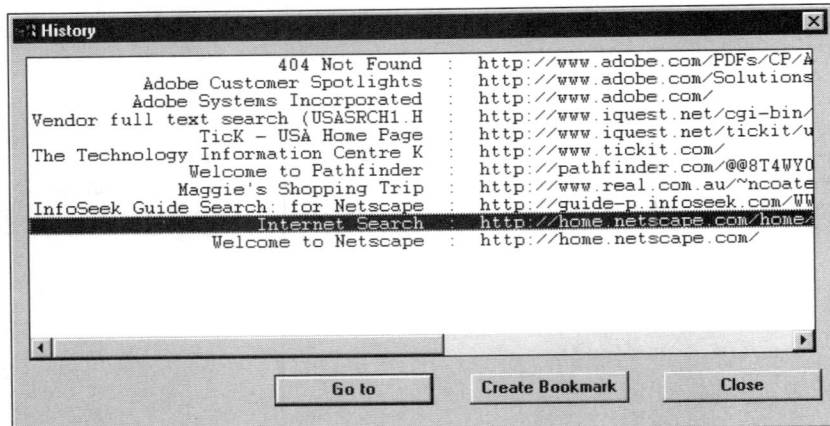

Figure 5-8: The History list provides a record of your recent Internet travels. Just click on Create Bookmark to move the file name and address.

Here's how you use Navigator History to place a bookmark:

1. Go to the Window item on the Control Bar and select History.
2. Highlight the site where you wish to create a bookmark.
3. Click on Create Bookmark.
4. Click on Close.

Your History item will be filed in the Bookmarks file.

Making Changes to Bookmarks

Notice as you go through these exercises that all information for Bookmarks is easily changed. In your Properties screen you will find several fields and a box in which to enter your descriptions of various sites. The box allows a fairly lengthy description, which is an option you may want to exercise. The nature of the Internet is that it is highly dynamic. The content of some sites changes often. The way you set up, organize, and maintain your Bookmarks and SmartMarks (see the SmartMarks discussion in the following segment) affects your productivity.

When you learn that a site has altered its content or has changed addresses or titles, it takes only a moment to make the corresponding changes in bookmarks.

1. Click on Bookmarks and open the menu.
2. Select Go to Bookmarks.
3. Select Item.
4. Select Properties.
5. Change the fields to include new information on the name of the site, the URL, or the description.
6. When you're done, click on OK.

Organizing Bookmarks

Bookmarks organization is pretty much a requirement for anyone wanting to maintain their sanity as netizens. A fact of Web life is that there is much to see and appreciate. The longer you are on, the more sites you'll find to enjoy and remember with Bookmarks.

The problem is, after a while your collection can begin to look like the white pages of the phone book: Just a long list of names and addresses with no real connection. But organization features in Navigator 2.0 help solve that.

Navigator 2.0 allows you to do more with Bookmarks than you could in previous versions of the software. You can take organization on the Navigator screen to hierarchical levels that resemble the threaded messages you get from e-mail and newsgroups. In Figure 5-9, you can see how sites can be categorized within logical folders.

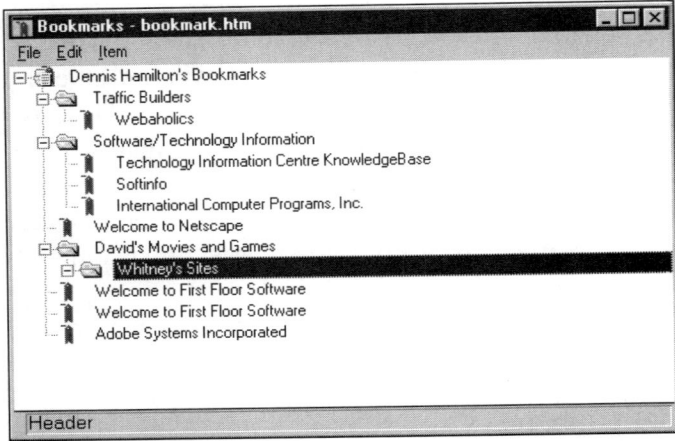

Figure 5-9: Organization facilities in Bookmarks let you group URLs into specific categories that are simple to access.

The hierarchical arrangement of the screen only shows you one level at a time, instead of displaying the entire file. The hierarchy is structured this way:

1. **Category header folders.** These are the broadest of categories and could contain literally hundreds of bookmarks. They are represented by folder icons. Like all folder icons, they display items contained within them when you click to open them.

2. **Secondary folders.** These are folders that you have the option of placing into your hierarchy. If you find yourself bookmarking a lot of pages, you may wish to utilize secondary folders; until you really mark a lot of pages under a single category header, however, it isn't necessary. Secondary folders also use folder icons, but are indented to the right of the category header folders.

3. **Separators.** These are dividing points that separate any of the folders.
4. **Bookmarks.** These are the names of the pages you have added to your file.

For example, you could create a hierarchy that looks something like this:

Category Header: Automobiles

Secondary Folders: Antique, Classic, Performance

Bookmarks: '57 Chevys

Once you know how you want to categorize your bookmarks, you can go to the menus under Bookmarks on the control bar and begin to define your library.

Making Folders and Separators

Creating your header folders is simple and can be done from your Navigator screen. Pay attention to the Properties frame, which contains the fields you will fill in to add all your folders, separators, and bookmarks.

1. Go to the Bookmarks menu and select Go to Bookmarks.
2. In the Bookmarks frame that appears, select the place in the Bookmark list where you wish to insert the new header folder. The new folder will appear below it.
3. From the Item menu, select Insert Folder.
4. In the Bookmark Properties window that appears, fill in the required name and description fields (see Figure 5-10).
5. Click on OK.

To create a secondary folder, highlight the header folder under which you want the secondary folder to appear. Then follow the same five-step sequence you followed to create a header folder. The secondary folder will appear indented to the right of the header folder, with the sites it contains offset to the right of the folder.

The other element in the hierarchy is the separator. This is a small icon that visually separates your folders and URLs. It's a good idea to use these icons judiciously. A good bookmark list is a model of organization with easy-to-understand headers, well-titled folders, and clearly-stated site names. A bad list can be more trouble than a long and unorganized list.

You can clutter things up with too many bookmarks and separators, or confuse issues with badly named folders that you have to open to have any idea what the contents are. The rule of the day in naming folders is clarity.

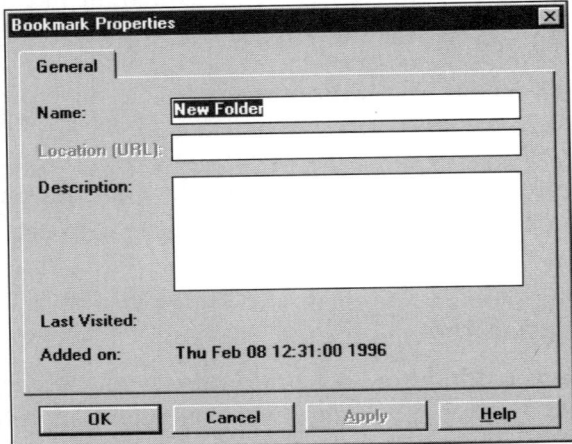

Figure 5-10: If you're just creating a header folder, the URL field will not be activated in the Properties frame when you fill in the information. If you're adding a site, it will.

Rearranging Your Bookmarks

Notwithstanding our most diligent efforts at organization, it is human nature to clutter. People do spring cleaning, have garage sales, and have to unclutter bookmark lists. Instead of a broom, however, you have drag-and-drop bookmarks, a handy feature of Navigator versions running on Windows 95.

Drag-and-drop is a popular feature of the graphical user interface found on Windows 95. Just as it is used to move files around by clicking, holding, and dragging them from folder to folder, you can drag-and-drop bookmarks and save yourself the more tedious renaming/update process.

If you want to move a single address from one place on your list to another, you begin from the Bookmarks list:

1. Open the category folder into which you want to place the new item.

2. Click on the item and drag it to the folder.

3. If there is a secondary folder beneath the category folder, open the category folder so that it displays the secondary folders. Then drag the item to the folder in where you want it to appear.

If you have an entire folder you wish to relocate, just click and drag the folder to either a new folder or a new location on the hierarchy tree. Moving the folder saves you from having to move the items within it one by one.

Using the Find Option

Like the Find File function in Windows 95, Netscape Navigator 2.0 has included a handy Find Bookmark facility to help you locate bookmarks that you can't seem to locate, no matter how organized you've tried to be. You don't even have to remember the complete name of the folder or site you're trying to find. The Find option locates those that contain the name or phrase you enter into the search field.

To find a bookmarked file, follow these steps:

1. Go to the Bookmarks menu and select Go to Bookmarks.

2. In the Bookmarks frame that appears, click on Edit and select the Find option (see Figure 5-11).

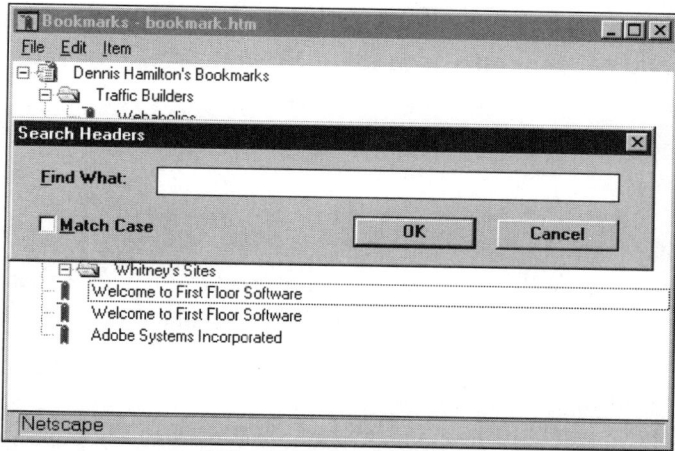

Figure 5-11: When your bookmarks list gets long enough that you've forgotten where an item is located, the Find option tracks it down by using the information you enter in this field.

3. In the search screen that pops up, enter the name of the needed item.

4. Click on OK.

The Find facility tracks down the item or folder and highlight it in the Bookmarks frame.

If you end up with a list of sites that contains the selected word or phrase, the Find option settles on the first one in the list. If that is not what you're seeking, click on Find Next and it moves to the next item with the characteristics you described.

Bookmarks Summarized

When the Bookmarks feature was first introduced on Netscape's early Navigator browser, it became a huge hit. It saved people from the numbingly tedious and error-prone process of keying and re-keying URLs; or, worse, trying to figure out where an address was taking them if they forgot the site name.

Now Bookmarks comes with new features that make the facility not merely a convenience (as the older one was), but an organizational necessity. While the Add Bookmark button is a fast and convenient way to get the name and address of a site into your Bookmark file, it is strongly recommended that you take the time to organize your folders and items into a page that represents the way you work — the sites you like for information, for laughs, for chat, for ideas. If you think of it as a personal reflection of your work and leisure life, 20 minutes of creating folders and dragging and dropping items into them can make your whole Internet experience vastly more satisfying. And productive.

SmartMarks

As you might infer from the name of this facility, SmartMarks is Bookmarks with a brain. While the Bookmarks facility is extremely useful, it still is a manually devised hierarchical tree that visually explains — and provides your links to — sites you liked. SmartMarks takes the whole concept of managing favorite sites several steps further.

What SmartMarks does is bring another level of organization to your Internet navigation. It elevates browsing beyond a technical exercise full of super-complicated URLs and sometimes tedious searches. Things begin to look more like the clearly headlined links that have been a strength of commercial services such as CompuServe. Navigator's Bookmarks takes a step in that direction, but SmartMarks races far ahead.

Where You Get SmartMarks

While you can download SmartMarks from Netscape's Web site, the software isn't automatically included in the Navigator suite of applications unless you purchase Netscape's PowerPack. The software was developed by First Floor, Inc., and made available through Netscape's facilities.

What SmartMarks Does

In a nutshell, SmartMarks watches your Web sites for you, then reports back to you about changes in them. Most people who bookmark their Web sites do so because they contain information that is useful. That information often changes (sometimes several times a day; and change will be more frequent with the advent of real-time updating on the Web). Web addresses change too, often with a forwarding notice that doesn't make itself known until you click to the vacant site. It is impractical for most people to devote a lot of time to monitoring changes at their favorite sites. SmartMarks, which has the capacity to manage literally thousands of bookmarks, was conceived to do it for you.

SmartMarks has a variety of other features as well. With this feature, you can

- Set the monitoring frequency to examine Web pages for changes.
- Receive automatic bulletins from Web sites and authors.
- Design HTML bulletins into your own Web pages.
- Get a point-and-click interface to most major search engines on the Web.
- Add customized descriptions to bookmarks.
- Add "smart" bookmarks directly from Navigator's Bookmarks menu.
- Double-click on any bookmark in SmartMarks to direct Navigator in that direction.
- Switch to SmartMarks from Navigator with a simple menu command.
- Import and export bookmark files.

The SmartMarks software comes with 300 preinstalled "smart" Web sites, which you can use to begin building your SmartMarks files.

Downloading SmartMarks

If you have purchased Netscape's PowerPack, you'll receive a copy of SmartMarks with it. Just insert the CD-ROM into the CD drive and run the standard setup.exe. The defaults allow the installation to proceed smoothly, though later you might wish to configure the software to start whenever Netscape starts.

If you want to download the software, go to: **http://www.netscape.com/comprod/smartmarks_install.html**

If you find this server busy, you can also download SmartMarks from the Netscape Home Page (**http://home.netscape.com**). Just follow the same download links you used to download Navigator, but when you come to the Select a Product box, check SmartMarks. One of these sites will enable you transfer a beta copy of SmartMarks to evaluate.

1. Download the SmartMarks File (sm10r2.exe).

2. Create a folder and place the downloaded file into it, then click on Run to open the self-extracting file.

3. Follow the default recommendations.

When SmartMarks is being installed, it opens a dialog box to ask whether you want your Navigator Bookmarks copied to the SmartMarks file. Unless you have some compelling reason not to do this, you should click on OK. This copies whatever bookmarks you have accumulated over to SmartMarks. Remember that after you have installed SmartMarks, it replaces your Bookmarks

You'll see the new software in your Programs list, which you open with the Start button.

Using SmartMarks

There is no question that, while Netscape Navigator's Bookmarks feature has been updated terrifically in Navigator 2.0, First Floor's SmartMarks is dramatically better. This is certainly why Netscape Communications has endorsed the product by making it available for downloading from Netscape's own servers. In essence, SmartMarks makes Navigator 2.0 even better, and that's easy for Netscape to embrace.

There is more to do in setting up SmartMarks addresses and files, but not a lot. And the return on investment in terms of information is unquestionably high. If you are going to work — or play — on the Internet at more than just a few selected sites, it is probably worth your while to get SmartMarks. If you're going to be a serious Internet user, its organization and monitoring facilities almost demand that you make the leap.

When you open SmartMarks, you see a Frames-type window called a Smart Window. From here you can perform the bulk of your SmartMarks management (after which it does most of its own). Figure 5-12 illustrates the arrangement of the Smart Window.

The frame on the left side contains the tree of folders that holds your site information. While you can hide it from view, it's a good idea to keep it open simply for quick navigation.

Creating a Folder

You can easily create a new folder to hold your "smart bookmarks." Like the organization you went through setting up Navigator's Bookmarks, you just need a little coherent logic to arrange items and folders along the lines of your work, leisure, and interests. The preinstalled folders in SmartMarks, which contain links to many of the Internet's most visited pages, show you how your folders and content items will appear and function.

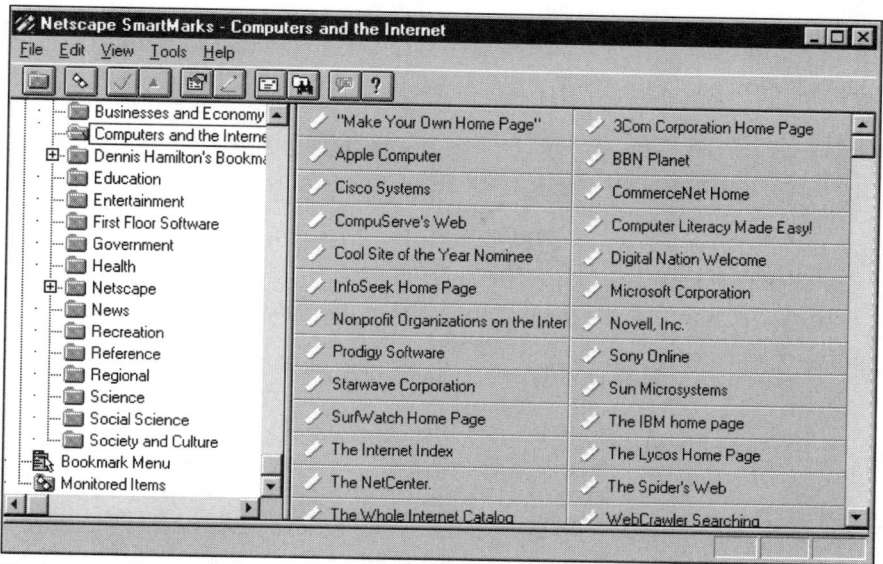

Figure 5-12: The layout for the Smart Window makes it simple to find, organize, and engage your "smart" bookmarks. When you open a folder in the left frame, its contents are displayed in the right frame.

1. Open your SmartMarks file.
2. Click on the Smart Folder icon in the frame; or click on File and select New Folder from the menu.
3. Enter the name you wish to give the folder in the Name field (see Figure 5-13).

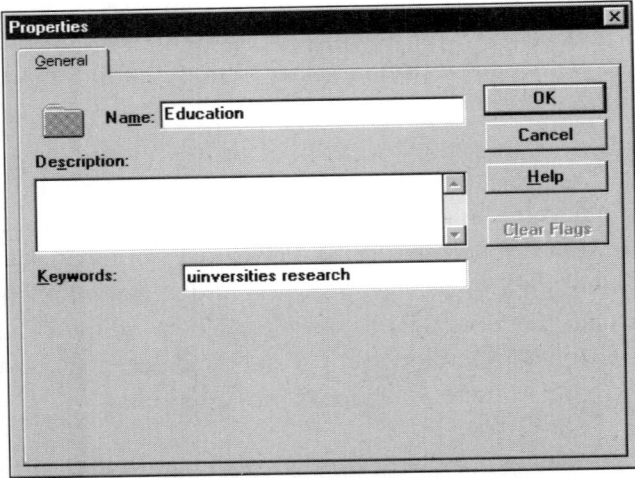

Figure 5-13: Even if you build a soundly organized library of bookmarks, entering keywords associated with the site or folder ensures that the file doesn't ever get lost.

4. Enter a description of what you will put into this folder in the Description box.
5. Click on Next at the bottom of the window. This opens a Keyword box.
6. Enter any important keywords that will help you locate the folder later.

Adding Addresses

After you have installed SmartMarks to your system, it replaces your Bookmarks command menu on the Navigator control bar. You have three new command line selections:

- Add SmartMark
- File SmartMark
- View SmartMark

It takes a little more time to add SmartMarks site information, but for the sites you truly wish to monitor, it's well worth a few seconds. It involves a single dialog box that can be invoked from the Bookmarks menu on your Navigator control bar (see Figure 5-14).

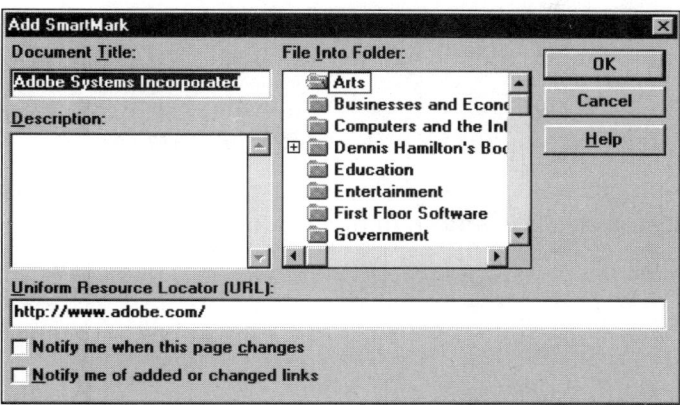

Figure 5-14: This dialog box opens when you select Add SmartMark.

If you select Add SmartMark, you simply add the site to the general list. You will not be adding any "smart" or descriptive properties. This is a tool used mostly for adding bookmarks when you're busy. It does not interrupt your Web browsing.

If you select File SmartMark, you open the Add SmartMark dialog box (see Figure 5-15).

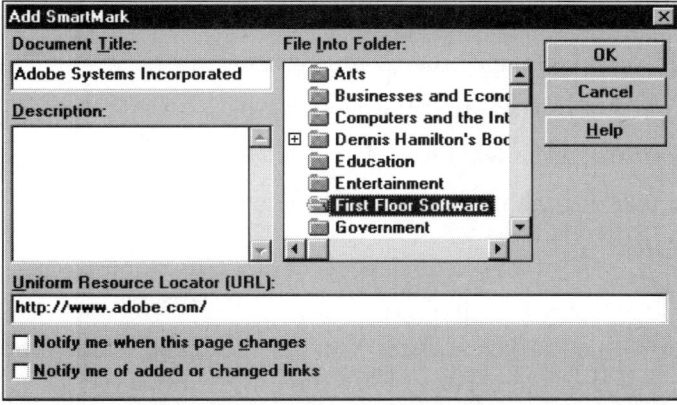

Figure 5-15: The Add SmartMark dialog box lets you decide to monitor the changes in Web site content and addresses automatically.

With the Add SmartMark dialog box on the screen, proceed with the following steps:

1. Enter a new title for the site if the one appearing in the window is long or inappropriate.

2. In the Description box, put as much descriptive information as you would need to understand the nature and value of the site later on.

3. Scroll down the folder list until you find one into which you would like to put the new SmartMark. Click on the folder to open it.

4. If you wish to be notified of content or address changes, check the appropriate boxes at the bottom of the window.

5. Click on OK.

If you select View SmartMarks, you get the main window with the hierarchical tree.

How SmartMarks Watches the Web

The niftiest feature of SmartMarks is its capability to spy on your favorite sites and then report back to you about what has changed in them. Anyone who has done any serious navigation knows it would be impossibly difficult to seriously review content at many Web sites on an ongoing basis. Some are sprawling sites, while others have pages that change addresses frequently. That's why the idea of an automatic monitor has so much appeal.

Here's how to establish monitoring with addresses in your file:

1. Open your main Netscape SmartMarks window.

2. Highlight the bookmark site you wish to have monitored.

3. Click on File and select Monitor Changes.

4. Click on either or both of the items in the dialog box.

5. Click on OK.

None of the 300 bookmarks that come with SmartMarks are set up to be monitored. As you come across them, you need to spend a few seconds checking off the content/address boxes. But the more sophisticated a navigator of the Web you become, the more you'll appreciate this feature.

Setting Your Monitoring Frequency

You can adjust the intervals at which SmartMarks checks on your designated Web sites. Checking often can be a waste of system resources; checking too infrequently can keep you out of the loop on important changes. Having a sense of the dynamics of your given pages — how often their key information is updated — can help you get a sense of the right interval. The default time is one hour, meaning that SmartMarks checks on things every 60 minutes, which could be too long if you spend time on pages that don't change.

1. From the Smart Window, click on Tools and select Preferences.
2. In the Preferences dialog box, select the tab marked Internet.
3. Choose your update frequency.
4. Click on OK.

SmartMarks Bulletins

One of the features that arrives with SmartMarks is its support of Bulletins, which are essentially messages that can be inserted into Web pages and routed to any SmartMarks users who have asked to monitor that page. It allows you to receive information about the changes that have taken place at that site. SmartMarks' monitoring feature, by itself, only informs you that a change has happened. Bulletins, when they are made available by the Web page developer, can tell you what those changes were.

First Floor Software, developer of SmartMarks, has a folder in the Smart Window tree. Opening it reveals the company's links, including one to a variety of sites that are using Bulletins. If you have trouble finding a site with this relatively new feature, you may want to check out this list just to get acquainted with the process. You can find the list at: **http://www.firstfloor.com/catalogs/bulletins.html**

Progressive JPEG

Anyone who has been on the Internet before, especially if they have sampled a lot of graphic images, probably is familiar with JPEG images. Even if you don't know the name, you have seen them.

JPEG — which stands for Joint Photographic Experts Group, a subgroup of the International Standards Organization — is a compression format that allows images to be reduced and expanded. All previous versions of Navigator supported simple baseline JPEG images, which are compressed bitmapped images. But Navigator 2.0 supports a new version of it called Progressive JPEG.

The difference between simple JPEG and progressive JPEG lies in the way in which the image is rendered onto your computer screen. Baseline JPEG paints the image one line at a time, exactly as it was scanned. Thus an image of a person would be painted line-by-line, starting with the top of the head and moving down. Each line would be fully rendered.

Progressive JPEG lays down complete images, one on top of another, each with increasing detail. Thus the viewer can see the entire (if incomplete, until the final layer) image from the beginning, without waiting for the often slow rendering of a baseline JPEG. If the image does not appear to be one they wish to wait for, they can click away from it.

For a side by side comparison of how these images work using Navigator, check out **http://www.in-touch.com/pjpeg.html**, shown in Figure 5-16.

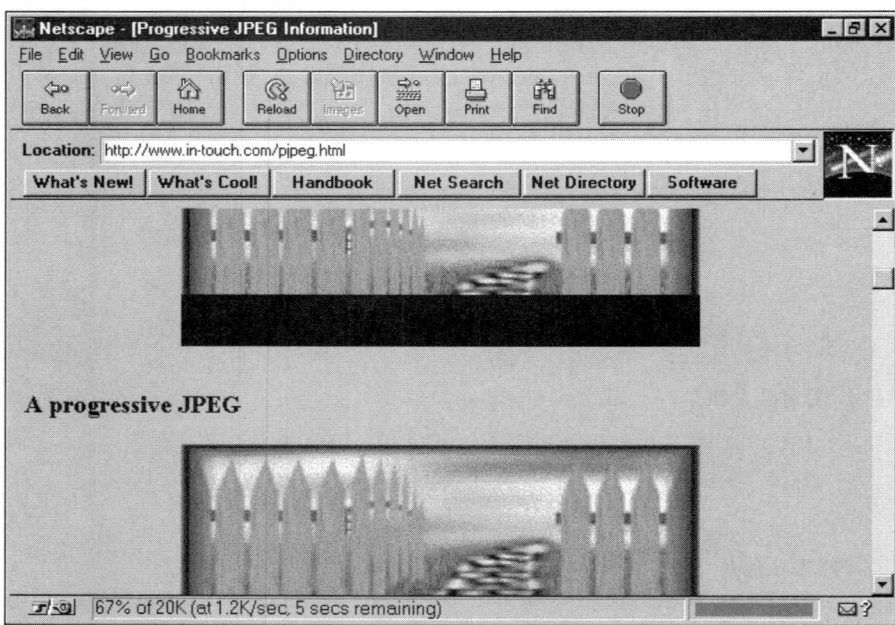

Figure 5-16: In a side by side look, progressive JPEG (bottom of screen) shows an entire, if incomplete, image; baseline JPEG (top of screen) loads line by line from the top of the image.

There does not appear to be a great speed advantage in progressive JPEG renderings, but rather a visual one, in that a version of the whole image can be seen right away. Other software and shareware available can enhance the progressive JPEG facilities. Generally, their features are designed for capturing and storing the JPEG image for reproduction (printing JPEG images without this support can be a disappointing exercise).

Navigator 2.0 supports both baseline and progressive JPEG images. Images you wish to view in progressive JPEG must be converted to that format. Navigator's support for progressive JPEG does not have to be configured.

Using Navigator's Chat

One of the quintessential tools of the Internet is the chatroom. There are thousands of them worldwide, all drawing in people who want to chat about whatever it is that interests them, inflames them, or otherwise animates them. From classic cars to Madonna, to computer problems, to math clubs, every special interest any soul ever imagined has enjoyed a chatroom.

What was harder to pull off was having a private chat in real time with a person or group of people who might meet regularly (for example, your company's sales group) or who might not ever meet again — in other words, a chatroom you could put up or shut down as needed. Navigator's Chat has the capability to do that and more.

Chat, a $24.95 complementary application for Navigator, has a graphical Windows interface to make it simple to use. To organize your chat, it can send, view, and share URLs with other chat users to alert them to the chat. You can host your own Internet talk show, share sites, give guided tours, or take part in more conventional chatroom activity. You can hold sales seminars, deliver training sessions, or communicate with partners or resellers. Chat offers the following benefits:

- A Web site can be shared with a colleague without the colleague having to manually enter the URL of that site.

- Multiple communication modes. Chat supports personal conversations (one to one), group conferences (many to many), and moderated auditorium (one to many).

- Multiple chatrooms allow users to participate in several chatrooms simultaneously.

Chat allows you to logon to any public IRC — Internet Relay Chat —
server on the Internet. IRC chatrooms allow multiple persons to participate
simultaneously in a discussion over a particular **channel**, or even multiple
channels. There is no restriction on the number of persons who can
participate in a given discussion or on the number of channels that can be
formed over IRC.

Downloading and Installing Chat

You can download Netscape Chat from any of the Netscape servers you
can reach from the company's home page (**http://home.netscape.com**).

1. From the download page, select your operating system (Chat works
    only with Windows, at this writing), location, and product. Choose
    Chat 1.0. The file number is nc32105.exe if you are running 32-bit
    Windows 95 or Windows NT; nc16105.exe if you are running
    Windows 3.1 or Windows 95 with a 16-bit WinSock stack.

2. Open a new folder in which the downloaded file will be stored.

3. When the file is downloaded, run setup.exe. Chat is a
    self-extracting file.

4. The Server Connection dialog box appears, as seen in Figure 5-17.

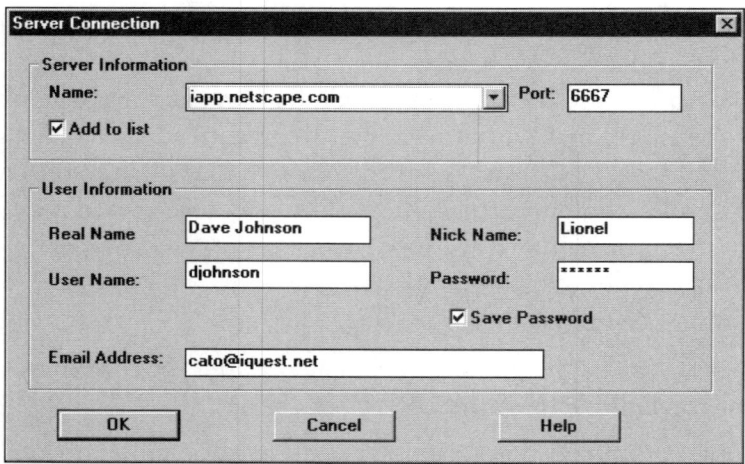

Figure 5-17: The Server Connection dialog box contains essential information for linking your
chats. The iapp.netscape.com and port number are default assignments and shouldn't be
changed. You can add others to the Server List later.

In the Server Connection dialog box you must enter the necessary information for login and dialog:

- **Real Name** is your actual name. You have the option later of adding it to any actual chats you engage in.

- **User Name** is the name you use with your ISP. Some IRC chat servers limit access only to those users who have registered. If you try to connect to one of these servers, then you must enter the user name that you used to register with that IRC server. This user name may or may not be the same one assigned to you by your ISP or company. Most IRC servers on the Internet don't enforce stringent access control, so most of the time you won't need to register.

- **Nick Name**; if you don't have one, pick one. This is the name that you use to identify yourself to other chat users. You may or may not want it to be a name different from your real name, but the choice is yours. Often chatroom users like to adopt a more anonymous identity. But if you're in a business meeting chat, you probably would want to use your own name.

- **Password**; enter the password you use for ISP access.

- **E-mail** is your actual e-mail address.

When you're done with your choices, click on OK.

The information you entered here won't automatically be revealed in a chat. That's all up to you. Each chat uses a dialog box to ask how much of your identity you wish to reveal. Even with only your nickname, you can still carry on an anonymous chat.

Adding Other IRC Servers

To create communications channels to servers from Chat, you must connect to either a Netscape Chat server or an IRC server. Table 5-1 is a list of server host names and port numbers to use. Select the servers you think you may like to sample, then enter the connection information into the Chat server connection dialog box when you're ready to connect.

Table 5-1: Server host names and port numbers

SERVER TYPE	HOST ADDRESS	PORT NUMBER
Australia/New Zealand		
IRC server	akl.nz.us.undernet.org	6667
IRC server	wollongong.nsw.au.undernet.org	6667
Canada		
IRC server	montreal.qu.ca.undernet.org	6667
Europe		
IRC server	caen.fr.eu.undernet.org	6667
IRC server	gothenburg.se.eu.undernet.org	6667
IRC server	oxford.uk.eu.undernet.org	6667
South America		
IRC server	irc.kanopus.com.br	6667
United States		
Netscape Chat server	iapp.netscape.com	6667
IRC server	austin.tx.us.undernet.org	6667
IRC server	manhattan.ks.us.undernet.org	6667
IRC server	milwaukee.wi.us.undernet.org	6667
IRC server	pittsburgh.pa.us.undernet.org	6667
IRC server	rochester.mi.us.undernet.org	6667
IRC server	sanjose.ca.us.undernet.org	6667
IRC server	tampa.fl.us.undernet.org	6667
IRC server	washington.dc.us.undernet.org	6667

There are literally thousands of chatrooms on the Internet, and you will find yourself gravitating toward those that interest you simply through the process of finding and bookmarking them.

Using Chat

When you wish to start or join a chat, you must start the Chat application by clicking on the program icon. This takes you to the chat options window named Conversation Channels (see Figure 5-18). At the time of this writing, the Create Chat function was disabled for all users, but it was expected that it would be enabled shortly. You still can enter Group Conversations and Private Conversations.

Group conversations are those in which more than two people are engaged in one of the forums. Personal conversations can be made up of as few as two people. Here is how to enter a group conversation:

1. Open the Netscape Chat window.
2. Click on File and select Group Conversation.

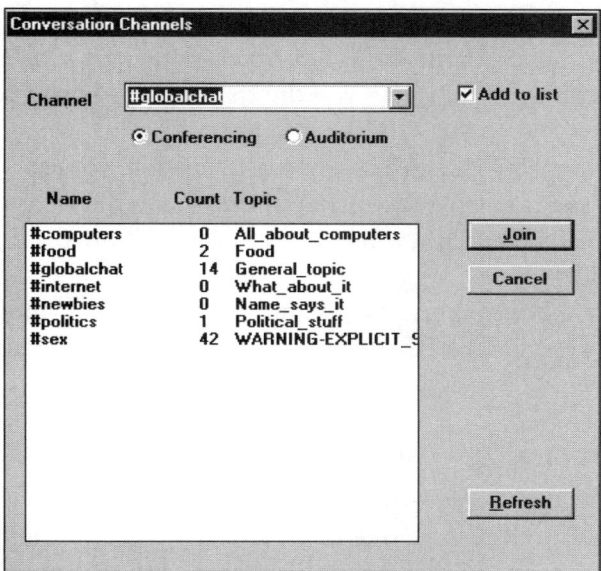

Figure 5-18: The Conversation Channels window allows you to select the channel you want to join. Highlight the channel, then click on Join.

3. This opens the Conversation Channels window (see Figure 5-18). You can look over the respective forums and find out what the subjects are and how many people are using the chatrooms. Make your selection by clicking on the desired chatroom.

4. Highlight the channel, then click on Join. This opens the dialog window that moves you into the chatroom (see Figure 5-19).

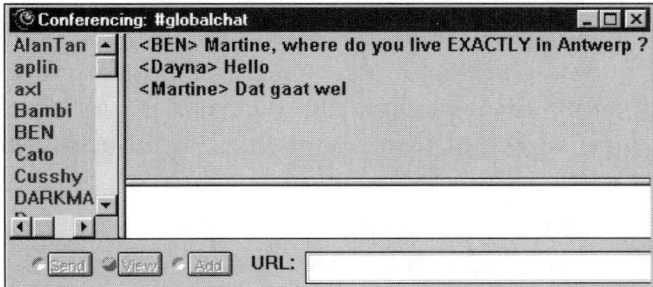

Figure 5-19: After you select the chatroom you want to enter, the dialog window appears. From here you can send and receive information in real time.

The frame on the left side of the dialog window shows you the nick-names (most often not the real names) of the persons taking part in the chat. The larger frame on the right shows you the chat record — who has said what.

To enter the chat, place your cursor into the text box. Write your entry — a greeting, a question, an answer, or whatever you feel is appropriate — and press the Enter key. Your comments are immediately posted in the chat window.

If you wish to send a URL to other chat members, you can do so at the bottom of the screen. Type in the complete URL, then click on the Send button next to the box.

Personal Conversations

One of the most appealing aspects of Navigator's Chat is having the capability to have a private chat, instead of merely joining a group one. You can leave a crowded chatroom and have a more intimate one-on-one with a single person. This is sometimes called **whispering**, because you are sending private messages to individuals who are engaged in one of the channel chats.

This capability affords you the chance to continue a completely private chat with someone or merely to send them a private message once in awhile in the midst of a group chat. Operation of the personal chat function is quite simple:

1. Click on File in the Netscape Chat window, then select Personal Conversation.

2. From the chat list that appears, select the name (or nickname) of the person you wish to engage in a private chat.

3. The Private Conversation window that appears next works similarly to the Group Conversation window. You enter your message exactly as you did for the group chat, then press enter. Only the person you designate receives the personal message.

4. Single-click on the chat list to remove the highlighted name when you are ready to return to the group chat.

Sending and Receiving URLs

In conversing with other people over the Internet, you often find a site or document or image you want them to see. Before Navigator 2.0, you could send them the address, which they could then key in themselves. Now you can send a live, clickable URL right in the messages you are sending them. At the bottom of the Chat dialog window, you will notice a box for sending URLs to the other people in the chatroom. Sending one is easy:

1. Place your cursor into the text box and write the entire Internet address.
2. Click on Send.

Unfortunately, this feature has some serious netiquette problems. Some chat users are constantly sending URLs to the people in the chatrooms. The problem is that Navigator and Chat automatically take you to any site displayed. This function in Chat is called Auto-View. If you get into a chat with a bunch of people who want to share their favorite site, you'll end up going crazy.

Chat's default is to go to any site that is sent, but you can disable the default. Just turn off the browser's Auto-View option by clicking on it from Chat's Browser line on the control bar (it is *highly* recommended you do this). Then you can select your own destinations by following these steps:

1. Make sure you are running Navigator.
2. Make sure the Browser⇨Enable choice is selected from your Chat control bar.
3. Click on the URL window to select the site you wish to visit.
4. Choose Browser⇨View URL.

This allows you to go only to the URLs you wish to visit, instead of being sent to places you have no interest in.

Using the Auditorium

The Chat's Auditorium is an interesting twist to the chatroom concept. Historically, a chatroom consisted of a group of people sending messages back and forth. There was usually no leader, no moderator, and no real structure. The Auditorium allows a speaker/audience relationship to exist instead of a random interaction.

The Auditorium is a moderated channel forum. It is useful for setting up events such as broadcasts, talk shows, seminars, meetings, and so on, when you have one or a few speakers and a high number of spectators.

The first person to create the auditorium is the moderator. The moderator then controls who can speak in the auditorium. If you join an auditorium session, you are not allowed to speak unless the moderator recognizes you (Chat notifies you of this, so don't think of your enforced silence as a system problem).

If you wish to set up an Auditorium event

1. Go to the main Chat window and select Auditorium.

2. Choose Grant Moderator.

3. When you wish to pass the microphone, click at the bottom of the menu.

Chat's Limitations and Potential

Chat has the potential to be a terrific addition to the Netscape product lineup. It is as close to true real-time interactivity as anything else on the market. Many of the chatrooms on the Internet unfortunately suffer from bottlenecked bandwidth, and the response times can be anything from 5 to 30 seconds, making coherent chat difficult at best. Chat's speed is an asset.

The product's versatility is also a plus. The capability to carry on private chats so simply is an addition that will take the product to bestseller status all by itself. The capability to create a chat, assuming it comes up to the specifications the company has laid out, will find a home with many people and businesses who have specific interests to discuss over the Internet.

The version tested for this book, Chat 1.0, has a great deal of potential, but also suffers from a few bugs and is a netiquette victim of the first order. Netscape should consider turning off the Auto-View option default. Some channels were tested and they turned out to be a blitz of one URL after another sent right to the screen — some of them extremely distasteful. If children, or even adults of moderate tastes, get caught in a public channel with the wrong crowd, they are likely to get offended quickly.

Chat 1.0 also crashed fairly often, sending back jittery screens that wouldn't respond to commands and had to be forced logged out (ctl-alt-del). Sometimes it just wouldn't connect to the server.

Still, even with the irritations, Chat is a product with tremendous potential. It adds greatly to Navigator's functionality as it is. When fully debugged, it will be invaluable for many users.

Navigator's Enhanced Security

The most frightening facet of the Internet is the prospect that someone could be electronically watching you — or, worse, stealing money, information, privacy, company secrets, or confidential messages from you. If any medium ever presented a specter of Big Brother in its maddest manifestation, it is this great assemblage of people, networks, and computers known as the Net. And the Internet itself does not provide security. That has been left to the people who use it.

Netscape made a good effort to thwart security weaknesses by inviting people to try to break its encryption and security schemes. Last year, a few computer experts — by using computer power that simply isn't available to most people, including supercomputers — did manage to decode one of Netscape's challenge documents. Netscape ignored the fact that almost no one could duplicate the feat and set about trying to correct the flaws. It would appear at this writing that they were successful. No further breakins have occurred.

One reason they wanted to shatter any notion of vulnerability was that they understand the commercial potential of the Internet. A few years ago, the Internet was regarded as an almost pristine medium for the sharing of information. Anyone who tried to actually sell something over it was **flamed**, meaning they received an avalanche of scathing e-mail condemning them for misusing the medium. But that attitude has changed.

As millions of new users flooded onto the Internet, commerce, security, and privacy became inevitable issues. People actually started wanting to transact business over the Net. It began with technology sales — for example, Netscape's sales of Navigator and its complementary applications is one of the great success stories in the history of business — which were a natural for online transactions. Now it's moved to electronic automobile showrooms, travel reservations, pizzas, and funerals.

Netscape has put a three-tier protection scheme into Navigator:

- **SSL Encryption.** By using Netscape's Secure Sockets Layer (SSL) protocol, a document is encrypted and transmitted on a secure channel to protect it from external viewers.

- **Certified Servers.** The Netscape Commerce Server, the primary host for transactions involving money and privacy, now requires certification from server administrators in order to use the security features. This shuts out imposters.

- **Data Integrity.** Techniques for thwarting vandals.

Clearly, the use of confidential forms and financial transactions dictated cooperation in security implementations — security on the sending and receiving ends of a transaction. Thus, both Navigator and Netscape's secure servers contain security features that work together by using the RSA public key cryptographic technology, which encodes and decodes messages by using two large random numbers. These numbers are the public key, which as its name implies is public; and the private key, which is confidential. Whatever is encoded with the public key can be be decoded only with the private key and vice versa.

Using the SSL Protocol

The SSL protocol delivers server authentication, data encryption, and message integrity. SSL operates in a kind of secure limbo, on a layer beneath application protocols such as HTTP, telnet, FTP, Gopher, and NNTP, and on a layer above the connection protocol TCP/IP. This strategy allows SSL to operate independently of — and out of the reach of — the Internet application protocols. With SSL implemented on both the client and server, Internet communications are transmitted in encrypted envelopes, ensuring your privacy.

It is impossible, for all practical purposes, to break the code. Because of more rigid security requirements, the U.S. domestic version of Navigator 2.0 has a 128-bit key, while the international version has 40-bit keys. A message encrypted with 40-bit RC4 takes an average of 64 MIPS-years to break (a 64-MIPS computer needs a year of dedicated processor time to break the message's encryption). The 128-bit U.S. domestic version provides protection exponentially more secure.

Getting a Digital Certificate

Server administrators who want to get digital authentication certificates have to apply to third-party providers such as VeriSign, a subsidiary of RSA Data Security, Inc., developers of the RSA cryptography technology and one of Netscape's business partners in security issues on the Internet. (Visit **http://www.rsa.com** for more information.)

Verisign is the major provider of certificates, although there are others. There are four classes of certificates:

- **Class 1.** Lowest level assurance, to be used for secure e-mail and normal browsing.

- **Class 2.** Somewhat broader access to advanced Web sites.
- **Class 3.** Higher assurance for larger transactions.
- **Class 4.** The highest level of identity assurance for high-end transactions.

Netscape Navigator 2.0 and Netscape Commerce Server deliver server authentication by using these signed digital certificates. A digital certificate verifies the connection between a server's public key and the server's identification. In that regard, it has been called an Internet driver's license. Cryptographic checks, by using digital signatures, ensure that information within a certificate can be trusted.

Netscape Navigator identifies secure documents in several ways. You can tell whether a document comes from a secure server by looking at the location (URL) field. If the URL begins with https:// (instead of http://), the document comes from a secure server (the *s* stands for secure). You need to use **https://** for HTTP URLs with SSL and **http://** for HTTP URLs without SSL.

You can also verify the security of a document by checking the security icon in the bottom-left corner of the Netscape Navigator window (see Figure 5-20) and the colorbar across the top of the content area. The security icon is a doorkey on a blue background to show secure documents and a broken doorkey on a gray background to show unsecured documents. The colorbar across the top of the content area is blue for secure and gray for unsecured. A mixed document containing both secured and unsecured information is displayed as secure. The unecured information is indicated by a mixed security icon. Some servers may permit you to access documents in an unsecured way, (using http://) permitting you to view mixed documents without icon substitution.

Several configurable notification dialog boxes inform you when you are entering or leaving a secure space, viewing a secure document that contains unsecured information, and by using an unsecured submission process. You'll always be warned if a secure URL is redirected to an unsecured location, or if you're submitting via a secure form by using an unsecured submission process. You can set alert display options by clicking on Options on the Navigator control bar and selecting Security Preferences. Figure 5-21 shows you the Security Preferences dialog box.

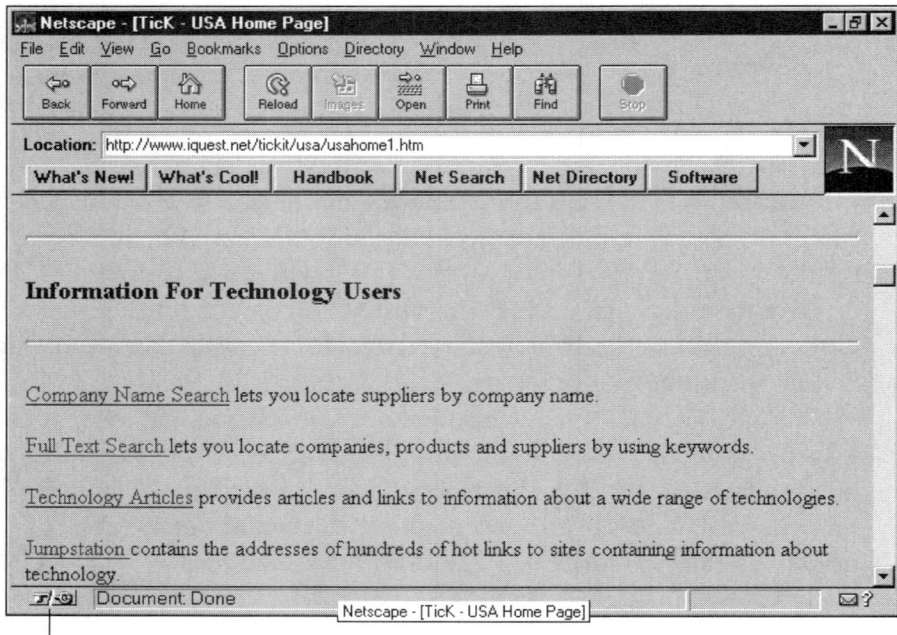

This broken key indicates an unsecured document

Figure 5-20: The key in the lower left-hand corner of the Navigator screen reveals the security level of the document you are viewing. A broken key such as this indicates an unsecured document. A solid key indicates a secure document.

The site certificates you accept for use are up to you. If you open the Security Preferences dialog box, you can click on the Site Certificates tab, as shown in Figure 5-22. The default here is to accept all certificates. Baring a technical problem with one of the certificates, this is the best way to proceed. However, you can delete any you wish by highlighting and clicking on the Delete Certificate button.

By clicking on the Edit Certificate button, you can view a dialog box that allows you to continue or discontinue connections to sites by using one of the certificates. It also lets you choose to view an alert dialog box whenever you come across a given site (see Figure 5-23).

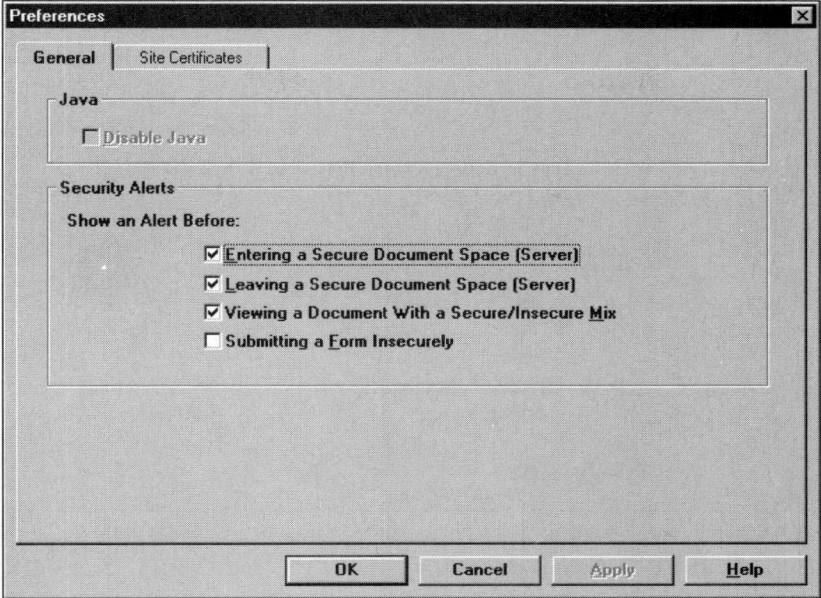

Figure 5-21: By using this dialog box, you can establish the alert options you wish to see in secure areas.

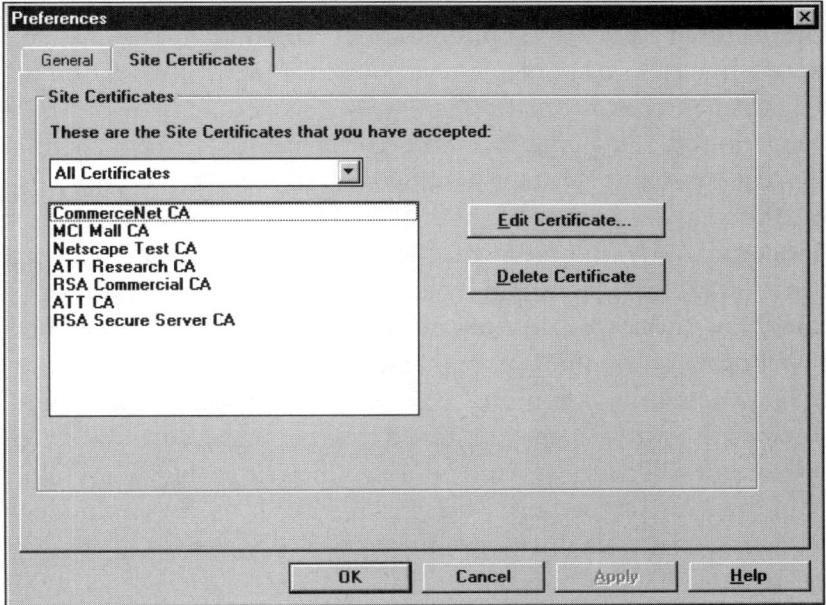

Figure 5-22: The only time you'd want to remove one of the certificates is if there was a technical problem with it.

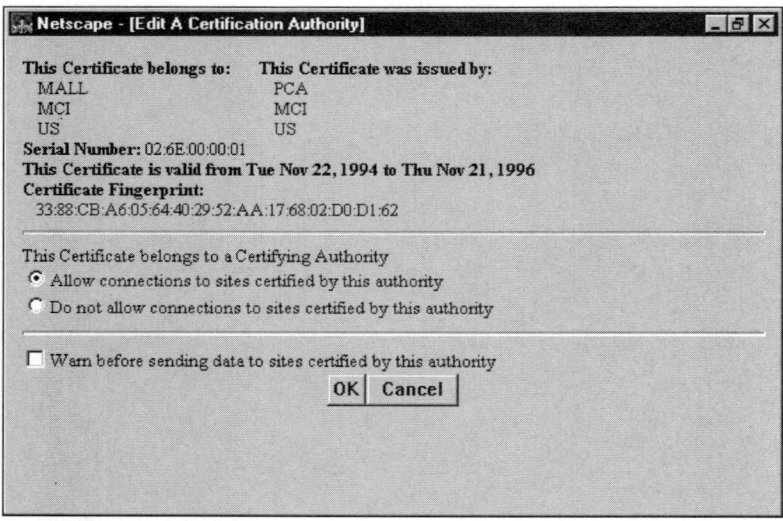

Figure 5-23: If you want to discontinue connections to sites by using one of the certificates, you must do it from this dialog box.

What to Expect from Navigator 2.0 Security

Navigator was endowed with a range of excellent security features. Certainly the strategists at Netscape Communications Corporation implemented these security features in order to give potential users one less reason to avoid the Internet and to give millions of businesses one more compelling reason to join it. The laying to rest of security fears is a psychological hurdle of the first order, and Netscape has done it quite well.

Like all security schemes, of course, Navigator's isn't perfect. The problem is not so much with the technology as it is with the people and organizations that use it. For example, by using Navigator's Secure Courier (**http://home.netscape.com/newsref/std/credit.html**), you could freely use your credit card number to purchase goods from Internet sites, the entire transaction away from the eyes and minds of potential intruders. Before you do that, though, you should have confidence that the server administrator will treat your card information as he should. The Golden Rule of Internet commerce isn't that much different from conventional transactions: Do business with good people.

Summary

The new features in Navigator 2.0, such as Frames, SmartMarks, and Chat, give you greater possibilities for how you and the users of pages you create can interact with images and other people. In addition, an ever-increasing supply of third-party plug-ins enhances the potential of Navigator. Support for the Java programming language and Adobe Acrobat are just two of the ways that Navigator makes information more accessible.

Improved security with this version of Navigator translates into more secure Internet users. That improved security may be one of the last barriers to the Internet becoming a global marketplace of immense proportions.

Chapter 6

The 60 Minute Navigator Test Run

onsider this chapter a travelogue. If you haven't yet gotten onto the Internet with Navigator 2.0, this chapter will take you through some exercises designed to help you make sure the software is working and that you are comfortable with it.

Whether you are experienced or not in things Internet, it's a good idea to do a test run with a highly functional new piece of software such as Navigator 2.0. Experienced users, especially those who have been using earlier versions of Navigator, will find the new exercise useful when comparing new features to old ones. There is enough commonality to keep them comfortable and enough evolution to keep them interested. For new users, Navigator 2.0 quite simply represents their first steps into a brave new world. Running through Navigator's different functions helps you to gain the comfort level necessary for a good Internet experience.

If you are a newbie, as those new to the Internet are called, it's a good idea to visit some newbie sites when you see them posted; they make great efforts to remove the confusion from sticky technical subjects. This chapter, in less than an hour, takes you onto the Internet, the World Wide Web, electronic mail, a newsgroup, file transfer, and it shows you some interesting things that you will want to explore further on your own.

Getting Started: The Dial Up

So you've installed your Navigator 2.0 software, configured your e-mail and newsgroups, downloaded your complementary applications, and now you want to go somewhere. This chapter assumes that you have successfully contacted your ISP and set up an Internet account. All that remains is for you to dial up the server.

If you have scripted automatic dial-up, just click on the Navigator 2.0 icon, which displays the wheel of a ship against a blue background. It automatically invokes your connection software and dials up your ISP's server without you having to do anything else.

If you don't have auto dial-up, click on your WinSock, MacTCP, or other connection icon. When you've been connected to the server, click on the Navigator 2.0 icon in your program group. It normally takes 10 to 30 seconds to establish a connection.

You know you have established a connection because the default image appears at Netscape's home page — **http://home.netscape.com**. Figure 6-1 shows you what this image looks like.

Figure 6-1: This is the first screen that appears when you have successfully connected to the Internet. When you first see the Netscape home page graphic, your journey in cyberspace will already have begun.

Incidentally, you can change the default page at any time by following these steps:

1. Click on Options on the Navigator control bar.

2. Open General Preferences to the Appearance tab.

3. Under Start within the Startup section, enter the new URL you want to open to. Navigator then opens to whatever screen you designate (but in the beginning, just use the Netscape page default).

If you haven't connected, a blank Navigator 2.0 control window appears, without the Netscape image in the primary frame. This means that you have not established a connection with your server.

If you cannot establish a connection, don't get anxious. Servers are sometimes momentarily busy or down, and you may have dialed up at the wrong moment. Try again to connect, then make certain to double check the following important connection points:

- Is your ISP account established?

- Have you configured your WinSock or Macintosh connection correctly with your user name, ISP telephone number, and password?

- Are you using the correct connectivity software for your version of Navigator?

Which Version to Use?

Remember, if you are using Windows 95 but not the 32-bit TCP/IP stack that comes with the new operating system (by using a 16-bit stack instead), you MUST download the Navigator 2.0 version for Windows 3.1, even though you're running Windows 95. To use the 32-bit version of Navigator, you must have a 32-bit TCP/IP stack. Many Windows 3.1 users used 16-bit stacks with their old Navigator 1.x software. When they upgraded to Windows 95, they did not configure the 32-bit stack, reasoning they didn't need another TCP/IP connection. When they downloaded the Navigator version designated "Windows 95," they automatically got the 32-bit version. It won't work without the 32-bit stack, but Navigator 2.0 for Windows 3.1 will.

Understanding URL Addresses

There are many ways to get somewhere on the World Wide Web. The key piece of information you need is the URL — the Uniform Resource Locator. This is that seemingly incomprehensible series of letters, punctuation, and numbers you see in the Location line just beneath Navigator's control bar. Fortunately, you will quickly learn that URLs are nowhere near as intimidating as they initially appear. Every part of those addresses has some specific meaning, and deciphering most of them (if you care to) isn't all that tricky.

The URL Translated

Here is what a URL looks like:

http://www.whitehouse.gov or **http://www.ibm.com**

Notice certain similarities in these two addresses. Here is what everything means:

- **http:** This stands for HyperText Transfer Protocol and indicates you are using http to access the resource. This usually means you will be using your Web browser to navigate.

- **www:** Not surprisingly, this stands for World Wide Web, the versatile text/graphics/sound medium that has catalyzed the growth of the Internet.

- **(domain entity):** The word that appears after www, or sometimes just after the twin slashes (//), generally denotes the domain entity of the page you are traveling to. For example, **http://www.IBM.com** tells you that you have traveled to IBM's home page. In this case, IBM is the domain entity. This part of the URL tells you the **domain name** of the entity.

- **/mainframe/software/client.html:** The remainder of the address gives you the path to extended pages beyond the home page. In this example, you would go to the section discussing mainframe computers and their software for clients. The html designation stands for HyperText Markup Language. This denotes additional files that have been added to the primary domain file, but which do not have their own domain name and therefore require HTML extensions.

Other Address Designations

You should become familiar with other designations. While the addresses sometimes look like gibberish, they actually can tell you a lot about the domain page you are looking at. The following designations indicate what type of organization you are dialing up:

- **.com** indicates a commercial organization, such as a company. **http://www.cocacola.com** quickly tells you that the Coca-Cola *company* is maintaining this site on the World Wide Web.

- **.edu** indicates an educational institution. For example, **http://www.indiana.edu** takes you to Indiana University.

- **.gov** indicates that you are about to journey to a government agency. The address for the White House, indicated at the beginning of this chapter, is one example.

- **.org** indicates a nonprofit organization.

- **.net** indicates an Internet Service Provider, or ISP. For example, **http://www.iquest.net** takes you to the Iquest home page.

You can also identify countries by using information found in the URL. The country information is denoted in two-character sets found in the latter part of the address. For example, **http://www.city.ac.uk/multimedia/**. If there is no two-character identifier, the domain server is most likely in the United States. A few of these country identifiers are

- **uk** for United Kingdom
- **ca** for Canada
- **jp** for Japan
- **cn** for China

So, while a URL may look like random letters drawn from an alphabet drum, every character has a precise meaning. And if you get even one character wrong, you won't get to your destination. Once you get the hang of looking at them, figuring out who they are and where they're from tells you a lot about where you're going.

Using the Navigator Controls

The Navigator 2.0 control bar is the main dashboard for Internet users. It contains all buttons and menus used to navigate, mail, download, and help. It controls the helper applications such as SmartMarks. It is the essential tool for moving easily through the Internet world.

As shown in Figure 6-2, the Navigator control bar is found at the top of the page. It consists of buttons with specific purposes, text controls with menus, and the Location field containing the URL of the site you are visiting.

Figure 6-2: There are more than 60 functions you can invoke from the control bar.

The Buttons

Navigator's nine buttons control functions that you are likely to use frequently:

- **Back** moves you back to the last page you viewed.
- **Forward** moves you ahead to a page you recently moved back from.
- **Home** returns you to your default home page from anywhere else you might be.
- **Reload** contacts the server to refresh the page you are viewing.
- **Images** loads images when invoked (you can automatically load images by clicking on Options and selecting Auto Load; doing this disables the button).
- **Open** brings up an Open Location window to enter another URL.
- **Print** prints the document or image you are viewing.
- **Find** provides a box for you to enter text you wish to find in a document.

The Menu Controls

The textual menu controls above the button bar contain dozens of functions that are useful to find, save, and store information. Take the time to get to know what each function does.

- **File.** One of the most important menus, File, controls the opening of documents, files, mail messages, plus your page setup and print functions.

- **Edit.** Like many edit menus, this menu enables you to undo a command, cut, copy, paste, and find information.

- **View.** View lets you reload and refresh pages, and shows you source HTML code revealing how the page was constructed.

- **Go.** Go allows you to move ahead to or back to pages you have visited, to stop loading a page, to return to your home page, or to visit any page listed from your current session.

- **Bookmarks.** As discussed in Chapter 5, this menu enables you to save site information for later recall. It also controls SmartMarks from the Bookmarks menu.

- **Options.** A vital menu that enables you to configure your news, e-mail, and network information, as well as design the way the Navigator screen will look.

- **Directory.** This menu duplicates what you see in button form below the Location window, plus it takes you to Netscape product pages and search engines.

- **Window.** This is the menu for calling up e-mail or newsgroups, plus your history list and address book. The bookmark list can also be called up from here.

- **Help.** A menu for finding help about Navigator and Netscape. There are links to Web-related tools here as well.

Going Places

Ready to enter your first URL? This test will help you understand how to write in your own addresses as you find them. You can enter a URL two ways: from the Navigator screen, click on File and select Open Location (see Figure 6-4); or highlight and delete the URL in Navigator's Location window beneath the control bar (see Figure 6-3).

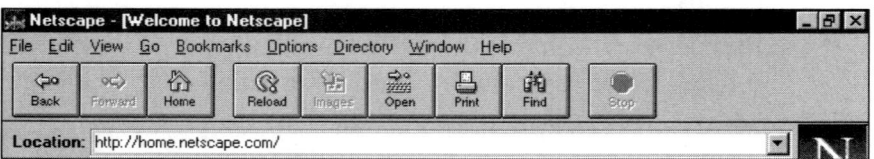

Figure 6-3: To go to a site, you can delete the address in the Location window, then write in a new URL and press enter. You do not need to write "http://" when using the Location window; but the full URL is required in the Open dialog box.

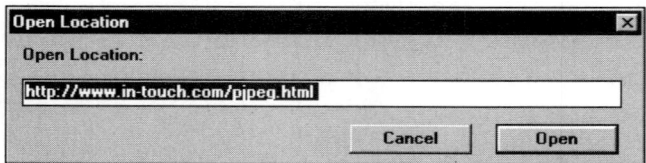

Figure 6-4: ...or you can open Location from the File menu and type in the URL.

After you've opened one of these boxes, you need to enter the address in the blank field. Try the following:

http://www.yahoo.com/

This is the address of a page you are likely to use a lot. Yahoo is one of the Internet's major **search engines** that allows users to enter keywords in their searches for specific information. If you successfully entered the right address, you should see the page in Figure 6-5.

If you find yourself at the Yahoo page, you've just successfully completed your first hypertext jump. In all likelihood, thousands of them lie ahead of you. If you find yourself still at the Netscape home page, try entering the Yahoo URL again. If that too fails, click on the Net Search button in the main Navigator screen. That should take you to the InfoSeek search page. If you arrive there, you most likely were entering the Yahoo URL incorrectly. Try again, making sure that every character and space is entered correctly. When you're successful, read on.

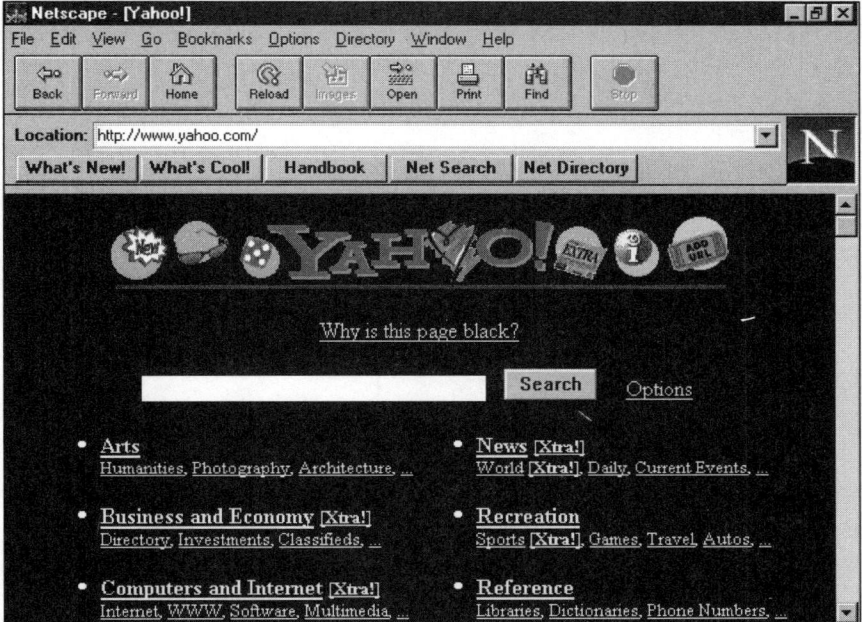

Figure 6-5: This is where you should be. The Yahoo search page is one of the best places to come to search for sites and documents on subjects of interest to you.

Printing from the Internet

One of the useful features of your Navigator software is that you can print what you see on the screen. If you're doing research, or you simply find images you like, a single command can print entire documents. An impact or daisy wheel printer only prints text. To print graphic images, you must have a laser or ink jet printer. If you were running one of these printers prior to setting up your Navigator 2.0 software, you probably don't need to make any adjustments; Navigator's set-up finds your printer and copies the information for its operation. After that, printing is simply a matter of finding a document you want hardcopy for, then following these steps:

1. Click on File from the Navigator main screen.
2. Select Print.
3. Designate the pages you wish to print (for example, "All" or specified pages).

4. Designate the number of copies you want in the lower right-hand box.

5. Click on OK in the Print dialog box (see Figure 6-6).

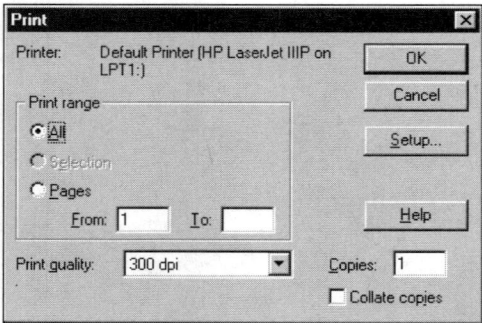

Figure 6-6: Your printer information should be visible in the Print dialog box; just click on OK to print any document you find on the Internet.

If you had a printer hooked up to your computer before you loaded Navigator 2.0, it should automatically print whatever pages you selected to that printer. If not, you need to do a normal printer setup to print pages off of the Internet.

Before you print any Internet documents, it's a good idea to get an idea of their length. Some Internet sites scroll their pages together into a single huge document that may be far more pages than you want to have pouring from your printer.

The best advice is to do the following:

1. Scroll down the page you think you want to print.

2. If it is in a long document, use the dialog box to instruct the printer to print only the designated pages (this will be an estimate on your part because they are usually not marked).

Testing Bookmarks and SmartMarks

Another way to get around to important places is by using your Bookmarks or SmartMarks. Here you have your categorized hierarchies that group subjects logically and provide you with clickable links to your favorite sites. Eventually they will become the predominant way you navigate around the Internet.

If you are using Navigator's Bookmarks and you have not downloaded SmartMarks (Chapter 5) to replace your Bookmarks, you need only read through the first part of this walkthrough. Bookmarks on Navigator 2.0 have been greatly enhanced. They allow you to create folders into which you can add site names and addresses. From them you can click quickly to any site in the Bookmark file, all without having to manually enter a URL. They make moving around to places of interest much simpler.

Linking to a Bookmarked Site

Here is a simple exercise to test Bookmarks' features. Bookmarks doesn't come with preloaded addresses, so you have to add one. You can add a bookmark by following these steps:

1. If you haven't loaded the Yahoo home page (**http://www.yahoo.com/**), do so now.
2. At the top of the Navigator control bar, click on Bookmarks to open the menu.
3. Click on Add Bookmark.
4. Next, click on the Home button on the control bar. This returns you to the Netscape home page.
5. Click on Bookmarks again, this time selecting View Bookmarks.
6. You should see the Yahoo entry. Double click on it.

This should take you back to the Yahoo home page without having to enter a URL anywhere. If you make the jump back to Yahoo, you successfully added your first bookmark and your Bookmarks function is working. When you come across pages you like, add them by clicking on Add Bookmark. Then organize them into logical folders when you have time.

Linking to a SmartMarked Site

If you downloaded and installed SmartMarks, it replaced your Bookmarks screens (unless you close it, it loads automatically whenever you load Navigator 2.0). Unlike Bookmarks, SmartMarks comes with more than 300 preloaded URLs ready for you to click to. To test SmartMarks, you need to open to the primary Netscape SmartMarks screen (see Figure 6-7).

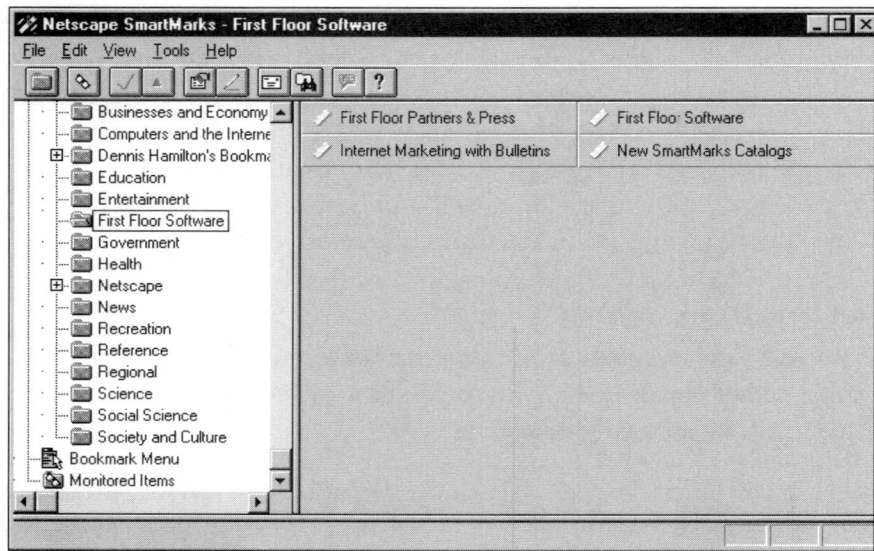

Figure 6-7: From this screen, select the First Floor Software folder for the test. In the right-hand window, double-click on First Floor Software.

1. Click on Bookmarks.
2. Select View SmartMarks.
3. Open the folder that says First Floor Software (the developers of SmartMarks).
4. In the right-hand frame, double-click on the First Floor Software tab.

If SmartMarks is working, you should find yourself at First Floor's home page, as shown in Figure 6-8.

You should do thorough testing of the SmartMarks sites that have been preloaded for you, just to get comfortable with the use of SmartMarks and familiar with the sites you really like. You also will want to add SmartMarks from the control bar, then practice organizing them in folders.

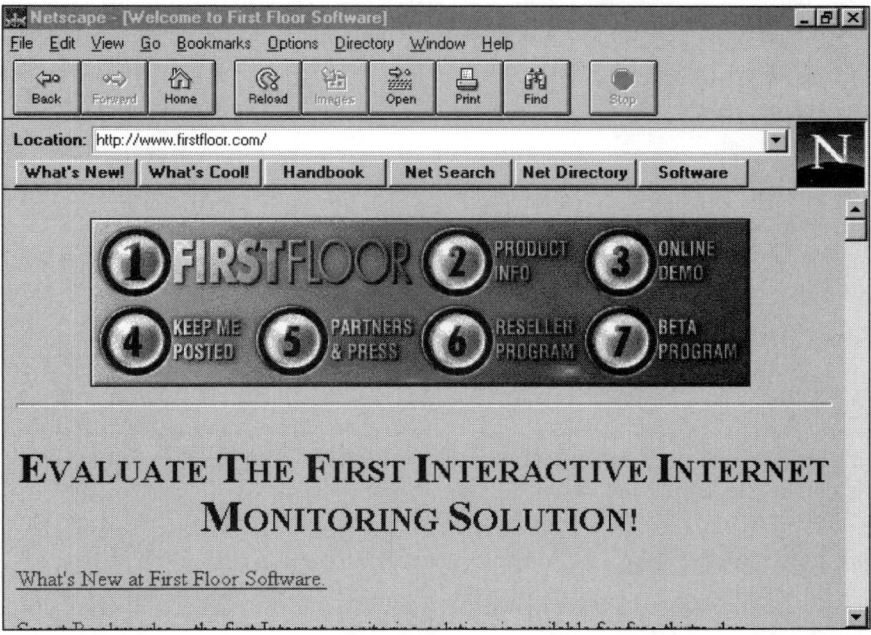

Figure 6-8: If this is the screen that appears in your Navigator window, SmartMarks has passed the test.

Sending E-Mail

No walkthrough of Navigator 2.0 would be complete without sending an e-mail letter. One of the Internet's most popular applications, e-mail is how you communicate with 30 million other netizens, request information from businesses and organizations, ask for help, provide support, and generally interact. The first letter you send in this test will be to Netscape Communications because the company has an automated response that will e-mail information back to you (telling you your e-mail is working). To test e-mail, follow these steps:

1. From the Navigator screen, click on File and select New Mail Message. The Message Composition screen appears, as illustrated in Figure 6-9.

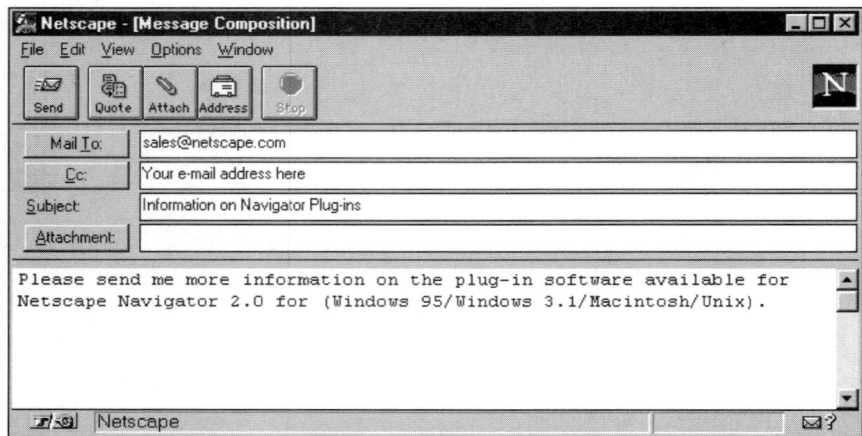

Figure 6-9: In this test, sending a carbon-copied letter to Netscape tells you whether your e-mail's Send, Cc, and Return functions are working properly.

2. In the Mail To field, enter: **sales@netscape.com**.

3. In the Cc field, enter your own e-mail address. This will send you a carbon copy of the message you are sending to Netscape and tell you whether the Cc function is working.

4. In the Subject line, enter: **Information on Navigator Plug-ins**.

5. In the Text window, type **Please send me more information on the plug-in software available for Netscape Navigator 2.0 for (Windows 95/Windows 3.1/Macintosh/Unix)**.

6. When you've completed the text, check to be certain that the addresses are correct, then click on the Send button on the control bar. You will often have your answer in minutes (although server or congestion problems can slow response time to hours in some cases, this tends to be the exception).

If the e-mail got through, you will have two messages in your e-mail delivery server: one from yourself that copied you on the message you sent; the other some background on the variety of Navigator plug-ins available (no salesman will call).

Joining a Newsgroup

In this section, we're going to post a message to a newsgroup. If you didn't perform this in the chapter dealing with newsgroups, you may want to take a moment and run through this exercise. If you have passions, curiosity, or passing interest in a subject, eventually you'll want to explore it with like minds inside a newsgroup. This practice session will help put you at ease.

This exercise assumes that you downloaded the list of available newsgroups. There are more than 10,000 of them, but they are structured in alphabetical order and nested within folders to make sure there is some logic to the groupings and order. If you have not yet downloaded the newsgroups list, you may wish to do so now. It takes several minutes if you have an average speed (14.4) modem, but it is something you need to do anyway when you're ready to check out newsgroups to which you want to subscribe. To load the names of the newsgroups, follow these steps:

1. Click on Options at the top of your Netscape News page.
2. Select Show All Newsgroups from the menu.
3. Click on OK.

When the download is complete, scroll down the list until you reach the folder labeled **alt.internet.** Click to open the folder as seen in Figure 6-10. There are, at this writing, 14 newsgroups within **alt.internet**, and they are useful for both asking and answering questions about the Internet. It's a good idea for any Internet user to subscribe to one or more of these, depending on your level of expertise and interest.

When you click to open the folder, notice that the 14 newsgroups appear in a column to the right of the folder. Scroll down the list until you reach **alt.internet.guru**.

1. Highlight **alt.internet.guru**.
2. Go to File and select New News Message.
3. Note that the message composition screen appears with the **alt.internet.guru** address already in the Newsgroups address box. In the Subject line, type **Re: Best sources for Netscape Navigator 2.0 Advice**.

4. Put your cursor into the message composition bow and write one or two sentences about seeking advice from newsgroup members about the best places to go if Navigator 2.0 problems come up.

5. Click on Send.

Your news message will be posted almost instantly. Within a (usually) short period of time, a person or persons from the newsgroup will respond with some information and advice. The **alt.internet.guru** newsgroup is not a moderated newsgroup, so your entry doesn't have to be judged on merits.

Take the time, when you have it, to explore the newsgroups you want to join. Once you've selected them, your News Server frame on the Netscape News window will only contain those newsgroups (instead of the whole list), and you can scan quickly through the list to learn what's new in your areas of interest.

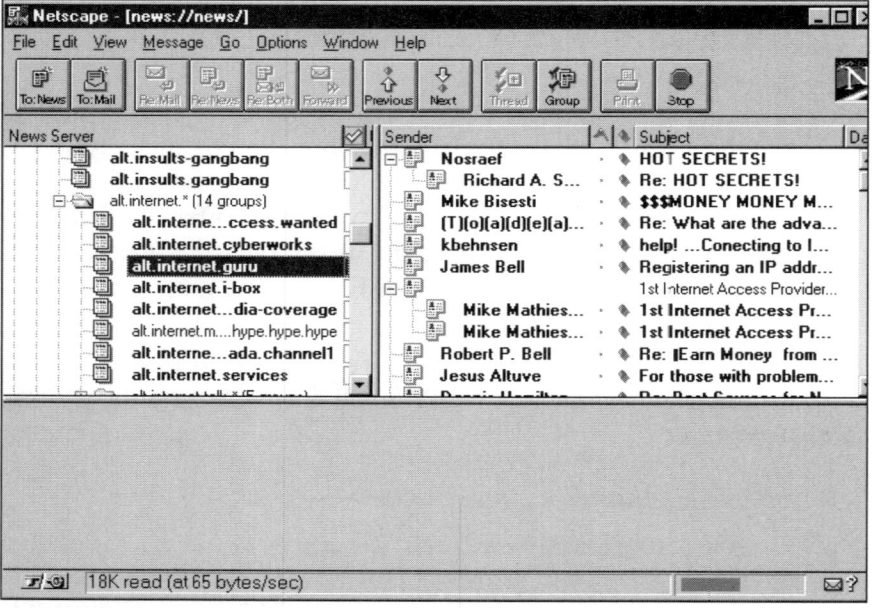

Figure 6-10: The alt.internet folder is a good one to become familiar with to solve problems that come up.

Using Navigator for File Transfer

If you had an earlier version of Netscape Navigator and followed the download instructions in Chapter 3, then you already have done some file transfer. If you loaded up an FTP application to download Netscape Navigator 2.0, then you've done file transfer. If you downloaded any of the plug-ins or helper applications described in this book, then you've done file transfer. But this segment assumes you have done none of that. The exercise here is to transfer a file by using Navigator 2.0.

Netscape Navigator has FTP facilities incorporated into it. You may have a separate piece of software such as WS_FTP, but for files of reasonable size available on the Internet, you probably won't need it if you're just downloading. Navigator's FTP facilities also allow you to send FTP files (although very early versions of Navigator 2.0 don't have this feature). Before this feature was incorporated, you would need to use Navigator's e-mail or newsgroup file attachment facilities to send a file anywhere. Now uploading is a matter of clicking on File from the main window and then selecting Upload File and designating an FTP location.

If the files that you are downloading are large, you may be better off using your separate FTP software (which downloads the files to a server) rather than Navigator's FTP (which downloads the files into RAM). Still, for many transfers, Navigator's FTP works well.

FTP allows you to see files on other computers that are available to you, then to take the necessary steps to download them to your computer. These kinds of files would include software, documents, graphics — anything you can see on the Web. Obviously, not every file on the Internet is meant to be downloaded, but virtually any file can be.

To get to an FTP site, you need to know the site's URL. URLs for FTP sites look slightly different from Web site URLs. For an exhaustive list of anonymous (meaning you don't have to identify yourself) FTP sites, go to **http://www.mid.net/FTP-LIST/** .

An anonymous FTP site might have a URL like this:
ftp://softinfo.com/
This indicates an anonymous site. If it is not anonymous, you would be required to use your user name and password. The URL might look this way:
ftp://username@ftp.softinfo.com/

In order to download a file from an FTP site, you must enter the URL of the site in the Location window. Often, you will find FTP links on Web pages, in which case you should just select the link to the page you want.

Navigator 2.0 is set up to log you in anonymously when it comes upon an FTP site. Most sites will accept this. The process is fairly standard after that, even if all FTP pages are not. Most FTP sites just require one or two clicks on the file you wish to download. Sometimes, as in Netscape's download site, you are prompted for more information. When this happens, the prompts are usually intuitive and easily followed:

1. Select the file you wish to transfer, usually by highlighting it.
2. Complete any version information you might be prompted for.
3. Select Download or hit enter.
4. Click on File and select Save As.
5. Name the file you are saving. The download progress bar tells you how long you have to wait, as shown in Figure 6-11.

Figure 6-11: The progress bar shows you the file size, how your download is progressing, and how long you have to wait.

When your download is complete, the progress bar disappears. You will find the file in your program directory under the name you gave it.

FTPing, it should be noted, is a **caveat downloader** situation. Some of the software is quite interesting; other files have been known to contain troublesome bugs and even viruses, which are programs that replicate inside your computer and can cause trouble. Before you download files into your computer, be certain you know the source and, if possible, the file you're getting. It is also a good idea to have anti-virus protection software running on your computer if you download many files.

Hypertext Links

At this point in the book, you have a good idea how hypertext links work. Each hypertext word on a page usually is colored blue (this color can be altered, but most Web page authors don't do it; when it is altered, the color always stands out from the rest of the text). It is by using hypertext links that you navigate quickly from point to point in a document, page to page at a site, and site to site on the Internet.

Virtually every page you come across on the Internet, and especially the World Wide Web, contains hypertext links. Each hypertext word takes you to a location that expands on the subject implied by the word.

For your test run, try out the links on Netscape's home page (**http:// home.netscape.com**):

1. If you have moved away from the home page, just click on the Home button on Navigator's control bar to return to Netscape.

2. Once there, select any of the blue links that look like they may interest you.

3. If you go to one that has no interest for you, click on the Back button until you return to the home page.

Summary

While this walkthrough gave you a chance to test some of the most important functions of Netscape Navigator 2.0, there is still a variety of applications to experience. For example, you can explore the increasing number of in-line plug-ins that enable you to see virtual reality pages, hear audio messages, play movies, and create your own Web pages (see Part II). We've only scratched the surface.

Nothing makes the experience of the Internet more productive than knowledge of what you can do. The easy-to-use controls in the form of button tools and menu commands make processes like sending e-mail and exploring newsgroups simple. Your practice jump using hypertext is all the training you need to become an accomplished Internet surfer. To keep up with all Navigator can do, check in regularly at the Netscape home page for information on the latest enhancement helper applications.

Part **Two**

Introducing Netscape Navigator Gold 2.0

- Netscape Navigator Gold 2.0 Basics
- Creating the 60 Minute Gold Page
- Inline Plug-Ins
- The Future of Netscape Navigator

Chapter 7

Netscape Navigator Gold 2.0 Basics

Netscape Navigator Gold 2.0 is the premier edition of the Netscape Navigator family of popular Internet navigation software. It incorporates all the features of the Netscape Navigator 2.0 browser, plus extensions and tools that allow users at almost any level of proficiency to design, author, and publish state-of-the-art HTML documents for the Internet and the World Wide Web. When you have achieved a familiarity with Navigator Gold 2.0 and the plug-in and helper applications that work with it, you will be able to create your own Web pages, pages that are professional, attractive, and effective. These pages can contain interactive multimedia; they can be filled with sophisticated graphics, virtual reality experiences, sounds, video, and animations. You can design them to exactly fit your needs and, almost effortlessly, publish them to the Internet.

Do You Need Navigator Gold?

Netscape Navigator Gold 2.0 is designed to provide both experienced and beginning content creators with simple, powerful tools, and it offers easy solutions to the problems of editing and publishing online documents.

Navigator Gold's WYSIWYG editing environment enables even first-time users to create dynamic online documents easily and publish them to local file systems and remote servers with little more than the push of a button. This can offer opportunities to many businesses and individuals to join in on the activity and promise of the WWW and the Internet and participate in its world-wide growth of opportunity.

For the experienced content creator, Netscape Navigator Gold has features for creating complex HTML documents:

- one-click image and Live Object insertion
- a raw document and script editor
- document and image format conversion
- sites can be developed with custom designs incorporating Java applets
- support for inline plug-ins for Adobe Acrobat, Macromedia Director, Progressive Networks Real Audio, and many, many others

Essentially, if you are a business person, an educator, a housewife, a student, or anyone interested in participating in the Internet's fast growing, worldwide phenomena of communication, information, and commerce (and you also enjoy having fun), this program is for you.

How Does Navigator Gold Work?

Since the beginning of their involvement in providing tools for the WWW, the folks at Netscape have been at the forefront of research and development of new ideas and tools for exploring, and stretching the envelope for participation, in the Web. Navigator Gold is the latest result of their efforts and the input derived from the many users of Netscape products who have contributed ideas, suggestions for improvements, and wish lists for new features and capabilities. The new extensions and features incorporated in Gold are designed with the user in mind.

By using the Navigator Gold Editor, you can compose documents for a variety of uses, and you can format text to suit your needs. With Navigator Gold's tools, you can apply paragraph and character styles to text, change font styles and color just as you would in your favorite word processing application, and then use these features to create pages that focus a reader's attention where you want it. With the Navigator Gold Editor, it is also easy to include objects in your pages: You can insert images, horizontal lines, and hyperlinks in the Web documents you create. You can also edit and include JavaScript in your documents. JavaScript is an open, cross-platform object scripting language for enterprise networks and the Internet.

Editing and Authoring

Special features have been added to Netscape Navigator Gold to facilitate the manipulation of text and the creation of new documents. You can now easily modify your documents by taking advantage of these features and others:

- **Add, remove, or modify text.** By clicking on any part of a downloaded Web page, you can immediately begin working with the text, the images, and also more elaborate items such as Netscape's Live Objects.

- **Compose documents for many purposes.** As easy as clicking a button, you can create a new page for printing an attractive handout, saving as a template for future pages, sending via e-mail, publishing, or posting to a newsgroup or to a Web server.

- **The WYSIWYG environment.** This environment frees you from the complexities of the HTML language and allows you to create pages as they will look online.

- **Document preview.** This feature eliminates the need to switch between an editor and the Navigator, so you can save editing time and effort.

True WYSIWYG Editing Environment

The fact that what you see is truly what you get offers time-saving advantages, as well as much needed facility for authoring and page layout operations. Editing features include

- **Drag and Drop.** The ability to easily insert text boxes, scrolling lists, pop-up lists, navigation buttons, and more enhances productivity and speeds up document creation and modification. Since both the editor and the browser are actually the same program, it is possible to drag an object (that is, an OLE object) from the browser window to the editor window. There you can save the object, together with all its code and with its links intact.

- **Text/Program Editing.** WYSIWYG capabilities provide a useful aid for writing Java-compatible scripts and HTML extensions, as well as text for stories or articles.

Layout and Page Presentation

While Netscape continues to pioneer new layout capabilities with the sophisticated options included in Navigator Gold, it has consistently maintained an open systems approach and adhered to standards. Open systems are based on published standards that are vendor independent, and a ready availability of published design specifications for hardware and software products done in a cooperative atmosphere. This is designed to foster the involvement of third-party manufacturers and developers to produce add-ons and enhancements to the system as a whole. All newly added capabilities in Netscape Navigator 2.0 have been created to be compatible with the standards published by the Internet Engineering Task Force and the World Wide Web Consortium. You can be assured of support for open standards.

Markup vs. Page Description Languages

Making Web pages that can be displayed on nearly any platform is achieved by using a markup language to create the documents, as opposed to using a page description language. Page description languages, like Adobe Postscript or Hewlett-Packard's PDL for example, are very exacting in the way that they describe how each item or element will appear on the page, regardless of the display device. If the page description language says that a document will be displayed in a 10-point Garamond font, then it must always appear that way. If your display or output device can handle the requirements of the document, you can see it as the author intended you to see it; if not, then you can't see it at all. Markup languages, like HTML, take into consideration that the viewer may be using any one of a number of computer platforms and display devices. Instead of defining how each letter should look on the page, markup languages use tags to identify the elements of the document, like the body text, section headings, and so on. Your display device (Web browser) will then display the document based on choices you have made in configuring the browser.

HTML Support

As it has been from the beginning for Netscape products, Netscape Navigator Gold continues to provide extensive HTML (HyperText Markup Language) support. New items supported in Gold are

- backgrounds
- tables
- subscript
- superscript
- extensive new paragraph alignment control (DIV and P)

Plus, there is implementation of some of the powerful new proposals to HTML 3 made by the Internet Engineering Task Force and the World Wide Web Consortium.

It is possible through the use of HTML to put things other than text and simple graphics in Web pages. Sound, video, and animation can be included to enhance and greatly sophisticate your Web page. Extensions can be added to those enhancements to include 3D and VRML virtual reality creations. Once the page is developed and published on the Web, all this multimedia can be accessed by anyone viewing the page online with a graphical Web browser running on a computer that can display video and play audio files.

While HTML is a flexible and easy-to-apply layout and formatting tool for designing complex and feature-rich pages, it does have its drawbacks. In particular, it isn't **What You See Is What You Get** (WYSIWYG). This means that editing a page in HTML requires that you view it through a browser to see what the page really looks like and then go back to the word processor or other text editor to make additions or changes. This can be slow and cumbersome, particularly if the page contains graphics or other slow-loading features. One of the really nice features of Navigator Gold is the ability to switch back and forth from the Netscape Navigator Gold Browser to the Netscape Navigator Gold Editor with the click of a mouse button. There is no need to reload the page at all. This great time-saving feature and others make Netscape Navigator Gold nearly the perfect tool for quickly and easily authoring feature-rich Web pages without the need to get down to the nitty gritty of working with HTML.

HTML Basics

Although you really don't need to know HTML to use the editor, it pays to be familiar with what's really going on inside HTML documents — especially if you're troubleshooting a Web page you're working on. If you aren't getting what you want, it can help a lot to be able to look at the file and the tags and understand what to do or find out what the problem may be. HTML has some real advantages in that its characters are all right on your keyboard and, for the most part, its use is straightforward. The following is a very short introduction to the way that HTML works. As you will learn shortly, the Netscape Navigator Gold Editor makes it easy for you by allowing you to write your text and format your page as though you were using a word processor. The Netscape Navigator Gold Editor then does the HTML tagging for you.

Formatting in HTML documents consists of tags of plain ASCII text instructions enclosed in angle brackets <>. A format area typically uses two tags: One at the beginning and another at the end. For example, to designate a particular line as a heading, you enclose the heading text inside tags that mark the beginning and end:

```
<H1>Learn HTML Quickly!</H1>
```

The tags correspond to the same sort of tags your word processor applies to text to format it in documents you produce there. For instance, in the example above, the <H1> tag marks the beginning of text to be considered a level 1 heading (Heading 1); the </H1> tag marks the end of the text heading. Instead of the usual manual way of inserting this tag, the editor lets you automatically apply an H1 format with the Properties⇨Paragraph command.

Major Features of Navigator Gold 2.0

Navigator Gold incorporates all the features of Navigator 2.0 plus some extras. These extras make it possible for you to participate in the world of online multimedia in ways not available to you before. Since the browser and the editor are both in the Navigator Gold package, some of the things we are discussing are common to both Navigator 2.0 and Navigator Gold. We focus in this section of the book on the features that will prove highly useful and desirable to the user who prefers Gold over the Navigator 2.0 plain browser.

Extensibility

Navigator Gold is highly extensible, with a range of configurable mechanisms like Application Programming Interfaces (APIs), support for the new inclusions in HTML 3.0, and some new MIME types that can enhance your Internet activities with additional software add-ons:

- **Inline Plug-Ins.** Software provided by third parties provides new capabilities for Netscape Navigator. (A player for Macromedia Director presentations, a viewer for Adobe Acrobat-format documents, and more than 30 other applications are available.)

- **Java Support.** Netscape is the premier platform for Java applets, which provide Web pages with a vast range of new functionality — including enhancements to live updating, two-way interaction, and platform-independent programmability.

- **Scripting Language Support.** Netscapes have has provided flexible, lightweight programmability via a Java-compatible scripting language and a macro-programmable API, which allows cross-platform scripting of events, objects, and actions.

- **Frames and targets.** These new features will dramatically change the look and feel of Web pages. Targeted windows permit a developer to cause another Netscape window to open when a particular link is clicked. There is also better support for scrolling text fields. That enhancement makes it easier for page developers to include live information like chat or stock quotes right in their Web page. Frames allow you to divide the window into separate scrollable areas, each with its own URL. You can make actions taken in one frame have an effect in the other. You can now create multiple frames on a single screen and control which frames are reloaded and which frames contain persistent logos, advertisements, or other useful HTML.

- **Object embeddings.** It is possible to insert a wide range of static and live objects, such as Macromedia Director movie clips, any OLE objects, and a host of new audio and video streaming technologies.

- **Inline Scripts.** Netscape Navigator Gold provides scripting support to connect objects and HTML together, thereby giving the developer rich control over events.

MIME and Helper Applications

One of the features of Netscape's Web browsers is that they are able to recognize whether the thing being requested is a graphic, a movie, an audio file, formatted text, or an animation. This is accomplished through the browser's recognition of files with Multipurpose Internet Mail Extensions (MIME). MIME types identify objects so that the Navigator knows whether or not it may directly display the item or if it must launch a helper application to handle the file. All items available on the World Wide Web have a MIME type associated with them. When you configure Navigator, you identify the helper application that Navigator is to launch to work with each MIME type.

Table 7-1: Common MIME types

TYPE/SUBTYPE	FILE EXTENSIONS	TYPE OF FILE
image/gif	.gif	GIF graphic
image/jpeg	.jpg, .jpeg, .jpe	JPEG graphic
image/pict	.pict	PICT graphic
image/tiff	.tiff, .tif	TIFF graphic
image/x-bitmap	.xbm	X-bitmap graphic
audio/basic	.au, .snd	Basic sound
audio/x-wav	.wav	WAV sound file
audio/x-aiff	.aiff, .aif	AIFF sound file
video/quicktime	.qt, .mov	QuickTime movie
video/mpeg	.mpeg, .mpg	MPEG movie
text/html	.html, .htm, .mdl	HTML file
text/plaintext	.txt	ASCII text file
application/rtf	.rtf	Microsoft's Rich Text Format file
application/mac-binhex40	.hqx	Binhex-encoded binary
application/macbin	.bin	MacBinary-encoded Macintosh binary
application/x-zip-compressed	.zip	Zip archive
application/x-stuffit	.sit	Stuffit archive
application/postscript	.ai, .eps, .ps	PostScript file
application/octet-stream	.exe, .bin	Executable file

The list of helper applications for which Navigator Gold is configured can be found by clicking on Options on the menu bar and selecting General Preferences from the pull-down menu in the browser (see Figure 7-1). The properties sheet, which appears when the Helper tab is selected, lists three things in the window:

- The MIME type, indicating what kind of object this is.

- The action to be taken by Navigator. This is a choice of either the helper application to be launched or directions to ask the user for instructions.

- The MIME file extension, an indication of how the helper application should handle the file.

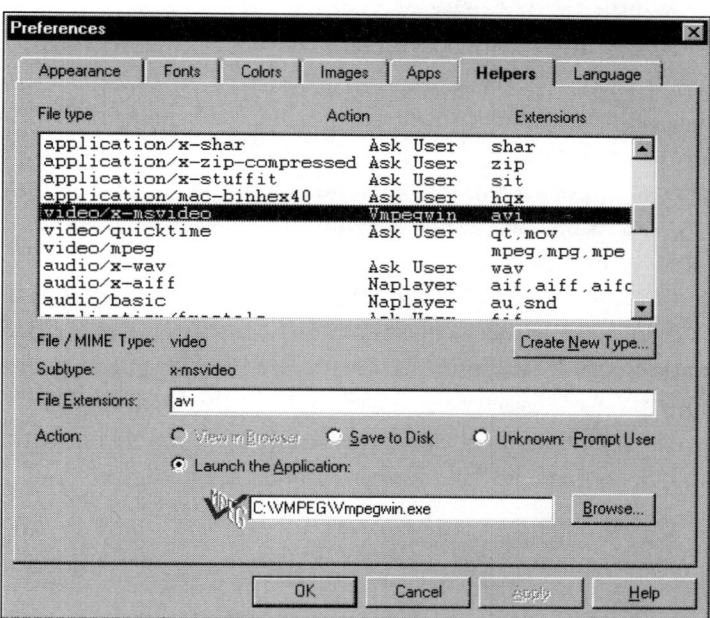

Figure 7-1: General Preferences Property sheet.

In general, all Web browsers handle MIME types in much the same way. The browser issues a connection request to the server indicating the object that it wants from the URL that you entered or the link that you clicked on. When it receives the request, the server looks at the object and determines what its MIME type is based on the file extension. The server then sends the object as a MIME-encoded data stream back to your browser. When the file gets there, your browser checks the MIME header to determine the MIME type of the item. Next, the browser checks the file against its MIME type mapping table to determine whether to display the file, launch a Helper application, or ask you what to do.

Netscape Navigator can directly display ASCII text, HTML files, and JPEG, GIF, and XBM graphics. If the file that you have is not one of these, then Navigator checks to see if you have configured a helper application that it might launch. If you have not configured a helper application, then Navigator asks if you want to save the item to a file or delete it from the temporary directory.

Data Streaming and Inline Plug-Ins

In addition to Helper applications, Navigator now supports the use of a newer kind of application called a plug-in. These third-party developed applications can perform different functions in the Navigator environment. Plug-ins can be launched to display information like a viewer, or they can be used to perform operations in background, such as compression or decompression. The thing that really sets plug-ins apart from helper applications is that plug-ins can be used to display information directly in the Navigator window. In the past, helper applications would display a QuickTime movie in the earlier versions of Navigator by launching the Helper application and displaying the movie in a different window. The new QuickTime plug-in displays the movie right in the browser.

For much more information about the available plug-ins and how they work with the Navigator Gold Editor and browser, see Chapter 9.

Realtime Data

You can now download more than just static text, sound, graphics, and movies from the Web. Newly developed and modified technologies have begun to rapidly boost the level of interaction on the Web to include realtime sound. By using **streaming** technologies, companies such as Progressive Networks have developed programs such as RealAudio, which is based on a new MIME type and an associated helper application that enables you to hear realtime sound. Instead of having to wait until the sound file downloads and then listen to it, you can listen to the sound in realtime as it downloads. This new technology has spawned a number of programs now available on the Web. Among them are several programs from National Public Radio and also some directed toward entertainment, news, technology, business, and comedy. The RealAudio helper application and instructions for loading it are found at http://www.prognet.com.

Ease of Use

The Netscape Navigator design has been enhanced and refined for Navigator Gold. The following features have been added or upgraded to provide ease of use and an improved look and feel for the new product:

- Highly configurable Graphical User Interface (GUI) advanced toolbar

- Bookmark facility, which better facilitates user abilities to maintain, index, and search a hierarchical list of favorite sites

- Pop-up, object-specific context menus

Performance

Recognizing the problem of trying to optimize performance over a low bandwidth transmission medium, Netscape designed Navigator for performance over low-bandwidth modems (14.4). Navigator Gold continues to pioneer performance improvements with

- **Multiple, simultaneous loading.** This makes it possible to download text, images, and files simultaneously. By doing this, it becomes possible to play audio, for instance, while a progressively rendered graphic downloads.

- **Solutions for document, video, and audio streaming.**

- **Intelligent 3-level persistent caching.** Netscape stores documents that you retrieve from the network on your machine in two ways: a RAM cache in memory and a disk cache for permanent storage. It also remembers where on the Web the original is. In fact, when you load one of the documents that you have downloaded from either the RAM cache or the disk cache, Netscape checks the time stamp of the document and checks to see if the one at the Web site is newer. Then it loads a new page for you, if necessary.

- **CD-ROM caching.** This provides quick access to CD-ROM-based media.

- **Native progressive-JPEG decompression.** With progressive rendering, you need to load less than 10% of the image for it to be recognizable.

- **Optimized client side image maps.** These controls can be interpreted locally and don't require server involvement or intervention.

- **Streaming audio and video support.** A variety of integrated plug-ins support the delivery of streamed data and allow the user to begin to experience the effect long before the entire object has been downloaded. This makes better use of download time and maintains the viewer's attention.

Windows Integration

Navigator Gold provides close integration with the Windows 95 environment through the following features provided either by Netscape or through third-party plug-ins:

- **OLE.** Embed Netscape Navigator Web pages into any OLE 2.0 container, including applications such as Microsoft Excel, WordPerfect, and Lotus Notes.

- **MAPI.** Use Microsoft Windows 95's Exchange messaging system as an alternative to Netscape Navigator's e-mail services.

- **Drag-and-Drop Desktop Integration.** Drag hyperlinks to Windows 95 folders and desktops to create easily accessible Internet shortcuts.

- **Microsoft's Dial-Up Networking.** This allows you to connect Netscape Navigator to service providers.

Summary

This chapter introduced you to the Netscape Navigator Gold 2.0 and outlined some of its features and capabilities that you may take advantage of to author and create your own Web content. The new functionality in the Navigator 2.0 browser, as well as the Navigator Gold Editor, introduce new and powerful tools. These tools help you combine the whole range of text and multimedia that you create on your page as easily as dragging and dropping an icon. These features are explained more fully in the following chapters as you learn more details about the Navigator Gold program and how it can be used to benefit you.

Chapter 8

Creating the 60 Minute Gold Page

In the last chapter, you got an overview of some of the features of Navigator Gold. You were introduced to some of the basic concepts of authoring a Web page and learned how Navigator can be extended through the helper applications and plug-ins. In this chapter, you are going to take a closer look at the editing features of Navigator Gold and learn how you can use its features and tools to create your own Web page.

Where Do You Begin?

A Web page is a document made up of text and graphics formatted in HyperText Markup Language (HTML) and containing embedded links to places within the document itself and, also, possibly to other pages or resources on the Web. These pages contain textual information often accompanied with graphic illustrations. Online, these pages are viewed with a browser, such as any of the Netscape family of browsers. Browsers are HTML interpreters. It is possible, in theory, to navigate across these links between documents and to "surf" the whole World Wide Web. However, in order for this to become reality, the Web pages created by you and other designers must contain properly formatted links and be in

HTML and clearly readable by HTML-browser software. The Netscape Navigator Gold Editor can help you create pages with attractive formats and content and links that work.

Navigator Gold Editor

When you first start Navigator Gold 2.0, you will be in a browser window (see Figure 8-1). Navigator Gold allows you to browse the pages on the World Wide Web and author your own Web pages. Navigator Gold also permits you to open multiple windows at the same time to facilitate using the various functions incorporated in the program. There are distinct windows for performing different tasks, and you may switch easily from one active window to another to address the task you want to perform. Since Navigator Gold includes the complete Navigator 2.0 browser, as well as the Navigator Gold Editor, you can open windows to access newsgroups and read electronic mail, in addition to browsing and editing. The browse and edit windows in Navigator Gold each have their own unique set of menu commands and toolbars designed with either the browsing or editing purpose in mind, respectively. It is easy to switch between browse and edit windows by using commands from each window's File menu or the toolbar.

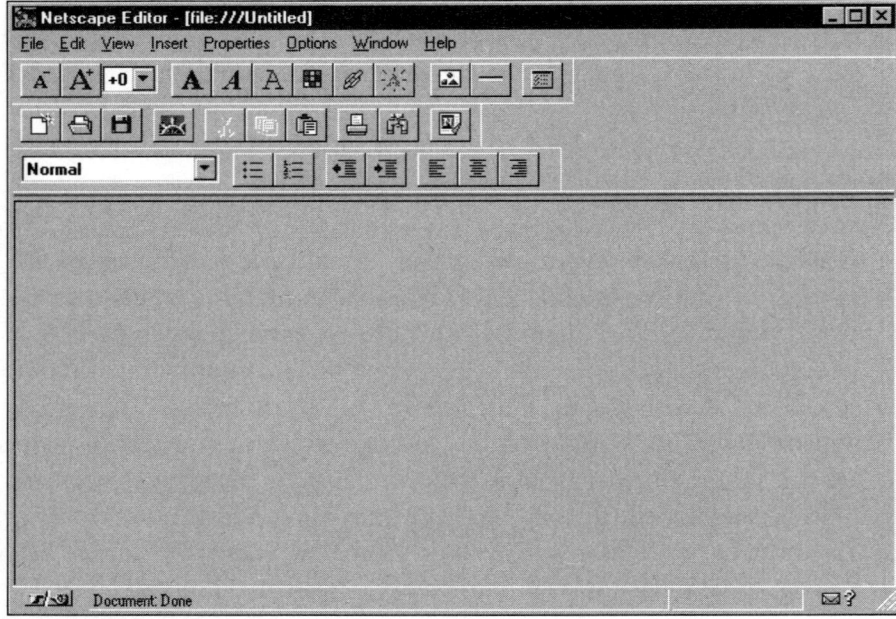

Figure 8-1: The main Navigator Gold Editor screen.

In the past, creating a Web page was a time-consuming process of editing HTML codes, then viewing the page by using a browser, then returning to the source file to make changes, then getting out the browser and viewing the page again, and on and on until you finally got it right. With the Navigator Gold Editor, creating or editing Web pages and working with HTML has been greatly simplified.

There are myriad advantages to creating HTML documents with the help of Navigator Gold's Editor. With the powerful features of Navigator Gold's Editor at your fingertips, it is not really necessary for you to understand the complexities of HTML to be able to create your own Web documents. You can work in a familiar, word-processing-like environment as you create your document. You can add, remove, and modify text easily by simply clicking on any part of a downloaded Web page and then going right to work with the text and images, again just as you would in a word processor or page layout program. The Editor supports drag-and-drop functionality, not only for text and images, but for OLE objects, Java applets, hyperlinks, and images from the Bookmarks, Mail, News, or Browse windows. You may move these to any document in the Editor.

Using the Editor's Functions and Tools

Along the top of the browser window is a menu bar. By selecting File and then New Document, you will find yourself in the Navigator Gold Editor. Take a moment to familiarize yourself with the overall look of this page. It contains a plethora of useful tools and commands.

Menus

The pull-down menus from the toolbar contain commands for all Netscape Navigator Gold 2.0 functions. In addition, pop-up menus are a handy way to get to frequently used commands. The commands you can get to are dependent on where you are when you right-click. For example, right-clicking while on a link provides you with commands to copy or modify the link. If you right-click while on an image, you'll have quick access to commands to save the image under a new name or display its properties.

Using the Toolbars

The three toolbars below the menus, File Edit, Paragraph Format, and Character Format, contain buttons corresponding to frequently used commands. Although it is possible to access the toolbar commands from the menus, it's generally quicker to use the toolbars. (See Figures 8-2, 8-3 and 8-4).

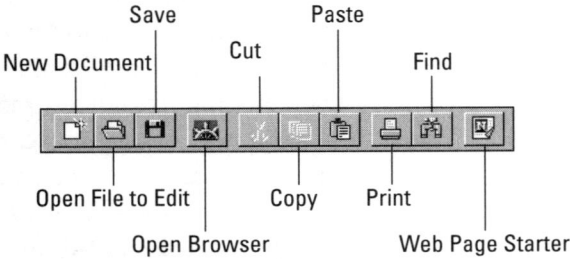

Figure 8-2: The File Edit toolbar.

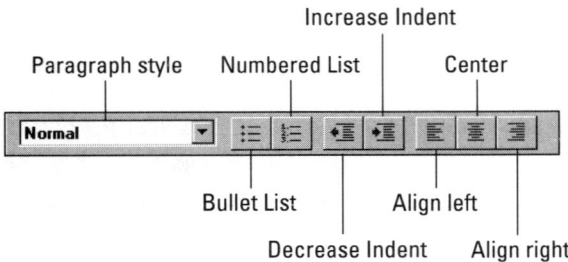

Figure 8-3: The Paragraph Format Toolbar.

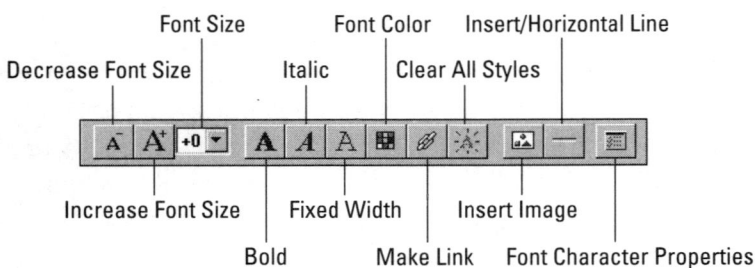

Figure 8-4: The Character Format Toolbar

Shortcut Menus

Shortcut menus are available to provide quick access to many of the Editor's features and functions (see Figure 8-5). For instance, if you right-click anywhere on the page in the Editor window, you get the pop-up menu that offers a shortcut to the Paragraph/List Properties Sheet, the Document Properties Sheet and the Links dialog box. Other shortcut menus offer assistance with and options for the Horizontal Line. Right-clicking on an image brings up the Image shortcut menu with quick access to the Image Property Sheet, the Save Image as... dialog box, the Paragraph/List properties sheet, the Document Properties Sheet, and the Create Link dialog box. Right-clicking on a link takes you to the Links shortcut menu. Of course these functions are accessible from the menu and toolbars as well, but the shortcut menus offer time-saving, quick access to the things that you need right on the page.

Figure 8-5: Shortcut menu.

Drag and Drop

Several drag-and-drop operations are available while using the Editor. You can

- Drag a link from a browse window and drop it in the edit window. This is just like inserting a link in the document you're editing.

- Drag a link from a Bookmarks, Mail, or News window and drop it in the edit window.

- Drag an image from a browse or mail window and drop it in the edit window. This is the easiest way to add images to your Web pages.

Creating a New Document

When you open Navigator Gold, you should be looking at the browser window. If you were linked to an Internet Service Provider (ISP) when you opened Navigator Gold 2.0, you are looking at the ISP's home page. If you opened the program without an ISP connection, you were prompted either to connect or load a document from the cache. If you elected not to connect, then the browser loaded the last cached version of your selected home page. Next, you'll open a new document so that you can begin using the Navigator Gold Editor to create a page.

From the File pull-down menu, select New Document. When you do this, another window opens displaying a blank page in the Editor (see Figure 8-6). The original browser window is still open, but it is behind the new page that you just created. You may minimize or close the browser window if you wish. You may also elect to leave it open to make it available to you if, for instance, you wish to drag things from it to drop on the new page in the Editor.

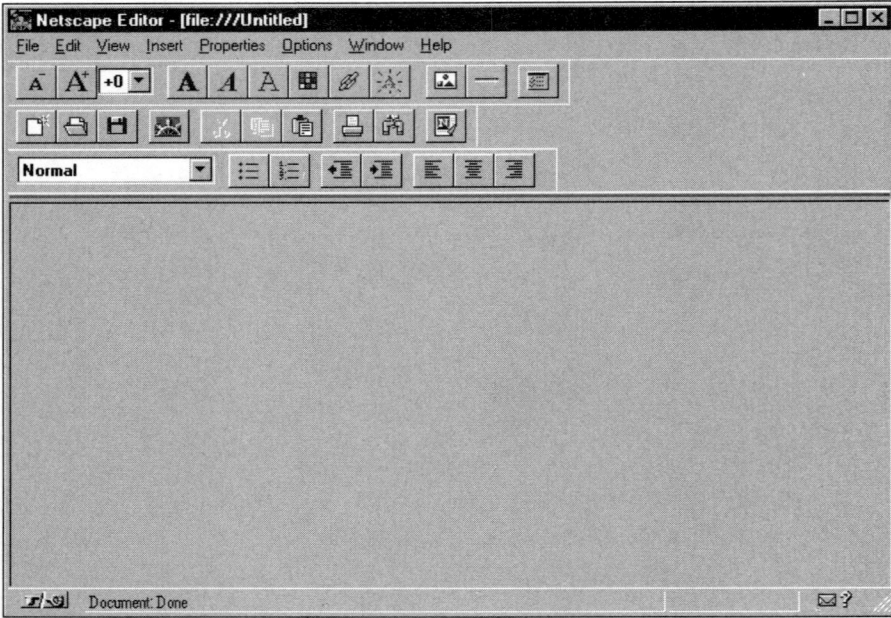

Figure 8-6: The Edit window ready to start a new document.

Editing a New Page

Now that you have a nice clean page in the Navigator Gold Editor window you can begin to create your first document. However, before you begin using the Editor to put in text and images to create a Web page, you should take a moment to familiarize yourself with the Navigator Gold Editor's tools and pull-down menus. The Editor's toolbars are equipped with tool tips. With tool tips, if you rest the mouse pointer for a moment on any of the tool bar buttons, a small pop-up flag identifies the tool by its function. Using the pull-down menus also offers you a choice of functions or opens up dialog windows for using the Editor's features. The pull-down menus also enable you to customize the Editor's features to enhance your documents' appearance and set preferences (see Figure 8-7).

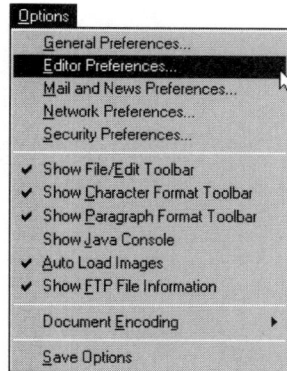

Figure 8-7: A Navigator Gold pull-down menu.

You can configure some of the edit window components, as well as how certain text elements appear in the window. For example, from the Options pull-down menu you can display or hide the File Edit, Paragraph Format, or Character Format toolbars, and use the properties sheet (which you can obtain by selecting Editor Preferences from the pull-down menu in the Options menu) to specify default settings for text and background colors for the Editor. To specify those choices for just the document you are working on, you can use the Properties/Document menu choice. The Options/General Preferences property sheet enables you to make choices about how Netscape Navigator Gold looks and how it works with plug-ins and helper applications.

The Navigator Gold Editor does two types of formatting: Paragraph formatting and character formatting. The Editor has a Paragraph Format toolbar and a Character Format toolbar, as well as pull-down menu items that make the business of formatting a page as easy as it is in your word processor. To demonstrate this, start your page with a title.

1. You can begin by clicking in the Editor window where you want to place the title and typing in the text exactly as you would in any word processor.

2. From the Paragraph Style window in the Editor's Paragraph Format toolbar select the Heading 1, H1 style (see Figure 8-8). When you do this, you will see that the Editor immediately applies the Heading 1 style and, although you don't see this part, it also applies the HTML coding for the H1 heading.

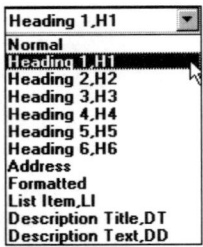

Figure 8-8: The Paragraph Style drop-down list.

Take a moment to look at the Style Window's pull-down list. Navigator Gold Editor applies HTML coding to your page for each of the formatting choices available to you from the list. (The same list of choices is also available from the Properties pull-down menu under Properties/Paragraph.) These are the styles currently supported in the Editor:

- **Heading** tags (<H1>) look like this when applied: <H1>Netscape Navigator Gold 2.0</H1> Headings are used to divide sections of text. HTML defines six heading levels. These are reflected in the six heading choices available from the Style Window list. The headings differ from regular text by their type size.

- The **Address** tag (<ADDRESS>) formats an address block, providing a means for people who view your Web pages to get in touch with you.

- The **Formatted** tag (<PRE>) corresponds to the preformatted tag in HTML. You will use this for text with special formatting that you wish to preserve.

- The **List** types all have the (<LI>) tag in common. The Navigator Gold Editor provides support for the following types:
  - Unnumbered <UL>
  - Numbered <OL>

  These additional list types may be manually added to HTML files created in Navigator Gold by inputting HTML code:
  - Block Quote <BLOCKQUOTE>
  - Directory <DIR>
  - Menu <MENU>

- The **Description Title** (<DT>) format corresponds to the Definition Term tag in HTML. You will use the Description Title tag for glossaries, definition lists, or other situations where left-justified short entries are followed by longer blocks of indented text.

- The **Description Text** (<DD>) tag corresponds to the Definition Description tag in HTML. You can use the Description Text tag for glossaries or other kinds of lists where you need to associate a single term or line with a block of indented text.

Along with the style selection tools, the Editor provides a set of toolbar buttons for the most common editing tasks, and it also allows various drag-and-drop operations. The three toolbars displayed on the top of the Navigator Gold Editor page are the Character Format toolbar, File Edit toolbar, and the Paragraph Format toolbar. These toolbars provide easy access to the tools you'll need to quickly construct and format your page (see Figure 8-9).

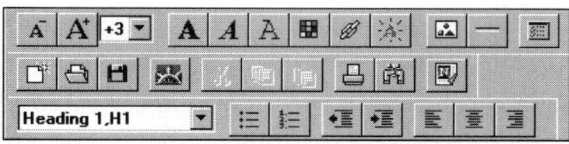

Figure 8-9: The Navigator Gold toolbars.

Text

Since you have begun to add text, you should be aware that there are several ways to put text on your page. You can continue to type it in and format it with the Editor's tools as you did with the title. The Editor works just like a word processor. You can also use the Edit menu's cut, copy, and paste commands, or the Window's Clipboard to copy text from almost any source and paste it into your document. Once the text has been placed in the document, the Editor's tools can be used to format it, color it, size it, change its font, and enhance it in other ways. The following is an overview of what can be done with the Navigator Gold Editor to incorporate text in your Web document.

Cut, Copy, and Paste

Since the Editor works like a word processor and supports use of the Windows Clipboard, you can enter text into your document by pasting it from almost any source, including a file displayed in your word processor or even from a Web document displayed in the browser. If you are copying text from the browser window, you can select the text that you want to copy and then use the Edit⇨Copy and Edit⇨Paste commands from the edit pull-down menu.

To use the Clipboard to copy and paste text, follow these steps:

1. First select the text to copy.
2. Press <Control> <c>on the keyboard to copy it.
3. After placing the cursor on the page where you want the text to appear, press <Control> <v> to paste it there.

Text can be moved from one place to another by pressing <Control> <x> to cut and <Control> <v> to paste.

Selecting Text

Text selection in the Editor is also very similar to most standard text Editors and word processors. Table 8-1 describes the methods for selecting text.

Table 8-1: Methods for selecting text

ACTION	RESULT
Double-clicking on a word	Selects the word
Double-clicking before a line	Selects the paragraph
Double-clicking after a line	Selects the last word or element in that line
Clicking before a line	Selects the entire line
Dragging the cursor over text	Extends the selection by the same unit as the initial selection (character, word, line, or paragraph)
Clicking at the beginning of the first sentence, holding down the shift key and clicking after the last sentence	Selects any size block of text

Character Formatting

Character styles can be applied to one or more characters, either within a paragraph or spanning parts of multiple paragraphs. The following character styles are supported in the Editor: Bold, Italic, Fixed width, Superscript, Subscript, and Blink.

To access the Character styles menu, click on the Properties menu and select Character. Some of the character styles are available on the Character Format toolbar as well, but you have to use the Properties menu to reach them all.

In addition to the Character styles mentioned above, Navigator Gold also supports Java script for both the client and the server. The options for switching in and out of Java script are also found in the Properties⇨ Character drop-down menu (see Figure 8-10).

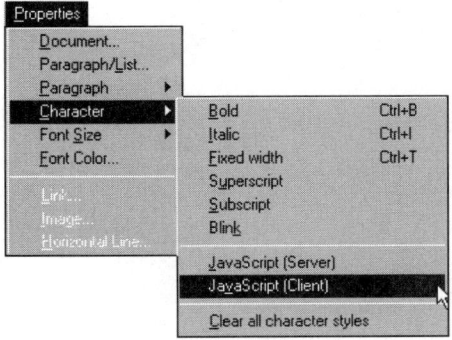

Figure 8-10: Character styles drop-down menu.

Fonts

Like most other graphical Web browsers, Navigator Gold 2.0 defaults to using a proportionally spaced font such as Times Roman for most of the text in Web documents. You can display a different font while viewing in the browse window. You do this in Navigator Gold the same way as you would in the Navigator 2.0 browser, by clicking on the Options menu and selecting General preferences. Next select the Fonts tab on the property sheet. When you do this, the Font dialog box will appear (see Figure 8-11). You can choose from all Windows fonts for the proportional font you wish to display. You can also choose from a selection of fixed fonts. Using different fonts can highlight things that you want to emphasize in your text, but a good presentation will be in a good readable font with few distractions. Remember, it is usually not a good idea to paint a picture by using all the colors in the paint set.

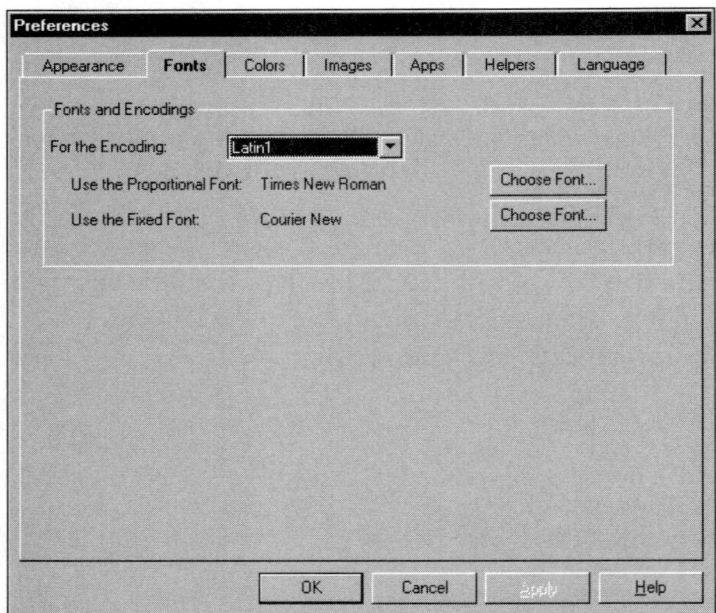

Figure 8-11: Selecting a different font in Gold.

Adding Color

Applying color to selected text is another excellent way to emphasize different parts of your Web page. To add color

1. Select the text whose color you want to change
2. Either press the Font color button on the Character Format toolbar or click on the Properties menu and select Font Color.

Either of these actions brings up the pop-up Font Color dialog box and you can select a color from the palette, or define your own custom color (see Figure 8-12).

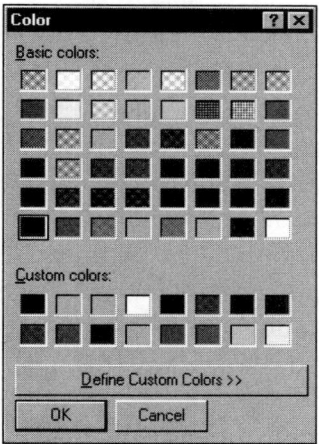

Figure 8-12: The font color dialog box.

Adjusting the Size

You can adjust font size in Navigator Gold either by using the Font Size drop-down list on the Character Format toolbar or by selecting Font Size from the Properties drop-down menu. If applied properly, changing the size of a font to emphasize a word or link can be used to draw the viewer's attention to a particular part of the page or text (see Figure 8-13).

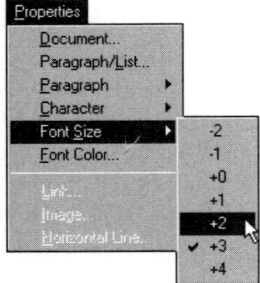

Figure 8-13: Adjusting the font size in Gold.

Applying Templates

Netscape has added another tool to the online documentation available to help you take advantage of Netscape and Netscape Gold's full potential. The Netscape Page Wizard, available online from Netscape, is an interactive Web page template that makes creating a fantastic-looking Web page with your Netscape Navigator Gold 2.0 Editor a piece of cake. It helps you organize your ideas and provides ready-to-use art, background textures, color, and rules so your page will have a professional look and feel.

Page Wizard only requires that you fill in the blanks, choose from the style selections, click the Create Page button, and your Web page will be generated automatically. Next, save your page into Netscape Navigator Gold and edit the content and format until you're happy with the final product. It is easy to find a home for your Web page: Any Navigator Gold Internet Service Provider can post your page to the Internet and issue it a URL (or address) so others can visit it.

The address for the Netscape Page Wizard is:
http://home.netscape.com/assist/net_sites/starter/wizard.html.

An alternate way of getting there is to choose Help from the Gold menu bar and then select Web Page Starter. This takes you to the Netscape Page Starter site. If you go halfway down the page, in the paragraph for the second step under *Three Easy Steps to Publishing Your Own Web Pages,* there is a link for Netscape's Page Wizard.

Elements of Style

Formatting your text and effectively using color goes a long way toward making your Web pages or presentations unique and interesting. Once you have added more things to your page, like images, horizontal lines, and links to other resources, you will begin to see why Web pages attract so much attention. These elements are the makings of a good Web page. The same rules of good document construction apply in Web pages, just like they do to other kinds of documents.

Graphics

Adding graphics to your page is perhaps the most effective way to provide eye-catching appeal and call attention to what you want the viewer to see. The addition of color and visual detail to your page makes it more pleasant to read and enhances the message you are trying to convey. The old adage about a picture being worth a thousand words can be successfully reiterated here.

In the last section, you learned how using the style and formatting tools can help to create a good textual presentation. In this section, we are going to examine the tools available to add graphics to polish the appearance of your page and improve its readability. Several graphical enhancements to your pages are available with Navigator Gold to improve the look and feel of your presentation.

Inserting Horizontal Lines

Using horizontal lines to separate and set off sections of the text is a simple but very effective way to add eye appeal to textually busy presentations. These simple graphics can be used to break the information into more manageable pieces for the reader's eyes to focus on and help keep the attention level you want. Horizontal lines may be created in several ways. The easiest way is to click the Horizontal line toolbar button on the Character Toolbar. The Editor places a horizontal line across the page at the point where the cursor is on the page. You can also insert a line by clicking on Insert and choosing Horizontal Line from the drop-down menu. Again, the line is placed on the page where the cursor rests.

The line that the Editor places on the page can be customized. To do this, place the cursor on the line and right-click to get the pop-up menu. Choose Horizontal Line Properties. In the properties sheet that appears, you may specify alignment, width, height, and whether or not to use 3D shading (see Figure 8-14).

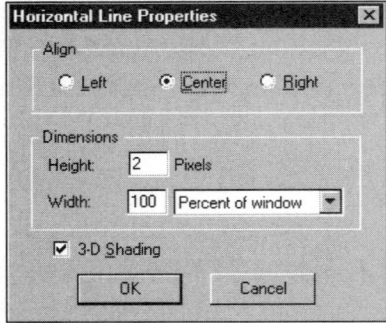

Figure 8-14: Creating horizontal lines.

Ten Tips for Designing Web Pages

1. Don't hurry. A little analysis of what message you want to convey beforehand will repay you greatly.

2. Know your prospective audience. Target the group of people that you want to reach and then start hanging out online with them until you know their interests.

3. Think first, then design. The more complex the message you wish to convey in your page, the more forethought that must go into the selection and formation of its content to make the design effective.

4. Organize what you are going to say. Outline your page so that you can see the best order of topics and content, write down the key idea or message that you are trying to convey, then list supporting points to make your case.

5. Keep it simple and elegant. Information in volumes can be as bad as not saying enough. Your audience wants to understand the message, but you may lose their interest if you inundate them with irrelevancies. Find that fine line between informing and rambling, and stay on the right side.

6. Help the reader remember what you want them to remember. Keep in mind that the audience for your page will not always embrace all that you have to say. When you organize and lay out your page's content, well-thought-out formatting places emphasis where it belongs. This emphasis helps guide the viewer toward that kernel of important information that you want him to take away after his visit.

7. Keep it appetizing. Don't mix up the food on the plate. Information in manageable pieces is more palatable and gives your readers an opportunity to look at the things that interest them and hold their attention better. Using headings to break up the content guides their eyes where you want them and keep things interesting.

8. White space is good. Leave room around the things on your page so that your readers' eyes are drawn to the things that you want them to look at. If your page is too busy, they may surf away to a more relaxing site.

9. Avoid jargon. Jargon is sometimes real 'naff'. Your message can be conveyed and better understood in clear concise language written to the level of the audience that you target. Your ideas should be what they remember and not just your obscure, albeit impressive, vocabulary.

10. Be happy. Unless the page you are doing is an advertisement for the funeral industry or a public service announcement about a very negative subject, the tone should be upbeat. Make your page a nice place to visit and fun loving Web surfers will visit it frequently.

Images

There are two ways that images are typically presented in Web pages. The most common way is as an inline image, where the picture actually displays with the Web page. A less common way is as a separate external link that you need to download apart from the Web page. You may have a specific need to have the image as a separate downloadable file, for example, if you want to make it an option for the reader to decide if they want to spend the time downloading a large file. However, for the most part you would want the images to display with the page to have the desired effect.

Computer images are a two-dimensional array of picture elements (pixels) on your monitor. An image can be as simple as one displayed on a monochrome monitor, where each pixel is simply on (monitor color) or off (black). In a more complex image, each pixel is capable of displaying a color chosen from a palette of millions of colors. Raw data graphic files containing information about images made up of millions of colors can easily be megabytes in size. Something is required to make graphics files manageable within the constraints of online file transfer bottlenecks. Even modem speeds of 28,800 baud only really transfer data at about 1.4 Kbps, which means that, without regard to pauses and fluctuation in the line speed, it will take a couple of minutes to download even a small graphic file. A full screen color image could take 15 minutes or more.

To help overcome the problems of graphic file size and unmanageable download times, graphic files are compressed. The two dimensional array of pixel values that describes the image is called a **raw bitmap** and it is possible to just save the image to a file with the file extension .BMP. The problem with this is that the **raw bitmap** file format is inefficient and it contains lots of wasted space. The file contains information about the location, state, and color of each pixel on the screen but without giving notice to the fact that much of the information is duplicated elsewhere in the file (For example, if a picture is of a green car many of the pixels that make up the image are probably exactly the same shade of green). In the compression scheme, the pixel's color information is listed only once and then it is necessary only to have information stored regarding it's location and state. Elaborate algorithmic functions keep track of adjacent pixel blocks with the same color value, and the size of the file is greatly reduced.

Most of the current Web browsers support either of the two image formats:

- GIF (CompuServe Graphics Interchange Format .GIF extension)
- JPEG (Joint Photographic Experts Group .JPG extension)

Both of these formats use built-in compression schemes. The difference between them is in the degree. GIF files are compressed by using **lossless compression**. With lossless compression, images are compressed only to the extent that they are always able to reproduce the original file when displayed without loss of image quality. The other method, **lossy compression**, is used by the JPEG formatted files. With lossy compression, the level of compression is selected when the file is created and the method of display of .jpg files is such that it only approximates the original color values and displays an image of lesser quality than the original. However, if image quality isn't very important, the file can be compressed to as little as ten percent of the original file size. This could be an important consideration in planning for download times for your page.

Inserting an Image from a File

To begin inserting an image into your Web document, follow these steps:

1. Choose the Open File toolbar button or open the File menu dropdown and choose Open File.

2. From the Open File window, choose the graphic file that you want to display and click on Open. If the file you selected is in a file format that the Editor can read, the picture or graphic appears in the editor window.

3. Press the Insert Image button on the Character Toolbar and you are shown the Image dialog box for your image. The Image dialog box can also be accessed through the Insert menu; click on the Insert Menu and choose Image.

4. You can fill in the blanks where needed (see Figure 8-15).

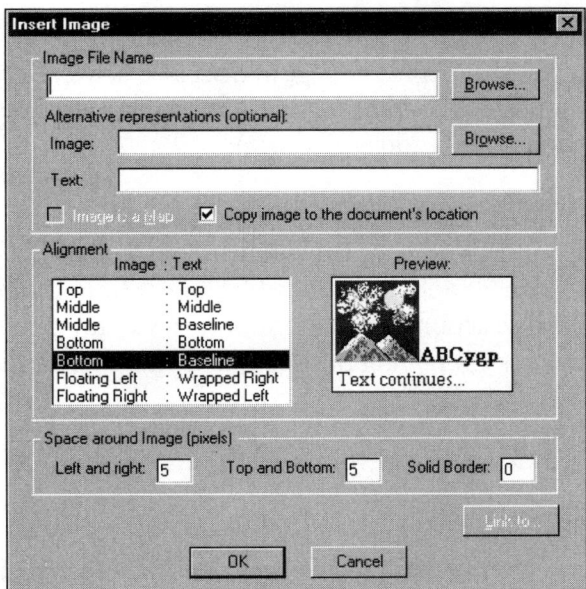

Figure 8-15: The Insert Image dialog box.

Inserting Graphics from the Web

Perhaps the easiest way to add an image in your Web document is to simply drag it from the browser window over to the editor window and drop it on the page you're editing. This is the same as copying the image. The browser window and the editor window can both be open at the same time and be resized so that you have easy access to the browser page, as well as a place on your editor page to drop the image. The browser can search local drives as well as the Net for files you want to use.

Creating Your Own Graphics

By using any of a number of readily available software graphics packages, you can create graphics yourself that you can include on your page. Just remember when you finish creating your graphic that you must export the graphic to a file format that the Netscape Navigator Editor can read. Then open your file in the Editor and select either the Insert Image button from the toolbar or select the Insert menu, then the Image command to get the Image Properties Sheet.

Editing an Existing Page

In addition to creating a page from a blank page as discussed above, elect to edit a page that you find on the Web. Editing text in the Editor works as it does in most word-processing applications. To begin

1. Open a page in the browse window that you want to edit.
2. Click the Edit tool on the Navigator Browser window toolbar (the one that looks like a pencil). Choosing Edit Document from the File menu performs the same action. The current browse window becomes an edit window containing the document you were viewing (see Figure 8-16).

You may also edit an existing file from your hard drive.

1. From the File menu, select Open File in Editor.
2. You are then be prompted to select the file from the File Open dialog window.
3. When you have selected the file that you want to edit, press Open. An edit window opens containing the specified file. The original browse window remains open, but behind the edit window (see Figure 8-17).

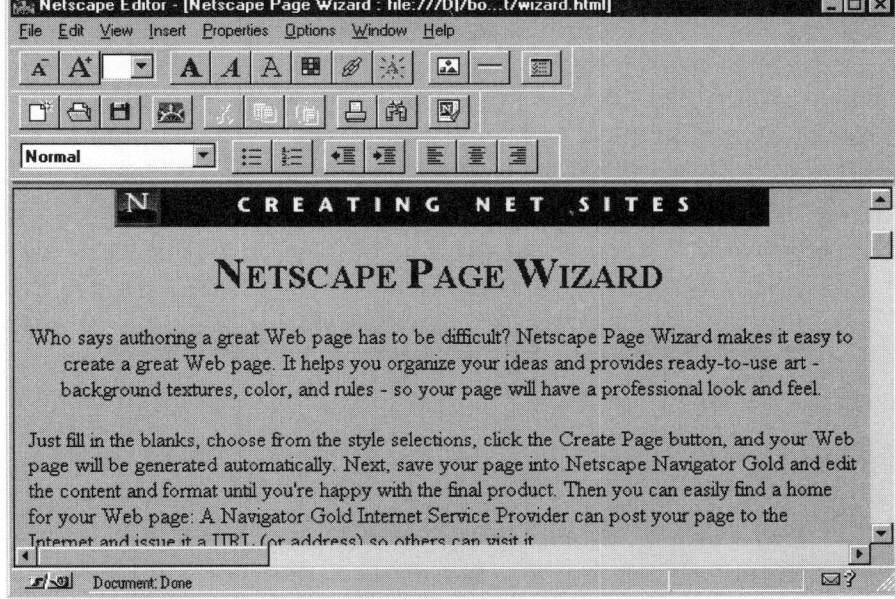

Figure 8-16: The Edit window ready to edit a document downloaded from the Web.

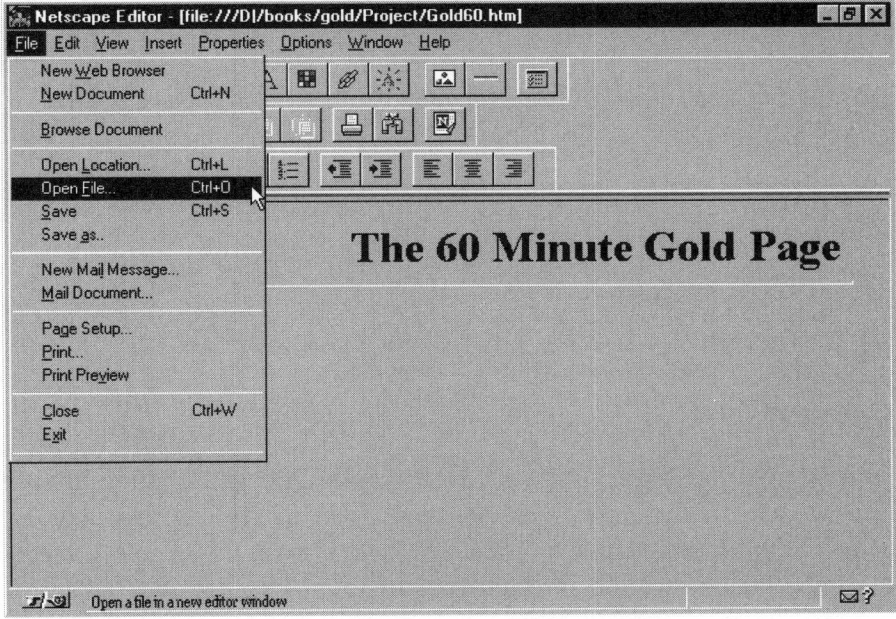

Figure 8-17: The Edit window ready to edit an existing document.

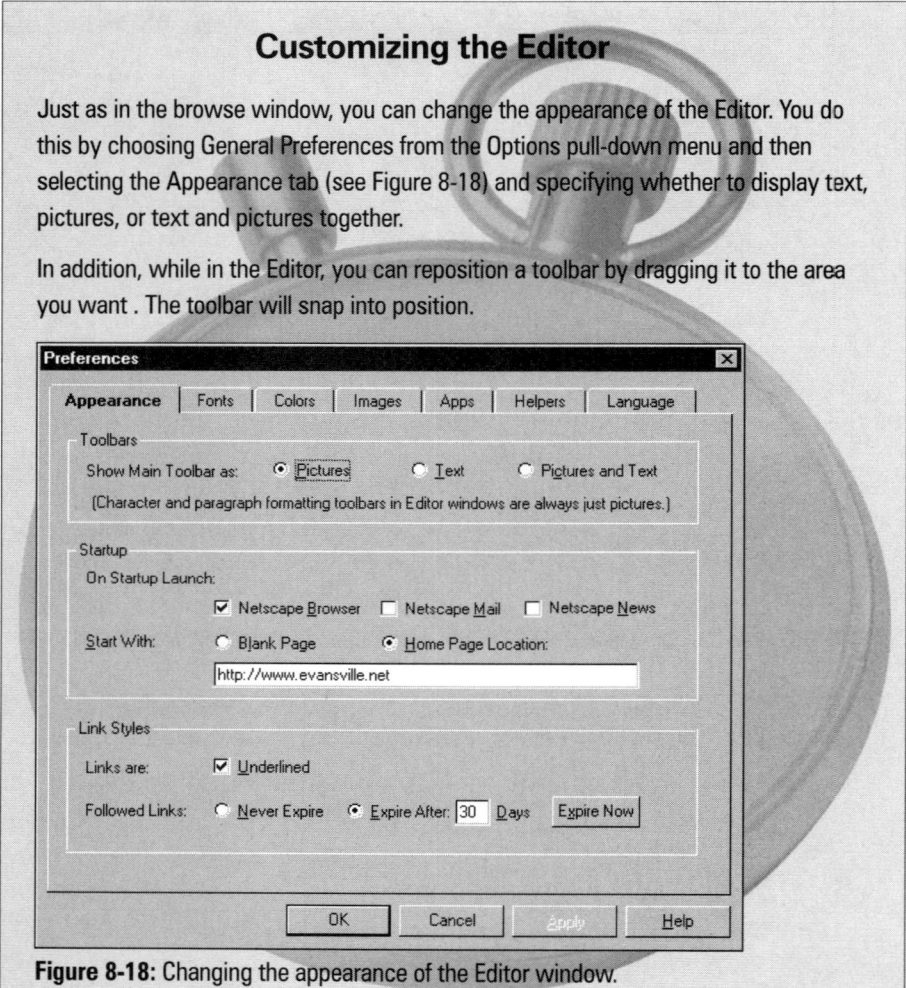

Customizing the Editor

Just as in the browse window, you can change the appearance of the Editor. You do this by choosing General Preferences from the Options pull-down menu and then selecting the Appearance tab (see Figure 8-18) and specifying whether to display text, pictures, or text and pictures together.

In addition, while in the Editor, you can reposition a toolbar by dragging it to the area you want . The toolbar will snap into position.

Figure 8-18: Changing the appearance of the Editor window.

Hypertext

It wasn't very long ago that hypertext and hyperlink documents were a new idea, but they are commonplace in computing today. Consider the MS Windows, Macintosh, and OS/2 Help systems, for example. Help typically displays highlighted areas that you can click on to access additional information. That other information might be contained elsewhere in the same file, or perhaps in another help file on your computer. On the

Web, hyperlinks access information on your own computer and potentially on any accessible computer on the Internet. The information you access, stored in computer files, can produce words, sounds, pictures, or even action video on your own computer.

URLs

Uniform Resource Locators, or URLs, are effectively street addresses for bits of information on the Internet. Most of the time, you can avoid trying to figure out your own URLs by simply navigating to the information you want to point to with your browser and then copying and pasting the long string of "stuff" into your link. But it's often useful to understand what a URL is all about and why it has to be so long and complex. Also, when you begin publishing your own information on the Web, you'll want to know something about URLs so that you can tell people how to find your Web page.

Most URLs have three parts: The **protocol**, the **host name**, and the **directory**. The protocol is how the document is accessed; that is, the type of program your browser will use to get the file. If the browser is using HTTP to get to the file, the protocol part is http. If the browser uses FTP, it's ftp, and so on.

Follow the example below to analyze the various parts of a URL.

http://www.teleport.com/~jdimick/cg.html

The host name is the system on the Internet where the information is stored, such as home.netscape.com. You can have the same host name but have different URLs with different protocols, for example

http://thesystem.com
ftp://thesystem.com
gopher://thesystem.com

These are all the same machine, but with three different information servers. As long as all three are installed on that system and available, there's no problem with them having the same names.

The host name part of the URL can also include a port number. The port number (preceded by a colon) is what tells your browser to open a connection of the appropriate protocol on a specific network port other than the default port for each protocol. The only time you'll really need a port number in a URL is if the server handling the information has been explicitly installed on that port. If a port number is necessary, it goes after the host name but before the directory.

Finally, the directory is the location of the file or other form of information on the host. The directory may be the actual directory and filename, or it can be a **pointer** or an **alias**, another indicator that the protocol uses to refer to the location of that information.

Creating links

As in most software operations, there are several ways to create links in your documents. Links may be created to link text, graphics, resources, other pages on the Web, files on your computer, or another computer on a Web.

Inserting Links

To create a link for your document, open the Insert menu and select Link, or press the Link button on the Character Format Toolbar. The Insert Link dialog box will appear. (See Figure 8-19).

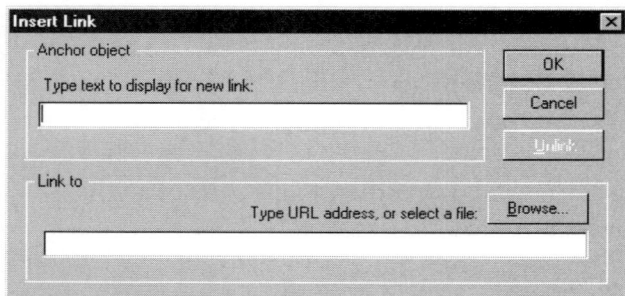

Figure 8-19. The Insert Link dialog box.

To insert the link into your page

1. In the Anchor text box, type the name of your link.
2. In the Link to text box, type the URL and click OK.

Dragging and Dropping Links

You can drag a link from a browser, Bookmarks, Mail, or News window and drop it on a document in the editor window.

Modifying Existing Links

To modify an existing link, choose Link from the Properties pull-down menu (or right-mouse click the link) to display the Modify Link dialog box (see Figure 8-20). You can specify a different URL for the current link or even unlink it from here. For example, if the location of the linked page has changed, you can update the specified URL so that clicking on that link doesn't produce an error message.

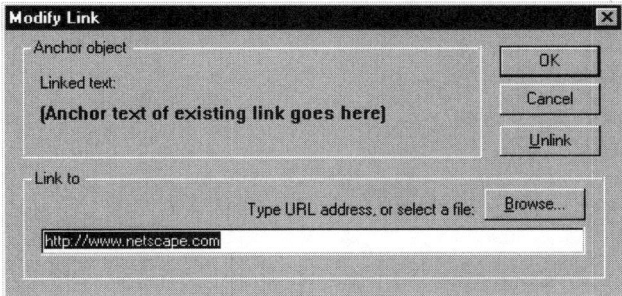

Figure 8-20: The Modify Link dialog box.

Summary

In this chapter, you looked in-depth at how the Navigator Gold Editor and tools work. You learned how to use the Editor to include text and graphics in your page. You examined the tools and how they are invoked through the menu and toolbars to modify links and attach them to a page. You learned how to apply templates and how to edit an existing page to change the content and add or remove links, objects, text, and graphics. You also looked at what constitutes a good design plan for creating your own page and got some hints about how to produce a good page, as well as some description of the pitfalls to avoid.

Now that you have an understanding of what options are available to you in Navigator Gold, you can begin to use the Editor to compose your own Navigator Gold pages. You may also edit your existing pages and update the content and liven them up with new graphics, sounds, and animations. The following chapter discusses what is available to you from third-party suppliers of plug-in applications for Navigator.

Chapter 9

Inline Plug-Ins

N etscape Navigator Gold 2.0's new enhancement features provide inline support for a large number of live objects. Developers can now deliver rich multimedia content through Internet sites. Navigator Gold's enhancement features enable users to view that content with plug-ins such as Adobe Acrobat Amber Reader and Macromedia Shockwave for Director right in the client window — all without launching any external helper applications. This chapter is an overview of the inline plug-in applications available for integration into Netscape Navigator Gold 2.0.

The Common Gateway Interface (CGI) was developed by the folks at the National Center for Supercomputer Applications (NCSA) at the University of Illinois at Urbana-Champaign. CGI is the standard mechanism in use on Web servers for the execution of programs that generate dynamic documents and send them to your browser. In other words, CGI provides a method for your browser to execute programs on remote servers using your input. You click on a spot on the page in your browser window, a graphic, or a send now box at the end of a form, and you generate a unique URL that your browser sends to the server. The server recognizes that the URL is not just for document retrieval but is intended to invoke a program on the server. The program is executed and the results are sent to the HTTP server and then returned to your browser for display.

The Netscape client API is a little different; it allows the server to cause programs to execute on your machine. These executable programs, which reside on your computer as plug-ins, use the API to interface with the programs on the server. Now not only can developers work interactive magic with the server, but they can direct that applications be downloaded and run on your client machine as well. This capability can greatly enhance your multimedia presentations with audio and video that you can embed in your pages for the user to view as the data is downloaded from the server.

A Word about Hypertext

The use of hypertext and hyperlinks in computer documents is quite common these days. The Help systems for MS Windows, Macintosh, and OS/2 are good examples. Help documents display highlighted areas that you can click on to access additional information, either contained elsewhere in the same file or perhaps in another help file on your computer. The linked information that you access can produce words, sounds, pictures, or even action video on your own computer. On the Web, hyperlinks can access information not only on your computer but potentially on any computer accessible on the Internet.

Application Programming Interface

It has long been a goal of developers to incorporate realtime functionality in their audio and video presentations. The low bandwidth modem connections over telephone lines present a barrier to moving the large amounts of data necessary for video and high quality audio presentations. **Streaming** is one of the more exciting developments on the Web for enhancing interactive multimedia. A good definition of streaming goes like this. When data is moving quickly from one piece of hardware to another, and it doesn't have to wait until it's all in one place for the destination device to do something with it, it's streaming. When your hard disk's data is being written to a tape backup device, it's streaming. When you're watching a QuickTime movie on the Internet, it's not streaming, because it has to be fully downloaded before you can play it.

Although the idea of streaming has been around for some time and the technology is not new, enhancements in modem technology and today's faster multimedia PC processors are bringing new forces to bear on the problem. Streaming data through multithreading technologies offers interesting possibilities. An example of one of the original uses of threading is the way that messages in a Usenet newsgroup are organized into a coherent conversation: Each additional reply to the original message is threaded onto the last posting in that context.

The method for streaming data such as audio or video is true client/server computing in action. The section that follows describes how the process works. Client/server computing is a process in which a client computer sends a request to a server machine for the performance of some activity. The server machine, after performing the function, sends the results back to the client. The power in client/server computing lies in the fact that both the client machine and the server machine may act as either a client, a server, or both in the transaction. This means that they may interact and leverage the computing power of both machines to get the job done.

In implementing the functions described above for applications associated with streaming, the client/server request-response paradigm is altered somewhat to facilitate realtime interaction. The client machine initiates a request to the server to download a page containing multimedia to the client machine browser. The audio file begins downloading from the server and then the server initiates a request to the client to launch the audio player application. The audio player application begins playing the audio as it is received. Multithreading technology allows all parts of the page to download simultaneously, so the graphics and text will be downloading while the audio is playing.

The Netscape Client API

The Netscape Client Application Programming Interface (NCAPI) provides the client half of the equation necessary to have true client/server interaction. This allows Navigator Gold to provide truly interactive Web content. The NCAPI supports two methods of handling dynamic data in multimedia enriched transactions, OLE (Object Linking and Embedding) and DDE (Dynamic Data Exchange). Netscape works through the API to provide support for interactive streaming applications.

Applet Utilities

Two utility applets assist you in embedding OLE controls in your pages. These controls help you to insert interactive applications created in program languages like Visual Basic scripting or Visual C++ on a page.

OLE Control

Vendor: ExCITE
Phone: (604) 291-3615
Fax: (604) 291-5679
E-mail: `excite@sfu.ca`
URL: `http://www.excite.sfu.ca/`

This plug-in, running under Windows 95, lets you embed OLE controls created using standard programming languages and development tools such as Visual C++, Visual Basic, and the MS Windows Game SDK as applets.

OpenScape

Vendor: Object Power Incorporated
Phone: (617) 876-0038
URL: `http://www.opower.com/`

The OpenScape plug-in delivers OLE/OCX compatibility. With OpenScape, you use a visual drag-and-drop environment together with Visual Basic scripting to build interactive applications. OpenScape Basic helps you to build forms in Visual Basic-compatible language and avoid the use of cumbersome HTML.

You can build your Home Page with the Visual Basic-compatible language without loss in performance. Forms that you build with OpenScape are reusable in Navigator 2.0.

Audio Players

Audio players have become one of the more popular plug-in applications, especially since the advent of **streaming** data technologies that allow you to listen in realtime to music and entertainment without having to first download the file. Coupled with emerging new video technologies, audio players are beginning to change the way we use the Internet. These plug-ins to Netscape Navigator are already beginning to enjoy support from a number of sites on the Web. That number is growing rapidly.

RealAudio

Vendor: Progressive Networks, Inc.

Address: 616 First Avenue, Suite 701
Seattle, WA 98104

URL: `http://www.realaudio.com/`

RealAudio provides live, on-demand, realtime audio over Internet connections of 14.4 Kbps or faster. RealAudio Version 2.0 is a powerful plug-in for Navigator with which you can customize and deliver audio enhancements to your page.

With the RealAudio 2.0 Player for Windows, you can listen to both live and prerecorded files in RealAudio format without downloading. Click on a RealAudio link from a World Wide Web page, and your RealAudio Player automatically opens and plays the file. See Figure 9-1.

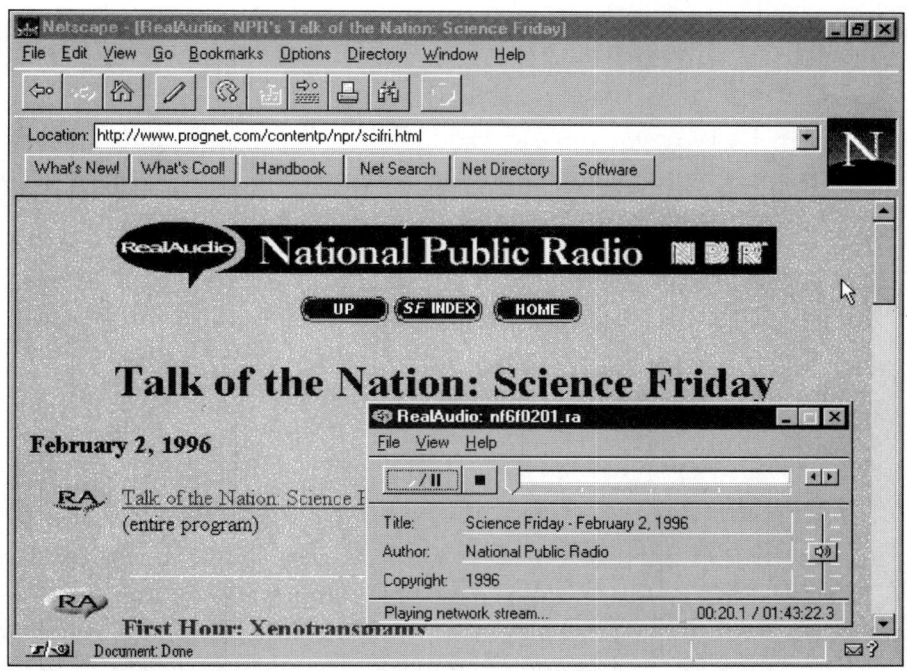

Figure 9-1: Playing a RealAudio file from National Public Radio.

After you have clicked on an audio file, you can continue to use your Web browser while playing the file. You can minimize the Player while you use other applications, and you can also choose to have the Player displayed in front of active applications. The Player continues to play the selected audio file until it is finished and does not interfere with other programs.

There are two RealAudio 2.0 Players for Windows available:

- **RealAudio 2.0 for Windows 95 and Windows NT**. This has been optimized to work with 32-bit Windows. It will not work with Win 32S.

- **RealAudio 2.0 for Windows 3.1 and 3.11.** This runs under 16-bit Windows. RealAudio 2.0 Players play two different algorithms:

The 14.4 algorithm provides mono AM quality sound, with 14.4 Kbps modems or better. **The 28.8 algorithm** provides mono FM quality sound, with 28.8 Kbps modems or better.

ToolVox

Vendor: Voxware, Inc.
Address: 172 Tamarack Circle
            Skillman, NJ 08558
Phone: (609) 497-1212
URL: `http://www.voxware.com/`

With ToolVox, you can easily add high-quality speech audio. ToolVox offers 53:1 compression ratios, more than three times the compression of first-generation Internet voice products.

TrueSpeech Player

Vendor: DSP Group, Inc.
Address: 3120 Scott Boulevard
            Santa Clara, CA 95054-3317
Phone: (408) 986-4300
Fax: (408) 986-4323
URL: `http://www.dspg.com/dspg.htm`

The TrueSpeech Player plays TrueSpeech over the Internet almost in real-time. It uses a low-bandwidth (8.5 Kbps) compression algorithm that supports streaming audio playback. It also utilizes a bookmarking ability that enables you to store and listen to your favorite sites directly from the Player. In addition, you may develop TrueSpeech Player-compatible content without the need for special server software.

The TrueSpeech encoder is bundled freely with Windows 95 and Windows NT.

Document/Presentation Viewers

Document/presentation viewer software enhances the functionality of Netscape to include a wider choice of file formats and access to different technologies. These programs facilitate viewing, downloading, and printing of Web documents. They also provide tools for reading and publishing documents to the Web in various file formats and offer new graphics handling capabilities.

Acrobat Amber Reader & Weblink

Vendor: Adobe Systems Incorporated
Address: 1585 Charleston Road
            P. O. Box 7900
            Mountain View, CA 94039-7900
Phone: (415) 961-4400
Adobe Customer Service: (800) 628-2320
Fax: (415) 961-3769
URL: http://www.adobe.com/

Amber is the code name for Adobe's newest update to the Acrobat Reader and Acrobat Exchange. Amber has been enhanced with several new features designed to optimize its performance on the Internet, and it integrates seamlessly with Web browsers to produce a speedy, page-at-a-time display. With the Amber version of Acrobat you can view, navigate, and print Portable Document Format (PDF) files in the Navigator window. PDF files offer design control for print-ready documents and many authoring applications.

Several pieces make up the 'Acrobat on the Internet' picture:

- The Adobe Acrobat Amber Reader.

- **Optimized** PDF files for progressive display and maximum file compression.

- **Weblinks** to connect your PDF files to other content on the Web.

Nonoptimized PDF files can still be viewed in the Netscape window (without page-at-a-time display) with the Amber Reader and Netscape Navigator 2.0 Version Beta 3 or better.

New Acrobat Amber features allow integration with Netscape Navigator Gold 2.0 to allow PDF files to be viewed seamlessly within the browser window (see Figure 9-2). Amber also has a new way to optimize PDF files for delivery on the Internet or online services. **Optimized** PDF files can be viewed a page at a time instead of waiting for the entire file to download.

The Weblink plug-in extends the link tool in Acrobat Exchange 2.0, Reader 2.1, and the Amber Reader to allow you to create and follow links containing URLs in PDF documents. This plug-in is included in the 2.1 release of Acrobat Reader and Exchange. Weblink is available without cost from several on-line services and from the Adobe World Wide Web Server at **http://www.adobe.com/** for use with Exchange 2.0.

At this writing, Amber is currently available only for Windows 95 and Windows NT.

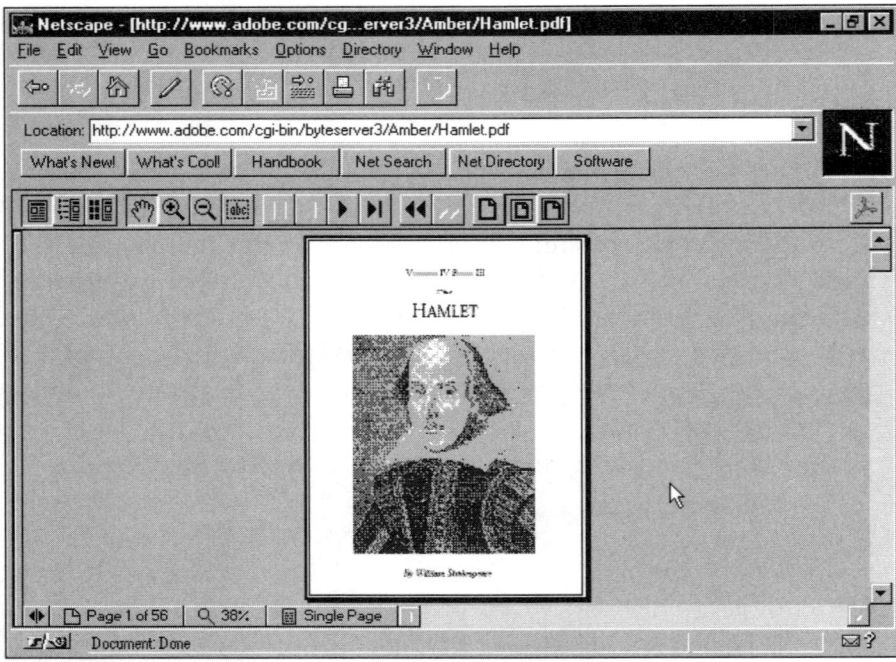

Figure 9-2: Viewing a PDF file in Netscape Navigator Gold.

For more information, you can contact Adobe at its fax request line (408-986-6587) or by e-mail at devsup-person@mv.us.adobe.com.

ASAP WebShow

Vendor: Software Publishing Corporation
Address: 111 North Market Street
               San Jose, CA 95113
Phone: (408) 537-3000
Fax: (408) 537-3500
URL: `http://www.spco.com/`
CompuServe: GO SPCFORUM

ASAP WebShow is a Netscape Navigator 2.0 plug-in presentation viewer. WebShow can be used for viewing, downloading, and printing reports and presentations. ASAP WebShow allows you to view any document created by SPC's ASAP WordPower report and presentation software package.

Authors of Web pages incorporating embedded ASAP WordPower presentations can take advantage of several parameters available in the plug-in. These parameters allow you to modify the appearance or functionality of the embedded windows (for example, the standard <EMBED> tag parameters of SRC, WIDTH, and HEIGHT).

Transmission times are estimated at a rate of three pages per second, a rate that is significantly faster than standard streaming rates. Graphically-rich pages with text, gradient colors, and graphical objects such as tables, pyramids, and organization charts can be saved in such small file sizes that the need for compression is eliminated. For example, thirty heavily-graphical pages occupy as little as 11K, permitting users with a 14.4 Kbps modem to download an entire report or presentation in under seven seconds.

What Is a PDF File?

The Adobe Portable Document Format (PDF) is a cross-platform, PostScript-based file format developed by Adobe. A PDF file can describe documents containing any combination of text, graphics, and images in a device-and-resolution-independent format. These documents can be one page or thousands of pages, very simple or extremely complex. The pages can make rich use of fonts, graphics, color, and images.

COREL VECTOR GRAPHICS CMX Viewer

Vendor: Corel Corporation
Address: 1600 Carling Avenue
             Ottawa, ON, Canada, K1Z 8R7
Phone: (613) 728-8200
Fax: (613) 761-9176
URL: http://www.corel.com/index.htm

With Corel Corporation's CMX Viewer, smooth vector graphics can be viewed online on the Net (see Figure 9-3). The CMX Open Standard is a vector-based graphical format intended to enhance the publishing of images on the Internet. The viewer is currently available only for Windows 95 and Windows NT.

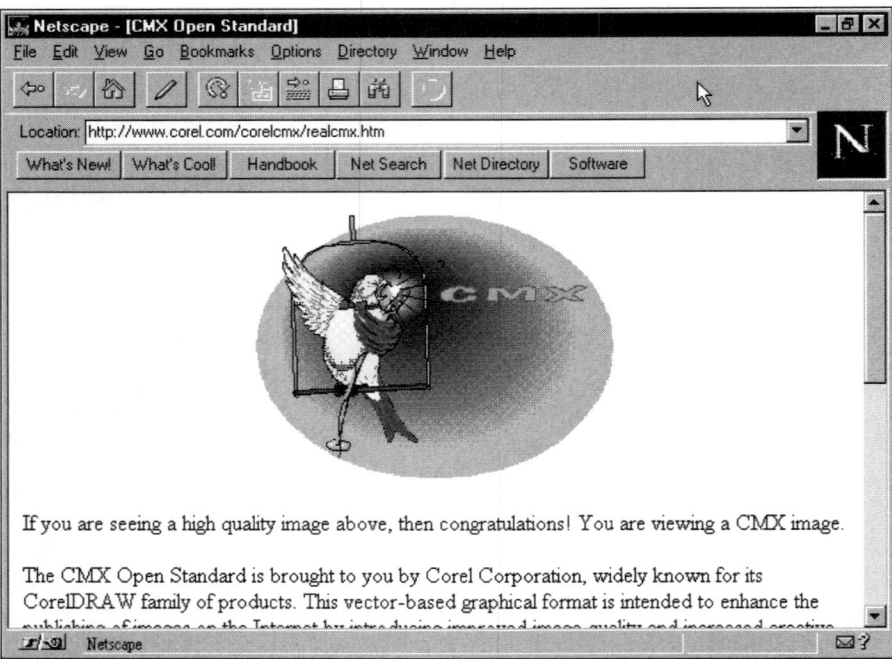

Figure 9-3: Viewing a CMX image over the Internet.

Image Quality

Vector formats allow for a richer, fuller representation of the image because they do not rely on pixels for their structure. Vector-based images consist of objects with defined properties. For example, if a user puts a picture of a circle in a drawing, he could go back later and change its orientation, color, and line thickness, or enlarge the image to any size and get smooth lines. Raster images as bitmapped graphics, on the other hand, are pixel-based. This means that, should a user put a circle into a drawing, it might not be possible for him to go back and edit it later and get smooth lines. Enlarging the image would merely increase the number of pixels, creating jagged edges. Vector images are perfect for projects such as logos, where the image is reusable and scaleable to any size without the problems associated with bitmaps.

Better Printout Quality

Vector graphics produce superior print output. When a bitmap image is sent to a printer, the image is likely to have output at a different resolution than the original. Vector graphics are unaffected by a printer's resolution. Vector graphics backgrounds are automatically transparent. This eliminates the need to rely on masking tools and additional steps to remove unwanted backgrounds.

At times, vector images are even more economical in terms of space. Vector formats such as CMX may use only 20 percent or so of the bandwidth that raster formats, such as GIF, do.

Innovative Technology

This viewer is the first open-standard vector format offered to Internet users. It gives users of Navigator Gold access to larger selections of clipart, such as the huge libraries found in products like CorelDRAW! or Corel GALLERY. The CMX Viewer opens the world of vector graphics to Internet users.

Vector formats such as CMX or CDR are widely used around the world. Corel's user base alone is estimated at 2.5 million. This viewer provides users of Navigator Gold the opportunity to publish a huge repository of graphic arts without losing the quality of the original illustration.

Publishing Web Pages

CMX graphics offer greater quality and control over the contents of your page. The CMX format is particularly suited for use with images that use gradient fills, such as the bleed at the top of a page. CMX is also useful with images that are repeatedly used in varying sizes, such as logos and product icons.

Envoy

Vendor: Tumbleweed Software
Address: 2000 Broadway
             Redwood City, CA 94063
Phone: (415) 363-7022
Fax: (415) 363-7024
E-mail: info@tumbleweed.com.
URL: http://www.twcorp.com/

Envoy is a portable document format designed for the electronic distribution and viewing of documents created with a broad range of authoring tools. Envoy created documents can match the original content, formatting, and graphics created within other authoring tools at a fraction of the original file sizes. The Envoy plug-in lets users view documents on the Internet exactly as they were designed: with all different fonts, graphics, and layouts. Tumbleweed Software offers the Envoy plug-in to view embedded graphics or entire pages from within Netscape Navigator on Windows 3.1, Windows 95, Macintosh, or the Power Mac.

Publishing in Envoy

You can publish in the Envoy format by printing your document from any application through the Envoy printer driver. The Envoy printer driver is included in both Envoy from Novell and Tumbleweed Publishing Essentials. You may also use the Tumbleweed Publisher for batch publishing of documents into Envoy and direct conversion from complex file types, such as PostScript. The Tumbleweed Publisher is included in Tumbleweed Publishing Essentials.

Post Envoy documents on your Web server just as you would HTML files. It's that easy. You must make sure that the content mapping table on your Web server maps the .evy extension to application/envoy. You can also embed Envoy documents in HTML pages.

Envoy enables the flexible electronic distribution of formatted documents. You can use any application to create your document and publish it
in Envoy. Here your customers can access it via the freely distributed
viewer, Web browser plug-ins, and customized viewers from third parties.
Envoy documents maintain visual fidelity with the original document.
They are also portable in that they can be read across multiple
computer platforms.

FIGleaf Inline

Vendor: Carberry Technology
Address: 600 Suffolk Street
            Lowell, MA 01854
Phone: (508) 970-5358
Fax: (508) 453-0336
E-mail: sales@ct.ebt.com
URL: http://www.ct.ebt.com/

Netscape Navigator users can dynamically zoom, pan, and scroll vector
(CGM) graphics and multiple raster formats, including GIF, JPEG, TIFF,
CCITT GP4, BMP, WMF, EPSF, Sun Raster, and other popular formats
with FIGleaf Inline.

FIGleaf Inline is a Netscape API-compliant graphics module that
operates as a plug-in to Netscape Navigator 2.0 and Navigator Gold 2.0.
FIGleaf Inline directly supports inline viewing, zooming, and panning of a
wide variety of popular vector and raster graphic file formats within the
Navigator 2.0 browser. With FIGleaf Inline, you can deliver all major
graphics file formats on the Web without the need for conversion to GIF
or JPEG format.

FIGleaf Inline provides support for Computer Graphic Metafile (CGM)
vector graphics within the Navigator 2.0 Web browser. CGM, the pending
vector graphic standard for the Web, enables highly detailed illustrations to
be displayed as vectors (line-art), instead of as raster bitmaps. In addition to
CGM, FIGleaf Inline supports the following file formats:

- Tagged Image File Format (TIFF)
- Encapsulated PostScript (EPSI/EPSF)
- CCITT Group 4 Type 1 (G4) and Type 2 (TG4)
- Microsoft Windows Bitmap (BMP) and Metafile (WMF)

- Portable Pixmap (PPM)
- Portable Greymap (PGM)
- Portable Bitmap (PBM)
- Sun Raster files (SUN)
- GIF
- JPEG

Shockwave for Director

Vendor: Macromedia, Incorporated
Address: 600 Townsend Street
            San Francisco, CA 94103
Phone: (415) 252-2000
            (800) 326-2128 (for product literature)
Fax: (415) 626-0554
URL: `http://www.macromedia.com/index.html`

You can integrate digital video movies, sound, animation, clickable buttons, links to URLs, and more within your presentation. The Shockwave plug-in enables you to import Macromedia Director presentations right into a Netscape Navigator window. Even complex multimedia can be made to run fast on low-end machines using Shockwave for Director. Its features can be used to greatly enhance your multimedia presentation.

Fast Network Delivery

Shockwave's use of advanced compression speeds delivery so movies load quickly. An additional plug-in supplements Shockwave's activities with Netscape Navigator: Afterburner post-processes Director source files to protect and compress content by 40 to 60 percent, for general LZ77 **lossless compression**.

Cross-Platform Multimedia

Director files are platform-independent, meaning that they play back across all platforms. This offers access to the greatest number of users with proven support, ranging from 386 PCs with Windows 3.1 to the Pentium Processor with Windows 95, from 68K series Macintosh to Power PC Macintosh, and even on UNIX platforms. Director movies play across the board (see Figure 9-4).

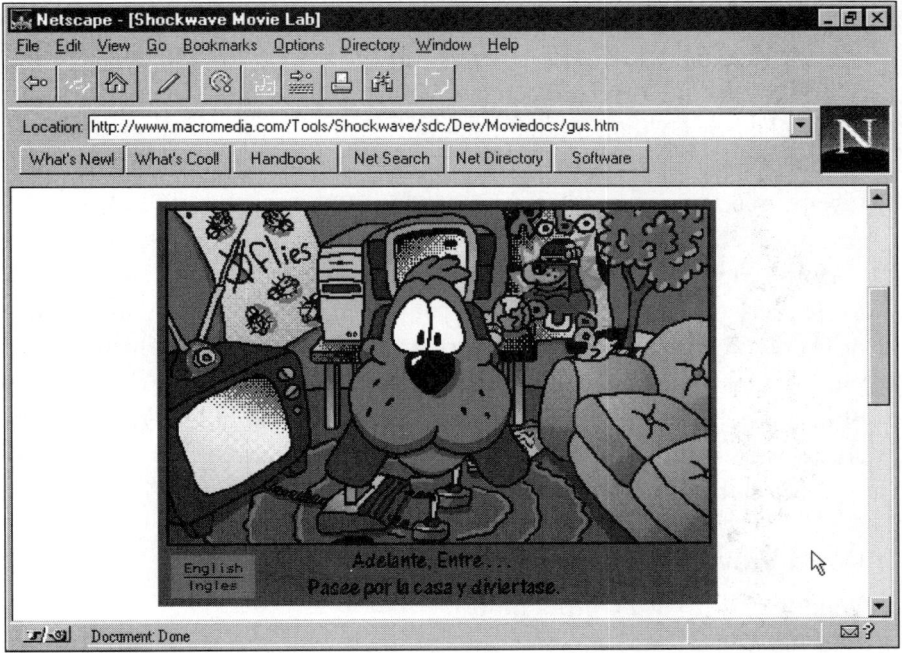

Figure 9-4: Viewing a Shockwave movie.

Hot Link through URLs

Shockwave integrates text pulled dynamically over the network, enabling users to integrate stock quotes and game scores into Director movies, for instance, or to facilitate multiplayer games. Using Network Lingo commands, users can hot link from Director movies to HTML pages. They can even link to other Director movies over the network and combine them to create large movies from smaller ones.

SoftSource

Vendor: SoftSource
Address: 301 W. Holly
           Bellingham, WA 98225
Phone: (360) 676-0999
           (800) 626-0999 (Sales)
Fax: (360) 671-1131
E-mail: softsales@softsource.com
URL: http://www.softsource.com/softsource/

SoftSource has two new plug-ins for enhancing Netscape Navigator —
one for viewing AutoCAD drawing and DXF files, and one for viewing
SVF files for CAD and general-purpose graphics. SVF is an acronym for
Simple Vector Format, a file format SoftSource jointly developed with
NCSA. These plug-ins are part of the ongoing steps SoftSource has taken
toward making architectural, engineering, and construction CAD data
easily available to all users.

Both plug-ins work with scaleable vector graphics, which allow the user
to magnify portions of the drawing or toggle layer visibility without multiple downloads. Thus, the zoom, pan, and layer visibility controls of either
plug-in make it a snap to explore even the most complex CAD drawings
online. The SVF plug-in also features navigation via HTML hyperlinks,
adding new options for applications or context that requires detailed,
structured information and graphics.

Word Viewer

Vendor: INSO Corporation
Address: 31 St. James Avenue
            Boston, MA 02116-4101
Phone: (617) 753-6500
Fax: (617) 753-6666
URL: http://www.inso.com/

View any Microsoft Word 6.0 or Microsoft Word 95 document from
inside Netscape Navigator with Inso's Word Viewer plug-in, based on Inso's
Quick View Plus viewing technology. This plug-in also enables you to copy
and print Word documents with all original formatting intact.

Video Players

Video players hold an attraction for most of us on the Web who are
waiting to be able to match quality of pictures and sound with that of
broadcast TV. The obstacles to be overcome in transmitting video over the
wire to our home computers in a fashion that allows us to watch video in
realtime may seem insurmountable. However, the new technologies
outlined on the following pages do have some promising attributes that
deserve attention.

PreVU

Vendor: InterVU, Inc.

URL: `http://www.intervu.com/`

PreVU provides streaming MPEG video for Netscape Navigator 2.0. PreVU allows you to play any MPEG video without MPEG hardware from a proprietary HTML server. PreVU provides a first-frame view right in the Navigator window, streaming viewing while downloading. PreVU also allows full-speed cached playback off your hard drive. PreVU is currently available for Windows 95 and NT (see Figure 9-5).

PreVU offers a good approach to Web video. Many players require that you download the entire video before you can view it. This can be a serious waste of both your time and Internet bandwidth if the video doesn't turn out to be what you wanted. Other closed-architecture video systems can show you the video while it's downloading, but they don't save the full video, and you can't quickly replay it. Also, some products degrade the video quality in order to get realtime speed.

Figure 9-5: Viewing an MPEG video with PreVU.

PreVU shows you the first frame before you download the entire video. You can then use this preview to help you select the video you want. You may also preview the video while downloading it to make sure you are only downloading the video you want. Full speed replay is available once the download is finished. PreVU's solutions save time and can greatly reduce the amount of Internet bandwidth required for video.

VDOLive

Vendor:	VDONet Corporation
Address:	2700 Augustine, Suite 261
	Santa Clara, CA 95054
Phone:	(408) 654-8400
Fax:	(408) 654-9447
Address:	599 Lexington Avenue, Suite 2300
	New York, NY 10022
Phone:	(212) 745-1126
Fax:	(212) 745-1139
E-mail:	info@vdolive.com
FTP:	ftp.vdolive.com
URL:	http://www.vdolive.com

VDOLive is a new technology, developed by VDONet Corporation of Santa Clara, California (USA), to transmit video and audio over the Internet or any other TCP/IP network. VDOLive software uses client/server architecture: The client is the VDOLive Player and the server is the VDOLive Server.

VDOLive compresses video images with lossless compression and doesn't compromise the quality on the receiving end. Of course, the speed of your connection determines the frame delivery rate: With a 28.8 Kbps modem, VDOLive runs in real time at 10 to 15 frames per second. Download times will also vary with the speed of your modem, but within most normal conditions, you can expect the following rates:

- 14.4 Kbps modem: up to 2 frames per second
- 28.8 Kbps modem: up to 10 frames per second
- ISDN line: up to 20 frames per second

VRML Players

Virtual reality is a part of life now, and its availability at more and more places on the Web is enriching the experience of traveling through the world of cyberspace. The technology has grown rapidly in the past few years, and it seems to have an assured future on the Net. These applications help make it easy for you to fly around cyberspace and visit the new worlds of interactive 3D. They may even make you want to take a shot at creating one of your own.

VRealm

Vendor: Integrated Data Systems, Inc.
Address: 6001 Chatham Center Drive, Suite 300
            Savannah, GA 31405
Phone: (912) 236-4374
Fax: (912) 236-6792
URL: http://www.ids-net.com/

VRealm, the VRML plug-in for Netscape 2.0 from Integrated Data Systems and Portable Graphics, fully supports VRML. VRealm makes available features such as object behaviors, gravity, collision detection, autopilot, and multimedia. It supports many navigation options and provides a user-friendly interface for navigation through VRML space.

VR Scout VRML

Vendor: Chaco Communications, Inc.
Address: 10164 Parkwood Drive, Suite 8
            Cupertino, CA 95014
Phone: (408) 996-1115
Fax: (408) 865-0571
URL: http://www.chaco.com/

Chaco's VR Scout VRML plug-in (see Figure 9-6) allows you to fly through 3D graphical scenes. Chaco's extremely fast viewers implement the full VRML 1.0 standard.

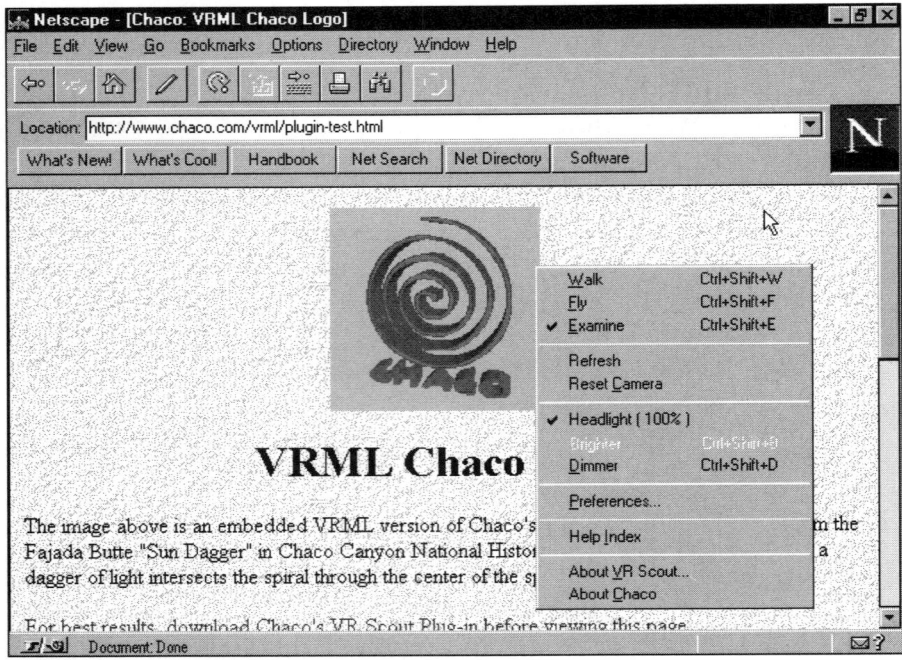

Figure 9-6: Viewing the embedded Chaco VRML logo

VR Scout 1.22 is a fast viewer for Virtual Reality Modeling Language (VRML) files. It has been rated by several independent industry sources as the most standards-compliant VRML viewer. VR Scout is more than four times faster than its predecessor, VR Scout 1.1. The VR Scout 1.22 works with Netscape Navigator 2.0 and Netscape Navigator Gold 2.0, as an embedded plug-in, so VRML files can be displayed just like GIFs, JPEGs, and HTML documents. VRML files can even be displayed inline in an HTML document.

VR Scout 1.22 supports all of VRML 1.0. The application uses Microsoft Reality Lab for fast software rendering and hardware acceleration. VR Scout also has many open inventor nodes, so many not-quite-compliant VRML files will still work. It can also handle GZIP and ZIP files automatically and transparently, and it uses multithreading so different aspects of a scene are downloaded simultaneously.

WebFX

Vendor: Paper Software, Inc.
Address: 4 Deming Street
            Woodstock, NY 12498
Phone: (914) 679-2440
Fax: (914) 679-4123
URL: http://www.paperinc.com/

WebFX is a high-performance, 3D VRML platform that lets you fly through VRML worlds on the Web and also run interactive, multiuser VRML applications written in Java. The WebFX plug-in features 3D text, background images, texture animation, morphing, viewpoints, collision detection, gravity, and RealAudio streaming sound.

The WebFX plug-in lets you fly through interconnected, three-dimensional worlds on the Internet with all the safety and comfort of Navigator. WebFX provides full VRML 1.0 compliance, progressive rendering, physics-based navigation, collision detection, animated viewpoints, GZIP support, level of detail, GIF, JPG, RGB, PNG, and BMP textures. WebFX also supports multiple nested inlines, 3D text, sprites, image backgrounds, and support for common open inventor nodes. With WebFX, you can view as many 3D files on the Internet as you want.

If you've racked up a lot of mileage playing Doom or Descent, you'll be familiar with WebFX navigation. The Doom model is used when walking or authoring, while the Descent model is used when flying.

WIRL Virtual Reality Browser

Vendor: VREAM, Inc.
Address: 2568 North Clark Street, Suite 250
            Chicago, IL 60614
Phone: (312) 477-0425
Fax: (312) 477-9702
E-mail: info@vream.com
URL: http://www.vream.com/

VREAM's new Windows 95 plug-in for Netscape Navigator 2.0 lets you experience interactive 3D worlds or applications within a Web page. WIRL fully supports VRML and extends it with support for object behaviors (such as motion, rotation, gravity, weight, elasticity, throw ability, and sound). It also supports logical cause-and-effect relationships, multimedia capabilities, and links to Windows applications.

VREAM's 3D browser, which is a Netscape Navigator plug-in, takes the emerging VRML standard to a new level. With its inline extensions architecture, WIRL allows Navigator users to experience fully interactive virtual reality on the Web, complete with complex object behaviors and logic functions. This adds a whole new dimension to the existing VRML specification, which does not yet support behaviors and logic functions.

Miscellaneous Plug-Ins

So many new things are out there these days that it is exciting to reflect on some of them that fit the regular pattern. The applications that are discussed in this section have a definite place in your Netscape Navigator bag of tricks. Lots of these applications are out there, many more than we have been able to introduce you to here.

3D F/X

Vendor: Asymetrix Corporation
Address: 110 110th Avenue, Suite 700
            Bellevue, WA 98004
Phone: (800) 448-6543 (Sales)
Fax: (206) 637-1504
URL: http://www.asymetrix.com:80/index.htm

Asymetrix 3D F/X provides you with easy-to-use graphics tools that let you create professionally rendered 3D images and animations.

3D F/X can be used to create attractive 3D images and logos for interactive learning programs, sales presentations, printed documents, CD-ROMs, desktop videos, information kiosks, and any other applications that can incorporate bitmaps and digital video files.

With the 3D F/X plug-in, you can instantly preview your 3D scenes and animations and analyze the color, surface, and transparency of objects. Solid model preview (not wireframes) eliminates the guesswork — so you know what your final output will look like.

The drag-and-drop interface lets you quickly create scenes by combining and modifying preset scene elements. You can select a starter scene from the 3D F/X catalog and either use the scene as it is or customize it. You can enrich your scene with backdrops, lighting, and other elements from the 3D F/X clip art catalog, and you can also drag and drop 3D models into it.

AnchorPage

Vendor: Iconovex Corporation
Address: 7900 Xerxes Avenue South, Suite 550
             Bloomington, MN 55431
Phone: (800) 943-0292
Fax: (612) 896-5101
E-mail: `74064.440@compuserve.com`
             `ICONOVEX@ix.netcom.com`
             `FYI@iconovex.com`
URL: `http://www.iconovex.com`

AnchorPage is an automatic indexing, abstracting, and hyperlinking software for the Web. It dramatically saves site maintenance time by automatically indexing, abstracting, and hyperlinking the key concepts and phrases in your HTML documents (see Figure 9-7). AnchorPage can also improve your site by introducing information and content-driven navigation for your page. Because your documents are inter/intralinked, visitors to your site are not merely linked to your documents; they can follow links within and between the documents.

AnchorPage extracts significant phrases and concepts from each of your World Wide Web documents and automatically inserts hypertext anchors for each of those phrases and concepts, then produces four navigational views of the document:

- Table of Contents view
- Phrase view
- Concept view
- Abstract view

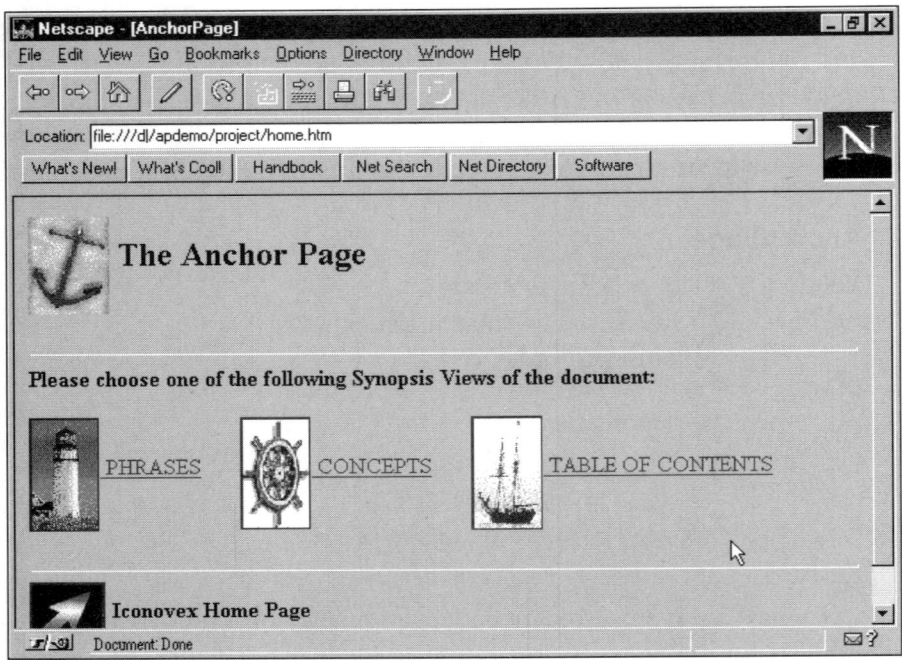

Figure 9-7: A completed AnchorPage index.

Navigational views represent different entry points into a document. The Table of Contents View presents the document headings and subheadings in outline form. The Abstract View presents abstracts of the significant concepts in the order in which they appear in the original document. The Concept View presents the significant concepts in context alphabetized according to the keywords they contain. The Phrase View is an alphabetical listing of the keywords and key phrases drawn from the concepts. These navigational views can then be linked to each other and to the presentation page, a view of the document in its presentation form.

EarthTime

Vendor:	Starfish Software
Address:	1700 Green Hills Road
	Scotts Valley, CA 95066
Phone:	(800) 765-7839
URL:	http://www.starfishsoftware.com/
America Online:	Keyword Starfish
CompuServe:	Go Starfish
Microsoft Network:	Go Word Starfish

The EarthTime plug-in from Starfish Software enables you to tell time around the world at a glance without leaving your browser (see Figure 9-8).

EarthTime, which was built for Windows 95/NT, shows you the local time and date in eight global locations. Choose from over 350 world capitals and commercial centers. The animated, worldwide map indicates daylight and darkness so you can plan the best time to make your calls. An essential tool for anyone doing business or making phone calls or navigating across time zones, EarthTime also adjusts for daylight savings time.

Formula One/NET

Vendor:	Visual Components, Inc.
Address:	15721 College Blvd.
	Lenexa, KS 66219
Phone:	(913) 599-6500
Fax:	(913) 599-6597
Fax Back Service:	(913) 599-6500, Option 5
E-mail:	Sales@visualcomp.com
URL:	http://www.visualcomp.com/

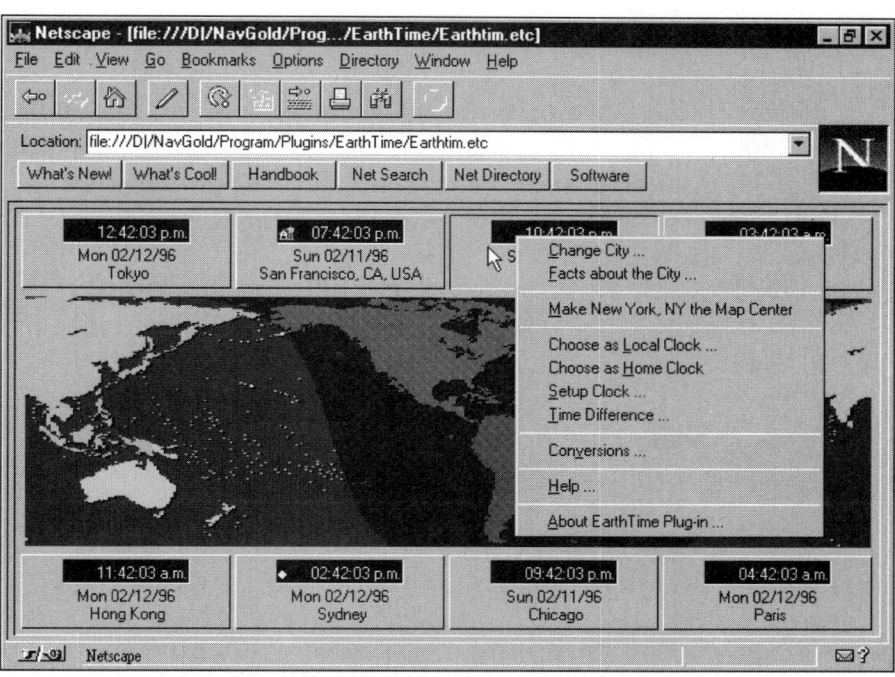

Figure 9-8: Viewing the EarthTime plug-in from Netscape Navigator Gold.

Formula One/NET is the first Excel-compatible spreadsheet with built-in Internet functionality. Worksheets can include live charts, links to URLs, formatted text and numbers, calculations, and clickable buttons and controls.

Globalink

Vendor: Globalink, Inc.
Address: 9302 Lee Highway
            Fairfax, VA 22031
Phone: (800) 255-5660 (Toll Free U.S. and Canada only)
            (703) 273-5600 (Local and International)
E-mail: info@globalink.com

The Language Assistant Series is designed for personal and home use. This complete suite of reference tools gives you instant help when writing, studying, or translating. The Language Assistant products have extensive grammar help, with complete conjugations for thousands of verbs and bilingual dictionaries. You can easily customize the dictionaries by adding new words and phrases or by modifying existing entries.

With this plug-in, you can add directions or text in different languages to your page, which can be selected by those viewing it. You can have sentences, paragraphs, or entire documents read to them in the languages supported by the program. You control the voice, speed, and pitch. Power Translator offers fast draft translations for business users. The core dictionary is built on single words, word phrases, alternate translations, and idioms. As a result, you can offer visitors to your site a choice of languages in which to have the text or audio presented to them.

Power Translator Deluxe programs also offer sound capability. Highlight a word, sentence, or the entire document and have it read to you in the language you select.

Lightning Strike

Vendor: Infinet Op
Address: P. O. Box 2562
            Denton, TX 76201
Phone: (817) 891-1538
URL: http://www.infinop.com/

Lightning Strike is an optimized wavelet image codec to compress your Web images; the product is ready to plug in to Navigator. It provides higher compression ratios, smaller image files, faster transmissions, and improved image quality.

WinFrame

Vendor:	Citrix Systems, Inc.
Address:	210 University Drive, Suite 800
	Coral Springs, FL 33071
Phone:	(800) 437-7503
Fax:	(954) 341-6880
E-mail:	Webmaster@citrix.com

WinFrame for Networks is the first complete TeleComputing platform for enterprise networks. WinFrame offers a solution to the problems you may face connecting employees, vendors, and customers to strategic Windows applications using any client over any kind of connection. With WinFrame, you can take 16- and 32-bit Windows applications anywhere. You'll realize wide-open possibilities for deploying Windows applications where you never thought possible.

With WinFrame, you can run high-bandwidth applications at LAN-speed over a dial-up connection. You can deliver 16- and 32-bit Windows applications to branch offices over low-cost switched or dedicated connections. You can deploy a wide mix of client/server, workgroup, and other strategic business applications across the enterprise network. You can also launch standard Windows applications right from your Web site and run Windows 95 and other 32-bit Windows applications from 16-bit platforms.

Summary

The collection of inline plug-ins discussed in this chapter all increase the power of Navigator to provide the broadest range of capabilities for experiencing and participating in the World Wide Web. Their ease of installation and configuration make it simple to incorporate these plug-ins into Navigator 2.0 and Navigator Gold 2.0. Once you have installed them you may begin using them immediately without a learning curve and with little more effort than clicking on a link in a Web page. As the popularity of the WWW grows, you may be certain that the demand for more ways to access the technology and take advantage of the online opportunities will spur the development of new technologies. This will only spawn more plug-in applications to incorporate into the Navigator toolbox.

Chapter 10

The Future of Netscape Navigator

I n this chapter, we look at a few of the exciting features that are on the horizon. You can stay informed with the latest news about these features when you visit the Netscape home page.

Throughout this book, we have talked about all that Navigator can help you do and the many added attractions of such features as the Plug-in and Helper applications. As Netscape continues to develop its powerful software, the number of add-ons supported will increase and new technologies will be added. In addition, security will continue to be an extremely important issue, and new releases will offer improved security. Netscape is also developing new Web site management tools that will help Webmasters manage their Web sites with greater ease.

Additional Development Options

New tools are constantly being added that enable Netscape developers to turn Navigator's basic Web browser into a more sophisticated application. Developers can include Java applets, JavaScript scripts, and many inline plug-ins, as discussed in Chapter 9. These options can be used to create pages that dance, sing, and respond intelligently to mouse click commands. The result of all this is that viewing the Internet through Navigator 2 is a richer experience.

Netscape JavaScript and Java Applets

Netscape's JavaScript is a reasonably simple interpreted language for people who want to control Navigator 2's customization but don't want to get involved with C++. JavaScript is very suitable for customization tasks such as building responses to events like user mouse clicks, or for local validation of HTML form fields.

You may integrate a number of predefined event handlers into your HTML pages with JavaScript to respond to events such as clicking a mouse, leaving an HTML page, or selecting a text field. Writing and testing scripts is fairly simple using the Navigator 2 browser. Scripts can be added to HTML pages by embedding the script source code into an HTML page by using the new <SCRIPT> tag. You can also add a script by putting the script source into an external file and by using the SRC option of the <SCRIPT> tag to read from the external file during execution. The script is executed by the JavaScript interpreter, a part of Navigator 2. Netscape's JavaScript interpreted scripting language can make interactive Web pages and inline plug-ins extend Navigator's support for new protocols and file formats. These options provide an integrated development environment.

Netscape's JavaScript scripting language is a good, if simple, way for developers to write programs to enhance Web pages. With JavaScript, you can write scripts that can communicate with plug-ins and applets.

Implementing JavaScript gives support for execution of Java programs, which means that Navigator can execute Java applets embedded in Web pages. Sun Microsystems's Java programming language is extensible and object-oriented. Although Java is similar to C++, it doesn't have pointers and is strongly typed. Sun excluded pointers from Java for security and error detection. From the security side, because Java programs don't have pointers, they can't reference arbitrary memory locations, some of which may contain private data such as a cached password. You can handle errors more easily without pointers because errant pointer references cause unpredictable program behavior. Now error conditions in your Java program are more likely to be caught by Navigator instead of giving you an error message.

Java applets, which are executed within the Web browser, are embedded in Web pages by using the HTML <EMBED> tag. Navigator 2.0 automatically downloads the applets to your machine. A Java runtime interpreter executes the applets within Navigator.

The number and complexity of Java applets and JavaScript scripts will continue to grow. Netscape provides a supportive environment that encourages developers to create exciting applications with these powerful tools.

Netscape Live3D Extensions

In February 1996, Netscape announced a technology called Netscape Live3D, which will enable developers to easily integrate Virtual Reality Markup Language (VRML) graphics into the Netscape software. Live3D extensions will offer new, powerful 3D capabilities to the Netscape software. Netscape is working with the Virtual Reality Markup Language (VRML) community to support the existing 3D graphics standards and to encourage development of new, 3D applications.

Netscape Live3D supports the Moving Worlds 3D VRML specification. Moving Worlds is the specification that is supported by more than 50 of the major technology companies, and it will probably be included in VRML 2.0. Support for this specification will promote new, powerful 3D VRML applications that will provide a rich graphical environment. Netscape Navigator users will be able to experience the Internet in live 3D.

Enhanced Security

Security is vital if the Internet is going to be used as a delivery tool for commercial promotion and information. The current release of Netscape offers enhanced security over previous releases. The SSL, Secure Sockets Layer, accessible to users of Navigator Gold, provides a way for developers to integrate high quality security into their applications. The key to this technology is SSL's emulation of the pervasive Sockets API (Application Programmers Interface). This API is supported by all major operating systems, including UNIX, Macintosh System 7, and Microsoft Windows. Programmers will be able to create a whole new class of secure applications easily, and Internet Service Providers will be able to provide security services.

SSL operates by layering an application protocol on top of the security protocol. The library establishes a connection with a remote host and then performs a security handshake. Once the security handshake is complete, the library then encrypts and decrypts data sent to and received from the remote host. All this is accomplished transparently.

The SSL library requires a reliable transfer protocol. For the UNIX, Macintosh, and PC environments, transfer protocol is commonly provided by TCP/IP, but it could as easily be Novell's IPX/SPX. The protocol independent nature of the WinSock 2.0 specification lends itself to expanding the scope of current SSL implementations.

Using this technology, a Navigator Gold application developer can quickly convert a client or server to its secure twin. By integrating this technology into the WinSock 2.0 specification, an end-user application developer can easily provide very strong security for an application. The application can simply enumerate the protocols supported by the system, and if any protocol provides SSL security, the programmer can enable security on arbitrary sockets. Adding SSL support results in almost no impact to the current specification for an ISP that chooses not to implement security. Basically, SSL support amounts to another capability that can be enumerated and then controlled through socket options.

Netscape continues to enhance its security features. A patched version of the Java Applet Security Manager has been released in response to potential security vulnerabilities. This patch prevents a Java applet from setting up a network connection with an invalid host computer. The next version of Navigator will offer additional security features.

LiveWire and LiveWire Pro Web Site Management Tools

Netscape is developing Web site management tools called LiveWire and LiveWire Pro. These tools provide a visual environment that makes it easier for Webmasters to manage their Web sites. LiveWire developers can build and manage applications for their networks and the Internet.

Netscape LiveWire includes the following components:

- Navigator Gold
- LiveWire Site Manager
- Java-compatible scripting language
- LiveWire server extensions
- LiveWire Server Front Panel

LiveWire Site Manager will make it easier for Webmasters to manage sites when common problems occur. Examples of these problems include links between pages that are broken or Uniform Resource Locators that are changed without the Webmaster's knowledge.

LiveWire Server Front Panel will include a set of pages and forms. These pages and forms act as a **front panel** to simplify the installation and monitoring of Internet applications.

Netscape LiveWire Pro includes the components of LiveWire and adds database connectivity. Developers will be able to integrate support for Structured Query Language (SQL) databases from Oracle, Informix, Microsoft, and Sybase. A single-user developer version of a relational database will also be provided.

Summary

Netscape continues to offer additional development options for its software. Netscape JavaScript and the integration of Java applets provide opportunities for very rich Internet content. Netscape Live 3D will enable Netscape developers to easily integrate VRML capabilities and Netscape users to view 3D content.

Netscape will continue to improve Internet security for Netscape users, which will encourage the growth of the Internet as a vehicle of commerce.

Netscape will provide Web site management tools, called LiveWire and LiveWire Pro. These tools will help Webmasters manage their Web sites more easily.

Appendix

Contents of the CD-ROM

This book/software package contains everything that you need to begin using Netscape Navigator 2. The CD-ROM contains the EarthLink TotalAccess Network software and Netscape Navigator 2. Once you install the EarthLink TotalAccess software and establish your account, you are ready to start using Navigator 2.

Installing EarthLink™ TotalAccess™ and Netscape Navigator 2 with Window 3.1x

Use the following instructions to install the software.

1. Insert the CD-ROM into the CD-ROM drive.
2. From the Windows Program Manager File menu, choose the Run option.
3. Type **d:\win3-1\setup.exe** and click on OK.
4. From the TotalAccess installation dialog box, select Install.
5. Follow the instructions to register your new EarthLink Network TotalAccess account.

6. Click on the Help button at any time during the process if you should need additional help.

7. Type the information requested on the screen to create a new account with EarthLink.

You are now ready to use the EarthLink software and Netscape Navigator 2!

Installing EarthLink™ *Total Access*™ *and Netscape Navigator with Windows 95*

Use the following instructions to install the software.

1. Click on the start button.

2. Click on Run

3. Type **d:\win95\setup** and click on OK. This launches Total Access™ installer. Follow the instructions given.

Glossary

alt newsgroup. A type of alternative newsgroup that does not follow the same traditions as the Big Seven newsgroups.

anonymous posting. Posting articles to a Usenet newsgroup anonymously.

anonymous remailer. A service that allows you to send e-mail or post Usenet articles anonymously.

applet. Nuggets of networked software included in HTML documents.

article. Used in many newsgroups to describe a variety of messages you might post. Obviously, it could be an article as you normally understand it — a discussion or analysis of a subject in some depth. In other cases, article could refer to a one-paragraph answer to someone's problem (you could also e-mail this response personally to the recipient, but posting it usually makes for a better dissemination of the solution).

attachment. A file that you include as part of an e-mail message.

AU. A format for storing sounds in files. File extension for files in the AU format.

backbone. This is the main artery of communications to which all of the other computers, networks, routers and other devices are attached. Many of today's ISP's use at least one T1 link as a backbone.

bandwidth. The amount of data that can travel through a circuit, measured in bits per second. The more bandwidth, the better.

Big Seven newsgroups. Newsgroups in the seven official newsgroup hierarchies (comp, sci, rec, soc, talk, news, and misc).

binary file. A file that contains information other than plain text. Binary files can contain graphics, sounds, video, programs, or other information.

Bookmark. A marker that indicates a spot that you may want to return to (for example, an interesting Internet site that you plan to visit again).

bounce. This is the process of returning an e-mail message to the sender because of delivery problems. Possible problems include bad e-mail addresses, an unavailable host, or typos.

browser. Software that uses special commands allowing users to move around the Internet just by clicking on highlighted *hypertext* words.

Chat. One of the most appealing aspects of Navigator's Chat is having the capability to have a private chat, instead of merely joining a group one. You can leave a crowded chatroom and have a more intimate one-on-one with a single person. This is sometimes called *whispering,* because you are sending private messages to individuals who are engaged in one of the channel chats.

client. The client is the computer that sends out requests over the Internet for something to be done. For example, the client computer sends a request to access a newsgroup or a Web page. The computer you operate at home or work generally is regarded as the client, because it is from there that you issue instructions to server computers. However, depending on whether you have Internet-accessible information on your computer, it could also be a server as well.

client application. These are the functional applications that work either inside Navigator or as a complement to it on your client computer. For example, you can send and receive e-mail right from the Navigator screen. You can access newsgroups, engage in chatroom conversations, and open portable documents via tools such as Adobe Acrobat Amber. All of these represent client applications that can be invoked from Navigator 2.0's screen.

com. The last part of the host name for a computer run by a business.

Common Gateway Interface (CGI). Developed by the folks at the National Center for Supercomputer Application (NCSA) at the University of Illinois at Champaign-Urbana. CGI is the standard mechanism in use on Web servers for the execution of programs which generate dynamic documents and send them to your browser. In other words, CGI provides a method for your browser to execute programs on remote servers using your input.

Cyberspace. A term that refers to a world in which computers and people coexist. The term first appeared in the science fiction book *Neuromancer,* written by William Gibson.

dial-up access. An Internet connection which uses a modem and is established over phone lines.

domain name. The name of your ISP's network. You will use it to send electronic mail, among other things. For example, if your provider is Iquest, the domain name might be iquest.com. Your e-mail name would then be something such as user ID@iquest.com.

download. To move a file from one computer to your own computer's hard drive. Many of the programs you'll find on the Internet must be downloaded in order to use them.

edu. The last part of the host name for a computer run by an educational organization, such as a university.

emoticon. A combination of keyboard characters that represent a facial expression or emotion. Emoticons are used to add expression in e-mail messages. The characters :-) are the emoticon for a smile (turn the page sideways to "see" it).

Eudora. An e-mail program that runs on Windows and Macintosh systems. A shareware version of Eudora is available on various FTP servers.

file transfer protocol (ftp). FTP is the protocol or set of commands used to translate file formats and send them from one place to another. More data is fired through the Internet every day via FTP than even e-mail (though the latter is a more common application, the former is used for much bigger transfers). Any serious user will most likely use FTP to send or receive all types of files.

flaming. Shooting your mouth off angrily in any online discussion.

Frames. A new feature in Netscape 2 that allows several screens to be presented in the Navigator window simultaneously. This often saves vast amounts of time lost switching back and forth among pages.

freeware. Refers to software that usually can be downloaded from one or more sites on the Internet or from FTP servers, and for which there is no cost. While the software is free, the support for it is often thin.

GIF. Graphics Interchange Format. A format for storing image files.

gov. The last part of the host name for a computer run by the U.S. Government.

hacker. A dedicated and talented programmer, and a vicious and irresponsible violater of computer security.

home page. A Web location that offers a "table of contents" for a group, individual, or organization. The address to a home page is specified by a URL.

HyperText Markup Language (HTML). The format language with which most Web pages are designed.

HTML editor. A program that helps you create Web pages.

HTTP. HyperText Transfer Protocol. The language that Web browsers use to talk with Web servers.

hypertext. A text document that contains hot spots (or links) to other documents. Hot spots allow users to move through the document to other documents in a nonlinear format.

Integrated Service Digital Network (ISDN). ISDN is a digital telephone system. Your current telephone system is probably an analog. An ISDN connection would give you a speed boost from the current top analog speed of 28.8 Kbps to the top digital speed of 128 Kbps. It usually costs more, but the jump in speed might be worth it for you. As a rule of thumb, anything you can do to speed up your Internet service is a good idea.

Internet. The network of interconnected networks in 70+ countries that uses TCP/IP networking communications protocol. The Internet is the largest network of computers in the world, providing e-mail, file transfer, news, remote login, and access to thousands of databases. Informally, the Internet is known as the Net.

Internet Protocol (IP) Address. With some 30 million Internet users worldwide, a numerical scheme had to be devised to identify each machine on the Net. This scheme is called the *Internet Protocol Address* (IP). There are more than four billion combinations, but that hasn't stopped the same number from being mistakenly issued to more than one person on a few occasions. You need to request that your ISP provide you with an IP address for your computer.

There are two types of IP addressing: dynamic and static. In all likelihood you will receive dynamic addressing from your ISP. If you are a dial-up user, which most individuals are, this means that the ISP's host computer will assign you a unique IP address for the particular session you are in. When you log off, that address will be available again. When you connect later, dynamic addressing gives you a new IP address.

In some rare circumstances, an ISP will provide you with a static IP address which will be used every time you log on to the Internet. But this is by far the exception and not the rule.

Internet Service Provider (ISP). A company that provides Internet access to individuals, organizations, and companies.

Internet Relay Chat (IRC). IRC is the CD radio of the Internet. It is the system that allows thousands of users to exchange messages in realtime (almost instantly) over the Internet.

Java. The fastest rising star in Internet programming is Java, an object-oriented programming language from Sun Microsystems. Navigator 2.0 — as well as Navigator Gold 2.0 — support Java and its applications (known as applets because they tend to be smaller than normal applications).

Java's applets are suited perfectly to the Web's diverse platforms. They can run on most of the computers that are linked to the Internet, a portability that has made them increasingly popular with developers who don't want to shut anyone out of their sites.

JavaScript. JavaScript lets developers script some action on the Web page — that is, it can sequence events or actions to happen whenever a given command is invoked. What this means for both new and experienced developers is that they don't have to resort to more complex coding and, instead, can quickly assemble a script to handle the action. JavaScript, as you probably inferred, is based loosely on Java.

JPEG. Graphic file format commonly used on the Internet.

linking. In hypertext and hypermedia (such as the World Wide Web), text or a picture that connects to other information. Selecting the link immediately displays the other information.

live objects. Refers to objects such as the URLs you can embed in e-mail, news, and chat, but also more visually dramatic applications called inline plug-ins, which enable you to view, for example, multimedia presentations created in Macromedia Director or documents published in Adobe Acrobat. Click on the embedded object and it will start automatically.

MIME. The MIME (Multipurpose Internet Mail Extensions) compliant newsreader gives you the ability to bring your news postings to life with URLs, live objects, and images.

Mozilla. The name for Netscape while it was in development.

MPEG. Moving Pictures Experts Group. A type of file that contains moving graphics; a movie.

multimedia. The integration of text, audio, sound, static graphic images, animation, and full-motion digital video.

NCSA Mosaic. The first Web graphical browser was built at the National Center for Supercomputing Applications (NCSA) and came to market in 1993, capturing two million users within a year. Suddenly, individuals and organizations could see, read, hear, navigate, and participate on the Internet in ways they could easily understand and creatively embrace.

netiquette. An informal list of rules that are the dos and don'ts of behavior when you are connected to the Internet. The unwritten rules of the road.

Netscape Gold. Navigator Gold 2 refers to Netscape's product for Web developers and authors. It has all of the features contained in Navigator 2, but also contains a toolbox of utilities designed specifically for Web publishing.

Netscape Navigator. Widely used Web browser that runs on Windows, Mac, and X Windows systems.

newbies. People who are new to the Internet.

newsgroups. Discussion forums that allow Internet members to discuss specific topics. Newsgroups also are referred to as mail groups, and you will find them available for just about every topic you can think of.

newsreaders. Think of these programs as special-interest access tools. They allow you to link into newsgroups and electronic bulletin boards (BBSs) where users discuss (sometimes with volcanic tension) specific subjects. There is a variety of newsreaders available, but one public domain application that can make your Internet news exploration worthwhile is called News Xpress.

org. The last part of the host name for a computer run by a nonprofit organization.

page. A screen on the World Wide Web. One page often contains links to other pages on the Web.

password. The secret combination of letters and numbers that you use to gain access to your Internet account on your public-access provider or local area network.

Point-to-Point Protocol (PPP). A TCP/IP protocol for transmitting data over serial transmission lines, such as telephone lines. This protocol is similar to SLIP; it operates on the link layer, however, and is slightly faster than SLIP.

Portable Document Format, or PDF. Provides a means of preserving the integrity and appearance of a precisely designed page as it is transferred from one point to another. Developed by Adobe and used widely.

Post Office Protocol (POP). This is a Retrieve Mail address that enables mail to come from the Internet to the ISP's customers.

realtime data. Data that is transferred as it happens, rather than delayed.

reload. A command used to retreive again the page you are currently looking at.

Serial Line Internet Protocol (SLIP). A TCP/IP protocol for transmitting data over serial transmission lines, such as telephone lines. With SLIP, your personal computer behaves like a machine that is directly connected to the Internet. Unfortunately, SLIP does not have error-checking capability.

server. This refers to the computer that is sending, or "serving up," the information that is being sent out over the Internet. It can refer to any sending computer on the route, meaning the computer of origination or the servers at your Internet service provider that provide the first link in the chain to you.

shareware. For example, Netscape Navigator 2.0. Refers to software that can be used free for a period of time, but then must be paid for.

shell access/shell account. This is a low-cost (as low as $5/month) account with an Internet Service Provider (ISP) that you'll see running only on terminal emulators by using UNIX command lines. Simply put, shell accounts are text-based, while SLIP/PPP accounts are graphical. These accounts are called shell because you aren't connected directly to the Internet. You send UNIX commands to the ISP host, which connects you to the Internet. Your PC just displays the communications between the ISP's computer and other hosts. There are Windows programs that can run over the shell's UNIX interfaces.

SmartMarks. An intelligent bookmarking tool that comes as a helper application for Navigator 2. It does for bookmarks what the Navigator did for newsreading and e-mail — it lets you organize them into logical groups. Even better, it monitors your designated Web sites and tells you if content or addresses have changed anywhere.

spamming. Posting the same (or nearly the same) article to many newsgroups, usually advertising something.

startup page. The Web page that appears when you run your browser.

streaming. Newly developed and modified technologies have begun to rapidly boost the level of interaction on the Web to include realtime sound. By using *streaming* technologies, companies like Progressive Networks have developed programs like RealAudio, which is based on a new MIME type and an associated helper application that will let you hear realtime sound. Instead of having to wait until the sound file downloads and then listen to it, it is possible to listen to the sound in realtime as it downloads.

surfing. Wandering around the Internet, browsing through the information that you find.

T1 line. A wiring specification that, in common use, denotes the type of phone-line connection that is used for data communications. A T1 line is capable of handling approximately 1.544 Mbps of data and is used for high-volume connections to the Internet.

T3 line. A phone system wiring specification that is used for extremely high-volume data communication needs. A T3 line is capable of handling data at approximately 45 Mbps. T3 lines, typically made of fiberoptic wire, make up the backbone of the Internet.

TCP/IP. The language of the Internet. TCP/IP (Transfer Control Protocol/Internet Protocol) is a protocol that allows computers on the Internet to communicate reliably.

threaded newsgroups. This feature greatly simplifies the process of sorting, reading and posting *threads,* which are series of responses to items that have been posted in the newsgroups. You can subscribe to a newsgroup as before, but instead of a loosely (if at all) organized list of articles and responses, you can quickly scan the articles and their threads (indented below them) by title.

Uniform Resource Locator (URL). The address that is used to refer to particular documents on the Web. An example is `http://www.music.sony.com/Music/MusicIndex.html`, which points to the initial page for Sony Music.

unsubscribe. The command that removes your name from the list of subscribers to a mailing list.

upload. To move a computer file from your computer to another, or from your computer to the Internet.

user ID. In the Internet addressing scheme, the portion of the address to the left of the @ sign.

Virtual Reality Modeling Language (VRML). VRML has opened up a world of possibilities for how Internet travelers will view and interact with sites on the Web. For those unfamiliar with virtual reality, it is the concept of putting you into a computerized virtual world and, by using graphical headsets to see and special gloves to manipulate objects in the virtual world, can perform functions, access information, shoot bad guys — anything that has been programmed.

WAV. A format for storing sounds in files. File extension for files in the WAV format.

Web. A nickname for the World Wide Web.

Web crawler. A program that creates an automated index to the World Wide Web, and a Web page that allows you to search the index.

Web server. A program that stores World Wide Web pages and responds to requests for them using HTTP.

WinSock. A WinSock-based connection (WinSock means "Windows Socket" and is the standard TCP/IP connection for Windows-based computers) still gives you the most flexibility with far less clumsiness and with only a little more cost.

World Wide Web (WWW). A hypertext menuing system that is accessed through the Internet.

World Wide Web page. Any file on the Net that is composed of ASCII text with HTML coding. A Web page may contain links to images, sound files, video clips, or other files.

Yahoo. A World Wide Web page that contains an excellent subject-oriented hierarchical index to Web pages and other Internet services.

ZIP file. A file that contains one or more compressed files, created by PKZIP, WinZip, or a compatible program.

Index

Symbols

IDG BOOKS WORLDWIDE, INC., END-USER LICENSE AGREEMENT

Read This. You should carefully read these terms and conditions before opening the software packet(s) included with this book ("Book"). This is a license agreement ("Agreement") between you and IDG Books Worldwide, Inc. ("IDGB"). By opening the accompanying software packet(s), you acknowledge that you have read and accept the following terms and conditions. If you do not agree and do not want to be bound by such terms and conditions, promptly return the Book and the unopened software packet(s) to the place you obtained them for a full refund.

1. **License Grant.** IDGB grants to you (either an individual or entity) a nonexclusive license to use one copy of the enclosed software program(s) (collectively, the "Software") solely for your own personal or business purposes on a single computer (whether a standard computer or a workstation component of a multi-user network). The Software is in use on a computer when it is loaded into temporary memory (i.e., RAM) or installed into permanent memory (e.g., hard disk, CD-ROM, or other storage device). IDGB reserves all rights not expressly granted herein.

2. **Ownership.** IDGB is the owner of all rights, titles, and interests, including copyright, in and to the compilation of the Software recorded on the CD-ROM. Copyright to the individual programs on the CD-ROM is owned by the author or other authorized copyright owner of each program. Ownership of the Software and all proprietary rights relating thereto remain with IDGB and its licensors.

3. **Restrictions on Use and Transfer.**

   (a) You may only (i) make one copy of the Software for backup or archival purposes, or (ii) transfer the Software to a single hard disk, provided that you keep the original for backup or archival purposes. You may not (i) rent or lease the Software, (ii) copy or reproduce the Software through a LAN or other network system or through any computer subscriber system or bulletin-board system, or (iii) modify, adapt, or create derivative works based on the Software.

(b) You may not reverse engineer, decompile, or disassemble the Software. You may transfer the Software and user documentation on a permanent basis, provided that the transferee agrees to accept the terms and conditions of this Agreement and you retain no copies. If the Software is an update or has been updated, any transfer must include the most recent update and all prior versions.

4. **Restrictions on Use of Individual Programs.** You must follow the individual requirements and restrictions detailed for each individual program in this Book. These limitations are contained in the individual license agreements recorded on the CD-ROM. These restrictions include a requirement that after using the program for the period of time specified in its text, the user must pay a registration fee or discontinue use. By opening the Software packet(s), you will be agreeing to abide by the licenses and restrictions for these individual programs. None of the material on this CD-ROM or listed in this Book may ever be distributed, in original or modified form, for commercial purposes.

5. **Limited Warranty.**

   (a) IDGB warrants that the Software and CD-ROM are free from defects in materials and workmanship under normal use for a period of sixty (60) days from the date of purchase of this Book. If IDGB receives notification within the warranty period of defects in materials or workmanship, IDGB will replace the defective CD-ROM.

   (b) IDGB AND THE AUTHOR OF THE BOOK DISCLAIM ALL OTHER WARRANTIES, EXPRESS OR IMPLIED, INCLUDING WITHOUT LIMITATION IMPLIED WARRANTIES OF MERCHANTABILITY AND FITNESS FOR A PARTICULAR PURPOSE, WITH RESPECT TO THE SOFTWARE, THE PROGRAMS, THE SOURCE CODE CONTAINED THEREIN, AND/OR THE TECHNIQUES DESCRIBED IN THIS BOOK. IDGB DOES NOT WARRANT THAT THE FUNCTIONS CONTAINED IN THE SOFTWARE WILL MEET YOUR REQUIREMENTS OR THAT THE OPERATION OF THE SOFTWARE WILL BE ERROR FREE.

(c) This limited warranty gives you specific legal rights, and you may have other rights which vary from jurisdiction to jurisdiction.

6. **Remedies.**

(a) IDGB's entire liability and your exclusive remedy for defects in materials and workmanship shall be limited to replacement of the Software, which is returned to IDGB at the address set forth below with a copy of your receipt. This Limited Warranty is void if failure of the Software has resulted from accident, abuse, or misapplication. Any replacement Software will be warranted for the remainder of the original warranty period or thirty (30) days, whichever is longer.

(b) In no event shall IDGB or the author be liable for any damages whatsoever (including without limitation damages for loss of business profits, business interruption, loss of business informa-tion, or any other pecuniary loss) arising out of the use of or inability to use the Book or the Software, even if IDGB has been advised of the possibility of such damages.

(c) Because some jurisdictions do not allow the exclusion or limita-tion of liability for consequential or incidental damages, the above limitation or exclusion may not apply to you.

7. **U.S. Government Restricted Rights.** Use, duplication, or disclosure of the Software by the U.S. Government is subject to restrictions stated in paragraph (c) (1) (ii) of the Rights in Technical Data and Computer Software clause of DFARS 252.227-7013, and in sub-paragraphs (a) through (d) of the Commercial Computer— Restricted Rights clause at FAR 52.227-19, and in similar clauses in the NASA FAR supplement, when applicable.

8. **General.** This Agreement constitutes the entire understanding of the parties, and revokes and supersedes all prior agreements, oral or written, between them and may not be modified or amended except in a writing signed by both parties hereto which specifically refers to this Agreement. This Agreement shall take precedence over any other documents that may be in conflict herewith. If any one or more provisions contained in this Agreement are held by any court or tribunal to be invalid, illegal or otherwise unenforceable, each and every other provision shall remain in full force and effect.

Installation Instructions

Please read installation instructions on back of this page.

Installation Instructions

Installing EarthLink 'TotalAccess' and Netscape Navigator 2 with Windows 3.1x

The CD-ROM that accompanies this book includes EarthLink TotalAccess and Netscape Navigator 2. Use the following instructions to install the software.

1. Insert the CD-ROM into the CD-ROM drive.

2. From the Windows Program Manager File menu, choose the Run option.

3. Type **d:\win3-1\setup.exe** and click on OK.

4. From the TotalAccess installation dialog box, select Install.

5. Follow the instructions to register your new EarthLink Network TotalAccess account.

6. Click on the Help button at any time during the process if you should need additional help.

7. Type the information requested on the screen to create a new account with EarthLink.

Installing with Windows 95

1. Click on the start button.

2. Click on Run.

3. Type **d:\win95\setup**.

You are now ready to use the EarthLink software and Netscape Navigator 2!

IDG BOOKS WORLDWIDE REGISTRATION CARD

RETURN THIS REGISTRATION CARD FOR FREE CATALOG

Title of this book: **60 Minute Guide to Netscape® 2**

My overall rating of this book: ❑ Very good [1] ❑ Good [2] ❑ Satisfactory [3] ❑ Fair [4] ❑ Poor [5]

How I first heard about this book:

❑ Found in bookstore; name: [6]　　　　　　　　　　　❑ Book review: [7]

❑ Advertisement: [8]　　　　　　　　　　　　　　　　❑ Catalog: [9]

❑ Word of mouth; heard about book from friend, co-worker, etc.: [10]　　❑ Other: [11]

What I liked most about this book:

What I would change, add, delete, etc., in future editions of this book:

Other comments:

Number of computer books I purchase in a year: ❑ 1 [12] ❑ 2-5 [13] ❑ 6-10 [14] ❑ More than 10 [15]

I would characterize my computer skills as: ❑ Beginner [16] ❑ Intermediate [17] ❑ Advanced [18] ❑ Professional [19]

I use ❑ DOS [20] ❑ Windows [21] ❑ OS/2 [22] ❑ Unix [23] ❑ Macintosh [24] ❑ Other: [25]_____

(please specify)

I would be interested in new books on the following subjects:
(please check all that apply, and use the spaces provided to identify specific software)

❑ Word processing: [26]　　　　　　　　　❑ Spreadsheets: [27]

❑ Data bases: [28]　　　　　　　　　　　　❑ Desktop publishing: [29]

❑ File Utilities: [30]　　　　　　　　　　　❑ Money management: [31]

❑ Networking: [32]　　　　　　　　　　　　❑ Programming languages: [33]

❑ Other: [34]

I use a PC at (please check all that apply): ❑ home [35] ❑ work [36] ❑ school [37] ❑ other: [38] _____

The disks I prefer to use are ❑ 5.25 [39] ❑ 3.5 [40] ❑ other: [41]_____

I have a CD ROM: ❑ yes [42] ❑ no [43]

I plan to buy or upgrade computer hardware this year: ❑ yes [44] ❑ no [45]

I plan to buy or upgrade computer software this year: ❑ yes [46] ❑ no [47]

Name:　　　　　　　　　　Business title: [48]　　　　　　Type of Business: [49]

Address (❑ home [50] ❑ work [51]/Company name: 　　　　　　　　　　　)

Street/Suite#

City [52]/State [53]/Zipcode [54]:　　　　　　Country [55]

❑ **I liked this book!** You may quote me by name in future
IDG Books Worldwide promotional materials.

My daytime phone number is _____

IDG BOOKS

THE WORLD OF
COMPUTER
KNOWLEDGE

❏ **YES!**

Please keep me informed about IDG's World of Computer Knowledge.
Send me the latest IDG Books catalog.